The Evolution of the Stock Market in China's Transitional Economy

ADVANCES IN CHINESE ECONOMIC STUDIES

Series Editor: Yanrui Wu, *Senior Lecturer in Economics, University of Western Australia, Australia*

The Chinese economy has been transformed dramatically in recent years. With its rapid economic growth and accession to the World Trade Organisation, China is emerging as an economic superpower. China's development experience provides valuable lessons to many countries in transition.

Advances in Chinese Economic Studies aims, as a series, to publish the best work on the Chinese economy by economists and other researchers throughout the world. It is intended to serve a wide readership including academics, students, business economists and other practitioners.

The Evolution of the Stock Market in China's Transitional Economy

Chien-Hsun Chen and Hui-Tzu Shih

Chung-Hua Institution for Economic Research, Taipei, Taiwan

ADVANCES IN CHINESE ECONOMIC STUDIES SERIES

Edward Elgar
Cheltenham, UK • Northampton, MA, USA

Published by
Edward Elgar Publishing Limited
Glensanda House
Montpellier Parade
Cheltenham
Glos GL50 1UA
UK

Edward Elgar Publishing, Inc.
136 West Street
Suite 202
Northampton
Massachusetts 01060
USA

A catalogue record for this book is available from the British Library

Library of Congress Cataloging in Publication Data

Chen, Chien-Hsun, 1933–
 The evolution of the stock market in China's transitional economy /
Chien-Hsun Chen and Hui-Tzu Shih.
  p. cm. – (Advances in Chinese economic studies series)
  Includes bibliographical references and index.
  1. Stock exchanges–China. 2. Free enterprise–China. I. Shih, Hui-Tzu.
II. Title. III. Series.

HG5782.C4315 2002
332.64'251–dc21   2002072191

ISBN 1–84376–059–2

Printed and bound in Great Britain by
Biddles Ltd, Guildford and King's Lynn

Contents

List of Figures   vii
List of Tables   ix
Preface   xii

1. Institutional Change and the Stock Market   1
    1.1 Institutional Transformation and the Resultant Changes
        to the Financing System
    1.2 The Emergence of the Stock Market in China

2. The Scale and Structure of China's Stock Market   24
    2.1 Types of Shares Traded, Equity Structure, Investor
        Structure and Intermediaries in China's Stock Market
    2.2 Regional Distribution and Industry Structure of Listed
        Companies
    2.3 Conclusions

3. Operational Efficiency and Regulatory System of the   55
    Chinese Stock Market
    3.1 Analysis of Stock Market Efficiency
    3.2 The Stock Market Regulation System

4. Operational Performance of Listed Companies   76
    4.1 The Relationship Between the Stock Market and the
        Reform of State-Owned Enterprises
    4.2 Exploration of the Relationship Between the Stock
        Market and Economic Development
    4.3 Conclusions

5. The Impact of China's WTO Accession on the Stock   110
    Market
    5.1 Analysis of the Level of Openness of the Stock Market
    5.2 The Impact of WTO Accession on Listed Companies

6.   Future Trends in the Evolution of China's Stock   158
      Market
      6.1   Institutional Prospects of China's Stock Market
      6.2   The Globalization of Financial Markets and the Reform
            of China's Stock Market

References   171
Index   183

Figures

1.1   The Fiscal Revenue Mechanism under the Centrally Planned
      Economy   5
2.1   Occupational Background of Investors   40
2.2   Educational Level of Stock Market Investors   40
2.3   Investors' Monthly Income   41
3.1   The Regulatory System in the Early Stages of China's Stock
      Market Development   62
3.2   The Transformation of China's Stock Market Regulatory
      System, 1992–98   64
4.1   Profitability Indicator (F1) – Industry Distribution   88
4.2   Liquidity Indicator (F2) – Industry Distribution   89
4.3   Stability Indicator (F3) – Industry Distribution   91
4.4   Management Performance Indicator (F4) – Industry Distribution   93
4.5   Growth Indicator (F5) – Industry Distribution   94
4.6   Distribution of ROE and Operating Revenue Growth Rate for
      Companies Listed on the Shanghai Stock Exchange – By
      Industry   96
4.7   Distribution of ROE and Operating Revenue Growth Rate for
      Companies Listed on the Shenzhen Stock Exchange – By
      Industry   97
4.8   Distribution of the Operating Revenue from the Core Business
      for Listed Companies Before and After Stock Market Listing
      on the Shanghai Stock Exchange   102
4.9   Distribution of the Operating Revenue from the Core Business
      for Listed Companies Before and After Stock Market Listing
      on the Shenzhen Stock Exchange   102
4.10 Distribution of Net Profit Growth Rate for Listed Companies
      Before and After Stock Market Listing on the Shanghai Stock
      Exchange   103
4.11 Distribution of Net Profit Growth Rate for Listed Companies
      Before and After Stock Market Listing on the Shenzhen Stock
      Exchange   103
4.12 Distribution of ROE for Listed Companies Before and After
      Stock Market Listing on the Shanghai Stock Exchange   104

4.13 Distribution of ROE for Listed Companies Before and After
      Stock Market Listing on the Shenzhen Stock Exchange   104
4.14 Distribution of EPS for Listed Companies Before and After
      Stock Market Listing on the Shanghai Stock Exchange   105
4.15 Distribution of EPS for Listed Companies Before and After
      Stock Market Listing on the Shenzhen Stock Exchange   105

Tables

1.1	The Transformation of the Financing System in China	4
1.2	Financial Data for Companies with Inadequate Assets	21
2.1	The Development of the Stock Market in China	25
2.2	A-Share Issues	29
2.3	Foreign Capital Raised through B-Share Issues	29
2.4	Issuing of H- and N-Shares	30
2.5	A-Share Market Trading Volume Statistics	31
2.6	A-Share Market Capitalization Statistics	31
2.7	B-Share Market Trading Volume	32
2.8	B-Share Market Capitalization	32
2.9	Equity Structure of Stocks Listed on China's Stock Markets	36
2.10	Distribution of A-Share Investors in 1999	38
2.11	Distribution of B-Share Investors in 1999	38
2.12	Comparison of Share Turnover Rates in Leading Stock Markets	39
2.13	Comparison of Fund and Share Trading on the Shanghai and Shenzhen Stock Exchanges	43
2.14	Chinese Securities and Futures Intermediary Institutions, 1994–99	44
2.15	Capitalization of Securities and Futures Intermediary Companies in China, 1997	46
2.16	Funding Source Structure of Chinese Securities Firms	46
2.17	Regional Distribution of Companies Listed on the Shanghai and Shenzhen Stock Exchanges	49
2.18	Number of Companies Newly Listed on the Shanghai and Shenzhen Stock Exchanges from Each Province, Municipality and Autonomous Region	50
2.19	A Comparison of Listed Companies in the Five Main Industry Sectors	51
3.1	Total Market Capitalization as a Proportion of GDP for Leading Stock Markets	56
3.2	Listed Companies in China – Profits Available for Dividends and Expenses, 1995–98	60
3.3	Risk Prevention Mechanisms Provided for by the Securities Law	70

4.1   Financing Structure of Chinese Enterprises   77
4.2   Sample Data Industry Categories   85
4.3   Chi-square Test Table   99
4.4   ANOVA Testing of the Impact of Stock Market Listing on
      Listed Companies' Operational Performance   100
4.5   ANOVA / LSM Testing of the Impact of Stock Market
      Listing on Listed Companies' Operational Performance   101
5.1   Estimates of the Scale of Foreign Involvement in the A-Share
      Market in China   116
5.2   Sino-American Bilateral Agreement – Agricultural Markets   118
5.3   Sino-American Bilateral Agreement – Industrial Product
      Markets   120
5.4   Sino-American Bilateral Agreement – Service Sector   122
5.5   The Impact of WTO Accession on China's Industries –
      Agriculture   135
5.6   The Impact of WTO Accession on China's Industries –
      Manufacturing and Light Industry   137
5.7   The Impact of WTO Accession on China's Industries –
      Textiles   138
5.8   The Impact of WTO Accession on China's Industries –
      Auto-manufacturing   139
5.9   The Impact of WTO Accession on China's Industries –
      Electromechanical   140
5.10 The Impact of WTO Accession on China's Industries –
      Chemicals   141
5.11 The Impact of WTO Accession on China's Industries –
      Pharmaceuticals   142
5.12 The Impact of WTO Accession on China's Industries –
      Service Industries   143
5.13 The Impact of WTO Accession on China's Industries –
      Telecommunications   144
5.14 The Impact of WTO Accession on China's Industries –
      Software   145
5.15 The Impact of WTO Accession on China's Industries –
      Banking   146
5.16 The Impact of WTO Accession on China's Industries –
      Securities   147
5.17 The Impact of WTO Accession on China's Industries –
      Insurance and Travel   148
5.18 Examples of Listed Companies in Industries which Enjoy
      Comparative Advantage   151

5.19 Examples of Companies with the Ability to Compete
     Successfully in International Markets   152
5.20 Industries and Listed Companies on which WTO Accession
     Will Have a Severe Impact   153

Preface

In the process of institutional transformation, within which China has moved gradually away from a centrally planned economy towards a market economy, the emphasis has been placed on the establishment of a sound system of property rights and a stable financial system. The establishment of the Shanghai Stock Exchange in December 1990 was a landmark in China's institutional transformation. During the continuing period of institutional transformation, if the transformation takes the form of the development of an inefficient system, with informal constraints such as culture, rules and values being difficult to change once formed, they could become an obstacle locking the institution into the original path of evolution. Other institutions displaying better performance would consequently be unable to emerge. An efficient institution can be beneficial to institutional transformation and the spontaneous evolution of society. With this in mind, this book considers the factors relating mainly to institutional change, such as changes in the financing system, the scale and structure of the stock market, operational efficiency and regulatory system of the stock market, operational performance of listed companies and changes in the external environment, such as China's accession into the World Trade Organization (WTO). This is used as the premise for analyzing the development of the stock market in China during the process of institutional transformation.

The book is split into six chapters. Chapter 1 examines the changes in the financing system and the emergence of the stock market under China's institutional transformation. Since 1978, institutional transformation in China has followed a process of gradualism, with the Chinese stock market displaying institutional transformation to an extent, and at a pace of change, rarely seen in the history of the world's stock markets. During the course of its development, the Chinese stock market has experienced speculation, dramatic fluctuations and violations of market regulations, which have been both frequent and of a diverse nature. As such, there is an urgent need for the establishment of a properly ordered and regulated market. As economic reform has progressed, the changes that have already taken place in China's financing system can be broadly divided into three stages – fiscal financing, bank financing and diversified financing. On the basis of the institutional change theory and the formation of the Chinese stock market, the emergence of the stock market can be classified into four stages, namely, the early stages of stock market development (1980–85), the period of development of formal stock market organization (1986–90), the period of systematization of the stock market (1991–95), the period of continued systematization (1996 and beyond).

Chapter 2 discusses the scale and structure of China's stock market. Although A-shares, B-shares and H-shares can all be freely traded, the trading markets for the three types of share are distinct and separate. There is too much speculation, and in the B-share market there is a serious problem with shares being issued at excessively low prices. Equity in the same company is artificially divided into state shares, legal person shares, public shares and internal (employee) shares, all with different rights. Owing to their limited knowledge, lack of experience and restricted access to information, individual investors tend to blindly follow the herd. Furthermore, the large number of securities companies, the small volume of underwriting business available, the lack of variety in products, and the low profit margins, all result in fierce competition between securities firms, leading to low efficiency and disorder. During the process of institutional transformation, the coastal eastern region was the first to be opened up, receiving preferential treatment in terms of being able to attract foreign capital and technology, and with respect to foreign trade, and so on; as a result, companies based in the eastern region account for a higher proportion of the listed companies. However, as more emphasis has come to be placed on the development of the western region, the proportion of companies located in the eastern region that are listed on the Shenzhen and Shanghai stock exchanges has fallen, while the proportion located in the middle and western regions has risen.

Chapter 3 explores the operational efficiency and regulatory system of the Chinese stock market. In this chapter, we investigate the state of development of the stock market in China from the point of view of the level of securitization and the frequency with which shares change hands. As far as the settlement system is concerned, at present, both the Shanghai and Shenzhen stock exchanges have their own independent settlement systems; the huge volume of share registration data involved are divided into two different unconnected systems, thus preventing the sharing of resources. This is not beneficial to the trading and settlement activities of investors and securities firms, as it reduces the efficiency of fund use and affects stock market operation. As far as financing risk disclosure is concerned, although the information disclosure system in China's stock markets is constantly being improved, and has made significant progress, it still has many deficiencies. The factors affecting stock prices are all reflected in the form of information and there is still much room for improvement in China's stock markets in terms of the accuracy, timeliness and openness of disclosure. The fundamental reason for the inefficiency of China's stock market is the weakness of the competitive mechanism, leading to imperfect competition and rent-seeking activity. Furthermore, giving the uneven quality of the participants in China's stock market, there is a need for the establishment of a powerful securities appraisal institution, along with the formation of a securities rating system and the division of shares into different classes, so as to ensure that investors' rights are protected.

Chapter 4 investigates the operational performance of listed companies, discussing first of all the relationship between the stock market and the reform of state-owned enterprises (SOEs), and then establishing financial indicators to evaluate the operational performance of listed companies. The development of the stock market will not only help to expand the financing channels available to enterprises, but it can also change enterprises' ownership structure and internal governance structure. However, there are still many weaknesses in the governance structure of China's SOEs. It is thus insufficient to rely on the development of the stock market to direct the course of SOE reform; this has to be combined with other measures to improve the governance structure of SOEs, and the creation of an environment favorable to privatization, if SOE reform is to provide genuine benefit. For enterprises in China's stock market, listing does not have any particular marked benefits with respect to their operational performance, and in fact operational performance tends to worsen. One of the reasons for this is that, in order to implement the initial public offering and secure stock market listing, companies tend to submit inflated figures in the financial statements they are required to provide; the real situation only begins to gradually unfold after the company has secured listing. Another reason may be the impact of poor corporate governance in Chinese companies. Regardless of whether one looks at the individual financial indicators of profitability, liquidity, stability, management performance and growth, or at a combination of these indicators, the only industries displaying good performance in China are public utilities, transportation and finance; that is to say, China's 'sunrise' industries. With regard to companies' operational performance after stock market listing, viewed on a regional listing basis, it is clear that in terms of management performance and growth indicators, the performance of companies listed on the Shanghai Stock Exchange is noticeably superior to that of companies listed on the Shenzhen Stock Exchange. Comparing the situation with respect to different types of shares, one can see that the growth performance of A-share listed companies is superior to that of B-share listed companies.

Chapter 5 illustrates the impact of China's WTO accession on the stock market, which will vary from industry to industry. Listed companies in labor-intensive and resource-intensive industries, such as textiles, clothing, food, home appliances and the electro-mechanical industry, will benefit considerably; however, they will also find themselves facing fierce competition. WTO accession will have a more serious impact on the more heavily protected agricultural sector and on capital-intensive industries such as autos, instruments, cotton, wheat, and so on.

Nevertheless, WTO accession will not be entirely without benefit to China's stock market. Once China has joined the WTO, listed companies will be able to improve their operational management through their experience of competition, thereby raising their overall competitiveness; those listed companies that lack markets or competitiveness will find themselves removed from the stock market, leaving only those enterprises which display strong performance and profitability. In this way, the overall quality of China's listed companies will rise, and the foundations underpinning the stock market will be strengthened.

Chapter 6 outlines the future trends in the evolution of China's stock market. The establishment of China's stock market and the reform of its operating environment have both been implemented on a gradual basis. The decision was made to rely on 'learning by doing' in the development of the stock market, which has resulted in a lack of concrete, long-term development plans. The trends favoring the development of a sound stock market under institutional transformation are to marketize share issues, introduce multiple level transaction, promote institutional investment and financial innovation, improve financial statements and the quality of listed companies, and subsequently strengthen the legal framework. In terms of globalization of financial markets, China's stock market itself needs to be reformed as rapidly as possible, in order to establish the sound structure and effective systems of the market, and to increase the level of stability by reducing both speculation and risk.

Finally, we would like to express our gratitude to Professor Frank G. Steindl, Regents Professor of Economics and Ardmore Professor of Business Administration, at the Department of Economics, Oklahoma State University for his encouragement and suggestions.

Chien-Hsun Chen and Hui-Tzu Shih

1. Institutional Change and the Stock Market

1.1 Institutional Transformation and the Resultant Changes to the Financing System

The re-establishment of the stock market in China was marked by the opening of the Shanghai Stock Exchange in December 1990, followed soon afterwards, in July 1991, with the establishment of the Shenzhen Stock Exchange. The background to the development of the stock market in China reveals a complex process of institutional transformation; China's stock market is not only a financing system, but it has also played an important part in the country's institutional change, which involved a move away from the former centrally planned economy to the use of market mechanisms for the allocation of resources. The stock market represents a high level of marketization of capital, and its development has come as a result of institutional transformation.

The operation of the stock market and its functions, including financing, allocation of funds, re-allocation of capital, transmission of information, price discovery, performance evaluation, placing of constraints on managers, and so on, comes as a result of the actions of the various different categories of market participants; these participants are themselves constrained by the existing institutions. The institutions have evolved through a process of institutional transformation, and only by careful analysis of this process of institutional transformation in the stock market can one gain an in-depth understanding of market operations and functions.

Market participants include the government, listed companies, investors, securities firms and stock exchanges. Institutional change alters the behavior of market participants, enabling the results and functions of market operations to achieve their expected objectives. As a stock market develops, institutional change comes to play an increasingly important role in the process of market development. Institutional factors have been very important in the development and operation of China's stock market, and institutional analysis therefore constitutes a vital element in the theoretical framework for a study of China's stock market.

North (1991) has suggested that institutions are the key factor in economic

1

growth, and that the presence or absence of an effective institution for increasing individual incentives is the most important element determining economic growth. Efficient organization is based on clear property rights; only when these exist are there any clear incentives for individuals to work and to invest. Institutional innovation derives from anticipated benefits within the existing institutions; these anticipated benefits are produced by the expansion of market scale, the development of new production technology and changes in the cost/benefit structure of existing institutions. However, owing to the need for economies of scale, it is also necessary to deal with the problems created by the internalization of externalities, risk avoidance, market failure, political pressure, and so on, which can create a situation where anticipated benefits cannot be achieved within the existing institution. Some people will take the lead in trying to overcome these obstacles in order to achieve the anticipated benefits. When the anticipated benefits are greater than the anticipated costs created by the obstacles, institutional innovation will occur.

Institutional transformation is also affected by the phenomenon of path dependence. When path dependence occurs based upon technological change, the adoption of the new technology often leads to a dramatic increase in returns. Assuming that the marginal return increases significantly, a self-enforcing mechanism will develop as a result of the following factors: (i) As output increases, the unit cost of large-scale fixed investment will fall; (ii) The learning effect; (iii) The coordination effect resulting from the adoption of similar technology by different producers; and (iv) The anticipation of further developments in fashion. Given that those technologies which are developed earlier can benefit from first-mover advantage, the companies which are able to develop a self-enforcing mechanism will have the advantage over competitors, otherwise potentially superior technology which is developed later may not be adopted by enough people, creating a vicious circle, or even a lock-in situation (Arthur, 1989).

North (1991, 1994) argues that path dependence also exists in institutional transformation. When institutions are characterized by rapidly increasing returns, the self-enforcing mechanism can exist within institutional change. In this way, the evolution of an institution can have one of two markedly different results. On the one hand, it may create a virtuous circle with rapid growth; on the other hand, it may lead to lock-in in an inefficient institution, resulting in decline and economic stagnation.

Unlike the shock therapy used in Russia, where price controls and interest rate controls were completely abolished, and wholesale privatization implemented, the institutional transformation of China since 1978 has followed the path of gradualism. Institutional transformation requires adjustment to household and enterprise behavior; gradual reform has the advantage of permitting gradual improvement and learning by doing, which makes it easier for households and enterprises to adjust their behavior. This is why institutional transformation has been more successful in China than in Russia (Smyth, 1998; Lau et al., 2000).

Since its establishment, the Chinese stock market has undergone institutional transformation of an extent and frequency rarely seen in the history of the world's stock markets. Institutions regulate human behavior, and human behavior decides how markets operate. This means that frequent changes in institutions are bound to result in frequent changes in the behavior of market participants, thereby also causing frequent change in the characteristics of market operation.

The establishment of efficient systems is an urgent problem facing China's stock market. During the course of its development, the Chinese stock market has experienced speculation, dramatic fluctuations and violations of market regulations, which have been both frequent and of a diverse nature. There is an urgent need for the establishment of a properly ordered and regulated market. Besides the need to establish formal regulations, there is also a need to cultivate informal rules, and to establish a strong mechanism for system implementation.

Analysis of the course of development of China's securities markets reveals that the bond market was the first to develop. The establishment of the Shanghai Stock Exchange in December 1990 was a major landmark in the development of the stock markets. As the various ancillary measures were established, the calls for the development of a direct financing market became increasingly vociferous; the stock market began to flourish and to develop rapidly within a very short space of time.[1] The development of B-shares (1992) and H-shares (1993), which foreign investors are permitted to purchase, subsequently helped to make the market more diversified. If we use market capitalization as a proportion of GDP to measure the level of securitization, we can see that in 1996 and 1997 the total market capitalization (A-shares) of the Shanghai and Shenzhen stock exchanges combined, came to Renminbi (RMB) 984.237 billion, accounting for 14.57 percent of GDP; in 1997, the figure reached RMB1,752.923 billion, 23.44 percent of GDP.[2] If one compares these figures with the 1992 figure of 3.93 percent, one can see how rapid the pace of growth had been. Although this is still significantly lower than the 54 percent level of securitization in the advanced nations, it is higher than the average level for developing nations (15 percent). In November 1999, agreement was finally reached on the bilateral negotiations between China and the USA, which augurs for even greater openness and transparency in China's stock market in the future. In order to gain a more in-depth understanding of the development of China's stock market, we will explore the changes in China's financing system, so as to be able to better understand the background to the transformation of the stock market. We will then go on to analyze the current state of development of China's stock market and the problems affecting it, so as to clarify the special characteristics of, and level of risk within, China's stock market.

As economic reform has progressed, the changes that have occurred in China's financing system can be broadly divided into three stages, fiscal financing, bank financing and diversified financing (see Table 1.1).

Table 1.1   The Transformation of the Financing System in China

	Planned economy 1952–78	Period of institutional transformation		
		1979–84	1985–92	1993–date
Fiscal financing system	Enjoys absolute dominance	Still dominant	Steady fall in the percentage of total financing provided by this system	Percentage of financing provided by this system continues to fall
Bank financing system	Banks provide small quantities of short-term loans to meet cash-flow and seasonal liquidity needs	Rapid development; the percentage of total financing provided by banks increases steadily	Dominant	Although the percentage of financing provided by banks is falling, bank financing remains dominant
Diversified financing system (securities financing)	Prohibited	Incubation stage	Small-scale; still getting off the ground	Rapid development, and becoming increasingly important

Source: Zhang, Changcai (1999).

1.1.1 Fiscal Financing

During the period of the centrally planned economy (1952–78), the financing system was dominated by fiscal financing. Only a limited amount of bank financing was permitted in order to meet short-term cash flow and seasonal liquidity needs.   Under the centrally planned economy, public finance was the main vehicle for the allocation of national income. Not only did the funding for administration, national defense, education and health derive from government allocation, funding for the economy and for the support of agriculture also derived from the government. Funds were concentrated at the government level before being distributed for the use of state-owned enterprises and individuals, in a classic example of a financing system dominated by fiscal financing (see Figure 1.1).

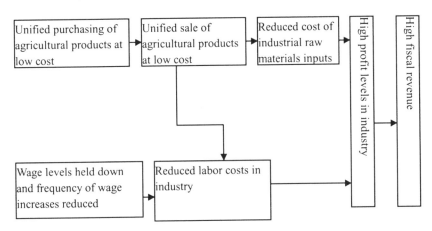

Source: Xu (1997).

Figure 1.1   The Fiscal Revenue Mechanism under the Centrally Planned Economy

Wages were held down under the centrally planned economy, while the income levels of urban and rural residents were determined by the disparity between the price of industrial and agricultural products, with the implementation of forced saving. In accordance with the 'unified revenue and unified expenditure' system, state-owned enterprises transferred all their profits upwards to the government; the funds were then distributed among the various industries and sectors requiring investment.

All investment activities were decided in accordance with government planning, and capital flows were not decided by the market. All investment derived from government allocation; banks merely provided small amounts of loans to meet state-owned enterprises' cash flow needs. The government was the largest savings entity, while also being the largest investment entity.

Over the period 1958 to 1978, fiscal revenue accounted, on average, for 37.2 percent of total national income. During this same period, 84 percent of the funds needed for capital investment by state-owned enterprises were provided from the national budget, in most cases requiring no repayment (Wang, Jianguo 1999).

The methods used for fiscal financing can be divided into: (i) Allocation from the national budget. Under the centrally planned economy, funds were allocated in accordance with the 'unified revenue and unified expenditure' system, with no repayment required; (ii) Government loans. Since there is no repayment requirement for capital investment included within the national budget, return on investment tended to be low and the government has found itself under a heavy fiscal burden. Beginning in 1979, a system was implemented on a trial basis in Shanghai and other provincial and municipal governments, whereby capital investment allocation was replaced by bank loans. By 1985, bank loans had replaced allocation throughout the country; however, this method ceased to be used in 1996; (iii) Investment instead of loans. Under this system, government investment was conducted through government-authorized investment companies, asset management companies, business groups, and so on; (iv) Policy-type bank loans. Policy banks in China (the State Development Bank of China, Agricultural Development Bank of China and Export-Import Bank of China) do not exist to make profits, but rather to implement the nation's economic policy, and furthermore, their fund sources are of a fiscal nature; (v) Special capital investment projects not included in the budget; and (vi) Fiscal subsidies (Zhang, Changcai 1999, pp. 46–8).

As both saving and investment were directed by the government, there were no problems regarding financing between those sectors making a profit and those making a loss. Under the fiscal financing system, the forced saving measures ensured that a high savings ratio could be maintained. In reality, the government's forced savings provided a guarantee of the future livelihood of China's citizens; government savings represented the funds required for housing of citizens, hospital care, pensions, education and unemployment benefit. The cost of fiscal financing was the obligation to provide these services and guarantees for the nation's citizens. Under the system of public ownership of property rights, state-owned enterprise financing was treated as cost-free funding, which made the efficiency of fund use even lower.

1.1.2 Bank Financing

The liberalization of the economic reform that began in 1979 led to changes in the national income allocation system which had previously been dominated by fiscal financing. The proportion of national income accounted for by central government fiscal revenue fell steadily and the national income structure was transformed into one in which wealth was concentrated among the people. The savings rate of China's citizens rose from 14.9 percent in 1978 to 56.2 percent in 1996; over this same period the government savings rate fell from 73.4 percent to 3.3 percent. The people became the main source of saving in society, while enterprises became the main source of investment. Financing between the capital-surplus sector (citizens) and the capital-deficit sector (enterprises) relied on specialized state-owned banks and the government continued to exercise control over the allocation of funds through the high level of control imposed on the four main state-owned banks (the Industrial and Commercial Bank of China, the Agricultural Bank of China, the Bank of China and the People's Construction Bank of China).

The fall in government revenue meant that the government was no longer in a position to meet the financing needs of state-owned enterprises; instead, they shifted over to a system of 'replacing allocation with loans' and gradually reduced the fiscal subsidies for loss-making state-owned enterprises so that state-owned enterprise financing became increasingly dependent on state-owned banks. However, the institutional transformation whereby state-owned banks became the main intermediary for financing resulted in many abuses, including: (i) Public ownership of property rights and soft budget constraints meant that state-owned enterprises did not take the cost of loans into consideration, and as a result, state-owned enterprises became heavily indebted; the average debt ratio for state-owned enterprises reached 70–80 percent, the vast majority of which was accounted for by loans from state-owned banks; and (ii) Being responsible for the making of policy loans, state-owned banks have some fiscal policy functions; since both state-owned banks and state-owned enterprises are owned by the state, moral hazard is created and as a result, the state-owned banks have accumulated large quantities of bad debts.

1.1.3 Diversified Financing

The reform of China's economic institutions requires the simultaneous establishment of an effective financial system. The long-standing reliance on the government and state-owned banks for financing of enterprises has to be changed, to create a situation in which the allocation function of production factor (capital) is determined by the market mechanism, and enterprises can engage in diversified financing in the market in accordance with their own needs. This diversified financing system takes the form of securities financing.

Since the early 1990s, China's stock market has developed rapidly and has assumed a particularly important role in the reform of state-owned enterprises.

As at the end of 1999, there were a total of 949 enterprises listed on the Shanghai and Shenzhen stock exchanges, and the combined market capitalization of the two exchanges accounted for 31.82 percent of GDP. With the rapid increase in the proportion of financing, the formation and expansion of enterprise capital has increasingly come to depend on the capital markets, and the stock market in particular. The diversified financing system will play the leading role in future institutional transformation.

1.2 The Emergence of the Stock Market in China

On the basis of the aforementioned institutional change theory and the formation of the Chinese stock market, the emergence of the stock market can be classified into four stages:[3]

1.2.1 The Early Stages of Stock Market Development (1980–85)

The implementation of the household responsibility system in 1979 led to a revitalization of the agricultural economy. Farmers' incomes rose, and the funds available to local governments, enterprises and individuals increased, creating an urgent need for investment channels. As enterprises gained more autonomy and as the reform of the investment system progressed, there was a pressing need for funds for innovation and development. As a result, a new financing system came into being. In order to deal with the problem of the shortage of funds, enterprise often sought to obtain funds internally from their employees, or made use of the issuing of corporate bonds. China's stock market thus developed gradually from the accumulation of capital within society and the issuing of corporate bonds.

In 1980, the Fushun Branch of the People's Bank of China issued shares on behalf of enterprises to the value of RMB2.11 million. This was the first recorded issuing of shares since the reform began. In July 1983, the Joint Investment Company of Baoan County in Shenzhen Municipality issued share certificates in Shenzhen. In July 1984, the Tianqiao Department Store of Beijing commissioned the Beijing Branch of the Industrial and Commercial Bank of China to issue shares on its behalf. In November 1984, the Fei Yue Stereo Company of Shanghai commissioned the Jingan Securities Division of the Shanghai Investment and Trust Company (a subsidiary of the Industrial and Commercial Bank of China) to issue irredeemable shares to the public on its behalf. Furthermore, when Yanzhong Enterprises of Shanghai was established in January 1985, its entire capital was raised through the issuing of shares to the general public.

During this period, in addition to Beijing, Shanghai and Shenzhen, the raising of capital through the issuing of shares also occurred in other parts of China such as Shenyang and Wuhan, raising the curtain on the development of the stock market in China. However, at that time, a comprehensive, properly regulated stock market had not been established. The main characteristics of China's stock market during this period were as follows: (i) The scale of issue and value of shares issued were low, for example, only RMB500,000 worth of Fei Yueh Stereo Company shares were issued; (ii) The majority of shares were issued internally within a company; (iii) Many of the shares issued had similar characteristics to bonds. The purpose of issuing the shares was to raise capital; investors could resell the shares back to the company at any time with all shares being repurchased by the company after a fixed period of time; for example, the shares issued by the Tianqiao Department Store were to be bought back after three years, with dividends to be paid every year. If the company made a profit, investors would receive a share of this; however, the shares could not be transferred; and (iv) Different categories of shares conferred different rights. Revenue allocation varied between corporate shareholders and individual shareholders, with individual shareholders having a higher earnings ratio than corporate shareholders; in some cases there was no provision for profit-sharing for the shares held by corporate shareholders.

Some of the ways in which institutional change occurred in this period were as follows. (i) Change in the incentive system. During this period, apart from the government bond market, there was no active promotion of stock market development by the government. The institution developed in an entirely voluntary manner, based on a change in the incentive system whereby the anticipated benefit was larger than the anticipated cost; (ii) Market regulation was dominated by informal constraints. No formal regulation system had yet been established within the securities financing system; for example, the legal framework had not been established. The raising of capital from society and the issuing of individual stocks was mainly affected by custom, tradition and other informal constraints; (iii) Instability with respect to market system change. During this period, since the anticipated benefits were affected by the system of a centrally planned economy and by the lack of clarity regarding ownership rights, the change to the market system was characterized by instability. In those regions where the market had reached a more mature stage of development, the securities financing system was more stable; (iv) The market system had only one function. The stock market financing system was limited to operating as a market of issue; there was no trading market, and financing was the main function of the market. Furthermore, there was no fixed group of investors, and the purpose of the system was unclear; it appeared to be mainly intended to secure profits from speculation; and (v) The operating costs of the market system were high. Owing to a lack of market knowledge and of the necessary techniques, the cost of implementing the new system was relatively high. Furthermore, the appearance of the stock market financing system led to conflict with the bank financing system, resulting in friction costs. Since the market organization was not yet properly formed, market transactions and behavior displayed a lack of order and organization, with high operating costs.

1.2.2   The Period of Development of Formal Stock Market Organization (1986–90)

During the course of institution transformation, the establishment of new systems may either be voluntary or arranged by the government. The stock market in China did not develop naturally in the way that it did in the advanced nations of the West; instead, its development was arranged by the Chinese government. The main role of the government was in the following areas: (i) Providing plans for systemic change and undertaking the creation of a stock market financing system; (ii) Promoting the change from private contracts to formal contracts; and (iii) Establishing property rights, reducing the implementation costs of the new system and improving the efficiency of the new system. In this way, the change in the Chinese stock market ceased to be incentive-based change and instead became compulsory.

As China's financial markets developed, specialized intermediary institutions began to appear. In 1985, approval was given for the establishment of China's first securities firm – the Shenzhen Special Economic Zone Securities Company. In 1987, in line with the process of financial reform and the development of the capital markets, the People's Bank of China (PBC) approved the establishment of financing companies in most provinces, autonomous regions, municipalities and the planned autonomous cities. A total of 38 financing companies were established throughout China; at the same time, stock market intermediary institutions were also developing rapidly. By the end of 1989, there were a total of 1,563 stock market intermediary institutions in China, including 63 securities firms, 743 over-the-counter (OTC) exchanges, and 757 securities transaction centers.

The motivation for institutional innovation was to reduce transaction costs, and the constant innovation in the stock market financing system in China can be seen as the result of the desire to achieve this aim. The transition from a dispersed OTC transaction system to a stock market based on stock exchanges was a milestone in the transformation of the stock market system, which was able to significantly reduce the transaction costs accompanying dispersed trading. By the end of 1990, there were 26 securities management institutions in Shanghai (including the stock exchange), as well as over 50 OTC transaction points. The total value of all securities issued, including government bonds, exceeded RMB10 billion, and more than 30 kinds of product had been launched; the total transaction volume came to over RMB3.5 billion.

The development of the Shanghai stock market during this period can be divided into three stages: (i) The initial stage (1984 – November 1986). In order to meet the financing needs of new business groups, corporate bonds and shares appeared in Shanghai once again. By the end of 1986, more than 1,500 enterprises in Shanghai had issued corporate bonds or shares, at a total value of RMB247 million. Beginning on 26 September 1986, the Jingan Securities Division (Shanghai) of the Industrial and Commercial Bank of China began to handle re-sale of shares for Yen Zhong Enterprises Ltd. and Fei Yue Stereo Ltd., although the transaction volume was less than RMB200,000; (ii) The formation stage (December 1986 – March 1988). During this stage, large and medium-sized enterprises began to become involved in the stock market. By the end of 1987, more than 1,700 companies in Shanghai had issued corporate bonds or shares, with a total value of over RMB1.7 billion. Eight securities trading points and agencies had been established in the city, and an OTC exchange was beginning to develop; (iii) The development stage (April 1988–90). The issue and transfer of treasury bonds began and these gradually became the main player in the secondary market. By the end of 1990, Shanghai had 25 securities management institutions, and more than 50 trading points throughout the city.

The development of the Shenzhen stock market can also be divided into two stages: (i) The initial stage (1987 – early 1990). When shares were first issued for Shenzhen Development Bank, the reaction of the public was muted; of the 500,000 available shares, only 79 percent were sold. Share sales also failed to reach the anticipated level with the issuing of shares in Wan Ke Ltd. at the end of 1988. The stock market did not start to take off until the first half of 1989, when the operational performance of several listed companies improved, and significant dividends were announced; (ii) The period of overheating (May 1990 – November 1990). The improving performance of listed companies meant that investing in shares now offered higher rewards. Furthermore, since the commodity market was weak and bank interest rates had fallen, society's capital began to flow into the stock market, causing share prices to rise.

1.2.3 The Period of Systematization of the Stock Market (1991–95)

1991 to 1995 was the period in which China's stock market became systematized. During this period, China established a system for joint stock company operation and the fundamental systems required by the stock market. Systems, which can be divided into formal and informal constraints, provide the 'rules of the game' for relations between people. With institutional change, informal constraints become more prevalent and affect the formation of formal constraints. A similar process occurred in the development of the stock market systems in China. During the evolution of the stock market over the period 1981 to 1991, while there were clear systems governing the issuing of government bonds, there had been no comprehensive, formal systems established to control the stock transaction market and the issuing of shares and bonds. Traditions and habitual ways of doing things were dominant; in other words, the market was dominated by informal constraints.

During the course of the market's evolution, a major effort was made to promote the formation of market organization; however, the stock market became regionalized and dispersed and a national market covering the whole of China did not develop. The period 1991 to 1992 was a period of rapid change in China's stock market systems. Changes occurred in stock market trading, settlement and the issuing of news, resulting in significant improvements in operational efficiency. These changes also made themselves felt in the following areas: (i) Share settlement gradually became more centralized, standardized and computerized; (ii) Share transactions gradually became characterized by computer inputting and automatic matching; and (iii) The issuing of news began to be more carefully regulated.

Formal constraints can increase the efficiency of informal constraints, reducing the costs of news issuing, monitoring and implementation. Formal constraints can also be used to revise and substitute for informal constraints, therefore it was inevitable that China's stock market would become more systematized. By the end of 1991, China's stock market already incorporated a comprehensive range of economic organizations including joint stock companies, investors, intermediary institutions and stock exchanges. These economic organizations were bound to take action, putting forward proposals for further institutional change, thereby bringing about the creation of formal institutional constraints. The scale of the stock market gradually expanded: over the period 1991 to 1995 the total number of shares issued came to 24.41 billion, with a total of RMB95.166 billion being raised. The cumulative transaction volume in the secondary market came to RMB1.6642 trillion, with market capitalization increasing from RMB3.058 billion in 1990 to RMB347.462 billion by 1995.

Also during this period, in October 1992, the State Council Securities Committee and the China Securities Regulatory Commission (CSRC) were established, creating a unified supervisory system for the stock market. In addition, a series of laws and regulations were introduced. These included the regulations governing alteration of the joint stock system and enterprise assets and accounting standards promulgated in 1992, and the Notification Concerning Improved Management of the Securities Market issued on 17 December 1992. In 1993, as part of the rectification of the financial system and the campaign against corruption, rectification was undertaken of the holding of shares by company employees in their own company, whilst government officials at county government level and above were also prohibited from buying and selling shares. On 22 April 1993, the Provisional Regulations Governing the Management of Share Issue and Trading were promulgated and came into effect. In June 1993, the government promulgated the Detailed Regulations Governing the Implementation of Disclosure by Companies Undertaking a Public Offering. On 7 July 1993, the Regulations Governing the Management of Shareholding by Company Employees were promulgated. In August 1993, the government promulgated the Regulations Governing the Actions of Securities and Exchanges Regulatory Commission Personnel. On 2 September 1993, the government announced the Provisional Regulations Governing the Preventing of Securities Fraud. In December 1993, the government formulated the Provisional Regulations Governing Share Allotment by Listed Companies. On 1 July 1994, the first series of sub-statutes under the Company Law came into effect, completing the initial stages of the establishment of the regulatory system and legal framework for China's stock market.

The changes occurring in China's stock market during this period can broadly be divided into the following categories: (i) Initially, the issuing of shares and subsequent transactions in them developed spontaneously from the actions of market participants. That is to say, the establishment of the stock market system was not wholly a compulsory process; (ii) The main motive force for change in the stock market system was citizens' desire to invest and their search for profits; (iii) The reduction of transaction costs was the fundamental reason for the replacement of one system by another. The reason that the black market was able to continue to exist after July 1990, and in fact succeeded in becoming the main exchange, was because it offered lower transaction costs than the OTC exchanges; (iv) The process whereby the stock market developed more systematic organization confirmed the division of labor between the securities industry and the banking industry. At the same time, as the organization of the stock market became more systematic, a legal framework was established for the stock market, and formal constraints gradually became dominant; and (v) Since the establishment of the Shanghai and Shenzhen stock exchanges, in terms of their transaction network, listed companies or investor, these have come to cover the whole country, providing China with a unified transaction system. Owing to this expansion of the Shanghai and Shenzhen stock exchanges and its whole country coverage, as well as the spread of modern communication technology making it possible to meet the needs of the stock market, there is no longer any need to establish another stock exchange; the direction which the future development of the stock market in China will take has thus been determined.

1.2.4 The Period of Continued Systematization (1996 and beyond)

Following the processes of organizational development and systematization, the general path of development of China's stock market system has already become clear. Path dependence determines the form taken by social, political and economic evolution in different countries. As a result of path dependence, as soon as institutional change moves onto a particular path, the self-enforcing mechanism will ensure that it stays on that path.

In terms of policy, the Chinese stock market has constantly displayed the regulatory dialectic whereby regulation begets more regulation. Generally speaking, after a period of development there is a need to clear up the structural problems that have accumulated; this is frequently implemented through regulatory policy. China is currently faced with the need to undertake a clear-up following the major expansion of the stock market that has occurred since 1996; for example, restrictions will be placed on listed companies' illicit funds and illicit operation (Fei et al., 2001a).

The characteristics of institutional change during the period of continued systematization have included the following: (i) Market development has continued to progress steadily, with market scale continuing to expand. Taking 1997 as an example, the total number of shares issued came to 26.383 billion, with a total of RMB132.5 billion being raised (equivalent to the total amount raised over the period 1991 to 1996). By 2000, China's stock market was expanding even more rapidly. During the period January to June 2000, a total of RMB82.25 billion was raised on the Shanghai and Shenzhen stock markets, with accumulated transaction volume coming to RMB349.67 billion, or 1.1 times the total transaction volume for the whole of 1999 (Ma, 2000); (ii) While market scale has been expanding, in order to prevent and ease market risk, there has been a further strengthening of market regulation; (iii) The Chinese stock market is formed by the Shanghai and Shenzhen stock exchanges; these two exchanges have maintained a relationship which combines competition with collaboration; and (iv) The systematization of the stock market has benefited the reform of the state-owned enterprises.

During this period, the most important examples of the implementation and on-going promotion of government measures, as well as the establishment of market regulations, have included the following:

Improvement of corporate governance among listed companies

On 26 March 1999, the China Securities Regulatory Commission promulgated the Suggestions as to How Companies Listed Overseas Can Further Improve Disclosure, whereby companies are now required to strictly fulfill their obligation to implement disclosure in accordance with the relevant regulations both in China and in the countries where they are listed. It was emphasized that all company directors will be required to bear an obligation with respect to honesty, to familiarize themselves with listing requirements both in China and overseas, to work to increase transparency within their company, and to improve the quality of information disclosure.[4] On 29 March that same year, the State Economic and Trade Commission and the China Securities Regulatory Commission issued a joint Opinion on the Further Promotion of Regulation of and Deepening of Reform of Companies Listed Overseas. The main provisions were as follows: (i) A company's management and its parent holding company must be separated. A holding company should exercise its shareholders' rights largely through the shareholders' meeting, in accordance with lawful procedures. The company's structures, and in particular the board of directors, management, finance and sales divisions should be independent from the holding company; (ii) There should be further reorganization of holding companies and the companies they control. Once the main business and assets of a state-owned holding company have been brought into the company, the responsibilities of the holding company should be gradually transferred or merged into another state-owned corporate entity. If, in addition to companies, a holding company owns other assets or businesses, they should reduce transactions among associates involving the companies, and avoid intra-industry competition. Holding companies' social functions and non-management assets should be gradually spun off, using auctions, mergers, transfers to local government, inclusion within the local social security system, and so on, in order to achieve efficient management; (iii) Company decision-making procedures need to be clarified, with a strengthening of the responsibilities of board directors; (iv) Companies should gradually establish a sound system of external board directors and independent board directors. Companies should increase the proportion of external board directors when the board is re-selected — external board directors should account for at least 50 percent of the seats on the board, and there should be at least two independent board directors (directors who are independent from the company's shareholders and do not hold positions within the company). Independent board directors should be able to report directly to the shareholders' meeting, the China Securities Regulatory Commission and other relevant agencies; (v) The secretary of the board should be able to properly fulfill the functions of the appointment; (vi) Enterprises should be kept separate from the government, with clear regulation of the relationship between shareholders and the company. The administrative subordination between companies and government agencies should be eliminated, and companies should be kept fully separate from the government with respect to assets, finance, personnel management, etc. Government agencies should not interfere in companies' production and management, nor should they require companies to pay them management fees or regulation fees of any kind. No shareholder agency or their representatives may go over the head of the shareholders' meeting to interfere in the company's production or management, or to appoint or remove the company's senior managers; and (vii) The stock market should be developed on the basis of properly regulated foundations, with a strengthening of stock market regulation. On 8 April 1999, the China Securities Regulatory Commission issued the Guidelines Regarding the Work of the Secretary of the Board of Directors of Companies Listed Overseas, which laid down regulations governing the status, main responsibilities, qualifications, scope of responsibility and legal obligations of the secretary of the board of directors (Wu, 2001).

Reduction in state-held shares

Attempts have been made to reduce the number of state-held shares using various different methods. These methods fall into seven broad categories: sale by allocation; buy-back; negotiated transfer; conversion of state-held shares to preferred stock; additional allocation; conversion to bonds; and the establishment of state-held share investment funds. At the end of 1999, an attempt was made to sell off the state-held shares in Zhongguo Jialing and Qian Tires through the sale by allocation method; however, as a result of pricing problems, the final results were far from ideal. Shen Neng provides a successful example of buy-back of state-held shares; however, the method of buy-back used placed severe restrictions on the listed company, highlighting the fact that this method is not universally applicable. Although there were a considerable number of examples of negotiated transfer of state-held shares in the stock market in 2000, this constituted only a superficial solution to the problem; it has not solved the fundamental problem of the liquidity of state-held shares. Planning is already underway to establish funds for reducing holdings of state-held shares; it can be anticipated that the establishment of these funds will constitute a major new effort to solve this problem in 2001 (Yang et al., 2001). On 11 June 2001, the China Securities Regulatory Commission announced that when listed companies issue additional shares, they must sell state-held shares equivalent to 10 percent of the total financing amount, in accordance with Article 5 of the Provisional Regulations for Reducing Holdings of State-held Shares. As a result of this measure, the stock market continued to fall; the China Securities Regulatory

Commission therefore announced on 22 October 2001 that implementation of this measure to reduce holdings of state-held shares was being suspended.

Provision of assistance for the listing of bank companies
In November 2000, the China Securities Regulatory Commission promulgated Parts One to Six of the Regulations Governing Disclosure for Companies Issuing Securities, which included special provisions regarding disclosure by financial enterprises for listing purposes. These Regulations helped to eliminate the obstacles to listing by banks. Not long after this, on 27 November, Minsheng Bank issued A-shares on the Shanghai Stock Exchange to the value of RMB350 million, thereby becoming the third bank in China to secure stock market listing (after Shenzhen Development Bank in 1991 and Pudong Development Bank in 1999).

Establishment of a new board for start-ups
The main obstacles currently affecting the development of China's high-tech industries are the fact that 80 percent of research results cannot be commercialized, and the fact that high-tech enterprises lack the funds they need to develop (Wang, Guoming 2001). The stock market has therefore established a new board for start-ups, targeting enterprises in high-risk industries. In mid-October 2000, the Shenzhen Stock Exchange announced that it would no longer accept new applications for A-share listing. At the same time, the Exchange published a series of consultancy documents entitled Market Rules for the Start-up Board, and subsequently announced that the technical preparations for the establishment of the new board had been completed. Once the new board has been established, in the primary market the new board and the main board will be sharing the market resources – potential listed companies. In the secondary market, the new board will be able to share some of the funds that would otherwise have gone to the main board. Furthermore, the new board is bound to serve as a model for the main board, and to create a diffusion effect, promoting the marketization of the main board's market (Mao, 2000). However, the new board for start-ups will still be affected by the management and technical risk affecting listed companies, moral hazard affecting listed companies, the risk of market manipulation and market operation risk (Wang, Kaiguo 2001).

If a new board for start-ups were to be created immediately, it would be established in Shenzhen, operating independently and taking the Growth Enterprise Market (GEM) board in Hong Kong as its model. In principle, the new board would not commence operation until a reasonable number of stocks had been secured for listing; it is possible that the board could begin operations by 2002. The existing Shanghai and Shenzhen stock exchanges can be expected to merge into a single main board (located in Shanghai) at some suitable point in the future. The main barriers to the establishment of the new board are the obstacles created by existing laws and regulations,[5] as well as inability to obtain the necessary legal protection; for example, the Regulations Governing the Issuing of Shares by Start-ups and the details of implementation for these regulations have yet to be promulgated.

On the basis of the information already available to the public, we can gain some idea of what a future new board for start-ups would look like. The board would target mainly high-tech enterprises and fast-growing small and medium enterprises (SMEs) in China. The threshold for listing would be relatively low, with the requirements in terms of total equity, scale of tangible assets, operational performance, and so on, being significantly lower than those of the main board. The qualifications for listing would be objective with simple review procedures; any enterprise which met the legal requirements for listing would be able to have an application for listing made directly by the public offering review committee formed of market experts. All equity would have full liquidity, in conformity with the principle of equal rights for the same shares. A guarantee system would be implemented, and disclosure obligations enhanced.

However, if in the process of reconstructing the stock market system, the protection of investors' rights is not adopted as the core element in market development, and instead, consideration is given only to supporting start-ups and providing an exit channel for venture capital, then the situation which occurred with the main board of 'shares for cash' would be repeated; investors' rights and confidence will gradually be eroded, and the new board would find itself in the embarrassing situation of having become as unpopular as new boards in other countries. The establishment of a new board will require a rigorous regulatory mechanism, with a higher level of regulation, stricter disclosure requirements, and more expected of listed companies. In this way, the abuses which have occurred with the main board can be mitigated on the new board, with the strengthening of regulation, prevention of excessive speculation, elimination of illicit market manipulation and the establishment of a mechanism whereby listed companies can withdraw, and the implementation of genuine marketization (Zhang and Liu, 2000; Yang and Wang, 2000; Yang et al., 2001).

Although the date for the launching of the second board has not yet been finalized, almost 2,000 companies are already planning to list on it (*Commercial Times*, 22 August 2000). Of these, the increasingly popular venture capital firms will be the most important element in the new board.[6] A considerable number of companies which have already listed on the main board are also interested in listing on the new board; however, the operational guidelines for the new board (which are constantly being revised) list seven categories of company which will not be permitted to list on it.[7] If this regulation is actually implemented, then many of the types of enterprise noted above will not be able to secure listing on the new board.

Opening up of the B-share market to domestic investors

On 20 February 2001, the China Securities Regulatory Commission made an announcement concerning the opening up of the B-share market to domestic investors. The B-share market was originally established for foreign investors; however, in reality domestic investors have come to dominate the market. The main reasons for this are as follows. Firstly, foreign investors and domestic investors have different attitudes. Foreign investors are used to a mature market environment, and to investing under highly regulated conditions. They tend to adopt a pessimistic attitude towards the various problems that affect China's stock market and to regard the level of risk as being too high; they have therefore tended to gradually withdraw from the B-share market. Chinese investors have grown up together with the market, and are accustomed to the high level of risk. When the B-share market offers a lower level of risk than the A-share market, they seek to enter the B-share market. Secondly, domestic and foreign investors have a different level of understanding of the political environment in China. Foreign investors often take a passive attitude towards government policy in China, whereas domestic investors, having been in the environment for an extended period, are able to take a more proactive attitude towards changes in government policy; they are often able to accurately forecast changes in government policy and are therefore more willing to risk investing in the B-share market.[8]

The opening up of the B-share market to domestic investors will affect China's stock market in three ways. Firstly, injecting additional vitality into the B-share market will facilitate the stable development of the stock market. Secondly, opening up the market will align the prices of A- and B-shares, thereby promoting the unification of the two markets. Thirdly, at present the choice of financial products available to Chinese investors is still very limited; this is particularly true for those citizens with foreign currency to invest. Opening up the B-share market will therefore provide investors with more choice and will help to spread risk and allow more people to benefit from the profits made by foreign-owned companies. In addition, the opening up of the B-share market will help in the process of making the stock market more tightly regulated.

Owing to the differences in the institutional environment for A-shares and B-shares, differences in investor attitudes and differences in the external environment, the two types of share display different prices, different rights, different dividends and the use of different accounting systems, creating an abnormal situation. The opening up of the B-share market should gradually solve these problems, helping put the Chinese stock market on the path towards properly regulated development (Jin, 2001).

The establishment of a de-listing mechanism

The establishment of a sound mechanism for de-listing would help to separate successful listed companies from those that have not been so successful, and would improve listed companies' operational performance. The China Securities Regulatory Commission and the Shanghai and Shenzhen stock exchanges have launched special treatment (ST) and particular treatment (PT) systems. The ST system is applied to those companies within which financial or other abnormalities have occurred for two consecutive years, such that it is difficult for investors to judge what the company's future prospects are, thereby creating a risk that investors' rights will be affected. The PT system is applied to those companies within which financial or other abnormalities have taken place for three consecutive years; the aim is to use restrictions on daily price fluctuation and trading time to prevent excessive speculation. However, the ST and PT systems only restrict trading in the stocks of companies within these specific categories; no comprehensive system of de-listing has been established in order to deal with cases where a company's operational performance continues to worsen, or where a serious violation of the law has occurred. Furthermore, the legal framework for securities business and other relevant legislation is not comprehensive, and since regulation is not sufficiently rigorous, this means that there is a serious problem in the stock market with respect to violations of regulations, and that it has not been possible to eradicate the danger of excessive speculation (Yuan, 2001).

Only when a sound de-listing system has been established, with a proper de-listing mechanism, supplemented with a rigorous regulation and penalty system, will it be possible to effectively prevent agency problems and bring the management of companies' within the scope of regulation, so that the operations of listed companies can be regulated and systematized. However, at present there is still a serious problem of over-emphasizing listing and not paying sufficient attention to de-listing. Although regulations have been established specifying the circumstances under which companies should be de-listed, with the exception of the temporary de-listing of Qiong Minyuan and the voluntary de-listing of Su Sanshan, in reality listing has been a permanent affair. The market has been full of companies with poor operational performance which should have been de-listed, creating a situation where 'bad money drives out good'. At present, many companies listed on the Shanghai and Shenzhen stock exchanges have debt ratios of 70 percent or higher and some companies' annual profits are insufficient even to meet the interest payments on their debt (Chen, Zhengrong 2001). Table 1.2 provides financial data on companies that have implemented asset restructuring for three consecutive years and yet still have insufficient assets to match their liabilities.

Table 1.2 Financial Data for Companies with Inadequate Assets

Name of company	Net assets per share (RMB)			Earnings per share (RMB)			Shareholders' equity (RMB million)		
	1998	1999	2000	1998	1999	2000	1998	1999	2000
PT Nong Shang She	-1.56	-7.73	-8.19	-1.68	-6.17	-0.46	-101.88	-504.32	-534.59
ST Yue Jin Man	3.37	-4.69	-7.05	-1.60	-1.64	-2.39	453.22	-629.79	-950.18
ST Zheng Baiwen	0.22	-6.58	-6.89	-2.54	-4.84	-0.31	43.75	-1,299.42	-1,360.47
PT Zhong Hao A	-2.01	-3.35	-3.73	-2.30	-0.82	-0.38	-316.51	-526.89	-585.88
PT Wang Dian	0.62	-1.75	-1.91	-0.88	-1.17	-0.16	99.47	-278.79	-304.54
ST Qiong Huaqiao	0.93	-1.67	-1.77	-0.30	-0.73	-0.07	193.53	-348.79	-369.57
ST Nan Yang	0.69	-0.54	-0.76	-0.63	-1.15	-0.22	171.93	-135.21	-189.57
ST Jin Li	1.22	-0.50	-0.43	-1.01	-0.87	0.07	80.37	-32.80	-28.45
ST Yong Jiu	1.08	-0.21	-0.32	-0.64	-1.28	-0.11	288.20	-54.07	-87.16
ST Shen Hua Yuan	1.33	-0.13	-0.32	-0.79	-0.84	-0.18	119.21	-11.77	-28.53

Source: Su (2001).

Clearly, for these companies net assets per share, earnings per share and shareholders' equity have all been falling, and in most cases falling by a considerable amount. If one looks for the reasons, it becomes clear that this is mainly because too much emphasis has been placed on asset management, at the expense of production management (Su, 2001). Nevertheless, the Shanghai Stock Exchange's refusal in April 2000 to grant an extension of the deadline for reorganization of PT Shui Xian indicates that the de-listing mechanism in China's stock market is finally starting to be used.[9]

Admission of funds to the stock market

According to the Insurance Law promulgated in 1995, the types of investment which insurance companies are permitted to undertake are limited to bank deposits, the purchase and sale of government bonds and bank debentures, and other forms of capital investment approved by the State Council. This means that participation in the stock market by insurance companies, pension funds and other contract-type savings institutions is restricted. However, in response to the pressures that WTO accession will bring, and the development needs of China's capital markets, China will be encouraging and working to cultivate institutional investors. In October 1999, the China Securities Regulatory Commission and Insurance Regulatory Commission gave permission for insurance companies to participate indirectly in the stock market through the purchase of securities investment funds, including secondary market investment funds and primary market investment fund allocation sales (Da Peng Securities Project Team, 2000). The government is now encouraging further development of open-end funds, and is aggressively promoting the participation of insurance funds and social insurance funds in the market, so that they can become the main institutional investors in the stock market as soon as possible.

In addition, China is considering the possibility of introducing the Qualified Foreigner Institutional Investor (QFII) system to allow foreign institutions to invest in the Chinese stock market. If this system is introduced, the range of investment channels will be significantly expanded, for example through the opportunity to participate in the management of pension funds and social insurance funds. At present, China is working hard to solve the problems affecting fund company operation, and is actively promoting open-end funds on a trial basis. In September 2000, the State Council decided to establish a 'National Social Insurance Fund' and a 'National Social Insurance Fund Management Committee', to come directly under the leadership of the State Council and to serve as the central government level agency for the supervision of social insurance funds throughout China. The Committee would also exercise control and supervision over the management committees of social insurance funds in China and over their non-government insurance fund activities. In addition, the legal framework for the introduction of social insurance funds into the stock market, including the Social Insurance Law, Trust Law, Investment Funds Law and Regulations Governing Endowment Insurance, is currently being formulated (Chen, Zhiyuan 2001; *Zhong Yin Wang*, 25 April 2001 and 9 May 2001).

Notes

1. Stock market transaction value as a proportion of GDP was 7 percent, 31 percent and 43 percent in 1995, 1996 and 1997 respectively, compared to only 0.2 percent in 1991; this shows how the market has gradually expanded since 1991.
2. This measure of securitization is based on total market capitalization, including shares reserved for the state and 'legal person shares', which cannot be freely traded; it is therefore not a wholly accurate measure of the level of securitization in China.
3. With regard to the Chinese stock market and institutional change, see Zou and Lin (1997), Zhang (1998), Chen (1998a), Hu (1999) and Southwest Financial and Economic University Project Team (1999).

4. Information disclosure includes: (i) Emphasizing disclosure of major events and transactions with affiliates; (ii) Exercising caution with respect to the disclosure of forecasts, disclosing major risks and latent dangers as appropriate; (iii) Strict adherence to both domestic and overseas requirements to produce regular reports, and proper coordination of disclosure in the different regions where a company is listed; (iv) Establishment of sound responsibility and internal coordination systems with respect to disclosure; (v) Strengthening of companies' self-introduction, and attaching of more importance to the reception of visitors. A company's chairman, president and key managers should proactively maintain contact and communication with investors and market analysts; (vi) Holding companies must perform the obligations with respect to disclosure. Holding companies, government departments and agencies may not interfere with a company's disclosure as required by law; and (vii) Regulation of disclosure by companies listed overseas should be strengthened (Wu, 2001).

5. For examples, while the revised Company Law permits the establishment of a new board for high-tech companies, when an enterprise undertakes business registration or has its registration altered, as technical achievements may be used to acquire shares at reduced value, in principle all shares must be paid for in cash or using tangible assets. This is not beneficial to the development of investment and financing intermediary service institutions. The Company Law also specifies that accumulated investment may not exceed 50 percent of a company's net worth, which restricts the development of venture capital and intermediary companies. Convertible bonds, and bonds which can be converted to preferred stock, lack legal guarantees, which prevents their free conversion, and constitutes a barrier to entry which makes it difficult for overseas venture capital firms to invest in China.

6. There are already several hundred venture capital firms in China, with almost 20 in Shenzhen alone, including Shenzhen Venture Capital Ltd., which was established by the government. Most venture capital firms have been established by securities firms and listed companies, and have started to invest in companies which are seeking listing on the new board (*Zhong Jing Wang*, 18 December 2000).

7. The seven categories of enterprise include: large-scale state enterprises; companies established by the spinning off of assets and businesses by large-scale state enterprises; companies established by the spinning off of assets and business by companies already listed on the main board; special-purpose companies with employee share-holding; enterprises with historical problems; companies directly or indirectly controlled by an employee shareholders' association; companies directly or indirectly controlled by a labor union (*Zhong Huan Zixun*, 6 August 2000).

8. Sun and Tong (2000) discovered that foreign investors tended to attach particular importance to the impact on share prices of macroeconomic variables such as exchange risk.

9. According to the regulations laid down by the China Securities Regulatory Commission and the warnings given by the Shanghai and Shenzhen stock exchanges to six companies including PT Shui Xian, PT Nong Shang She and PT Wang Dian, 'If approval is not obtained from the stock exchange at the end of the grace period, the company will be de-listed, and the stock exchange will cease to provide special PT transfer service'.

2. The Scale and Structure of China's Stock Market

The series of policy measures that have been adopted in China demonstrate the government's desire to keep apart the country's money market and capital market, ensuring that the operations of the two sectors are distinctly separated. We can see from the chronology of the development of China's stock market that bonds were the first type of security to be traded, followed by A-shares, B-shares, H-shares and N-shares (see Table 2.1). By 2000, the total market capitalization of China's stock market came to RMB4,774.432 billion, or approximately 18.27 percent of the market capitalization of the Tokyo Stock Exchange. This is lower than the market capitalization of the Hong Kong Stock Exchange, but higher than that of Taiwan, South Korea or Singapore. The level of financing in the primary market more than doubled in 2000, with the total amount of capital raised coming to RMB210.37 billion, 123 percent higher than in 1999. The price index in the secondary market also reached new highs several times during 2000, with market scale constantly expanding; the total transaction volume came to RMB6,082.666 billion in 2000, 94 percent higher than the previous year, representing the third highest in Asia, exceeding the figures for Hong Kong and South Korea and surpassed only by the market volumes of Tokyo and Taiwan.

In the first quarter of 2001, the combined transaction volume for the Shanghai and Shenzhen stock exchanges came to RMB1,005.9 billion, 47 percent lower than in the same period the previous year. At the end of 2000, the Shanghai composite index and Shenzhen composite index were 52 percent higher and 58 percent higher respectively than at the start of the year, and the number of accounts opened by investors had increased by 29.5 percent since the beginning of the year (Sun and Zhang, 2001).

By April 2001, the total number of listed companies in China had grown to 1,123, surpassing the figures for Hong Kong, South Korea, Taiwan and Singapore and second only to Tokyo in the Asia region. A total of 89 companies had listed both A-shares and B-shares on either the Shenzhen or Shanghai exchange; 989 companies had listed only A-shares; 24 companies had listed only B-shares; and 55 companies had listed H-shares overseas.

Table 2.1   The Development of the Stock Market in China

1981	Issuing of treasury bonds begins.
1987	Issuing of financial debentures begins, along with the issuing of convertible bonds by local enterprises.
1988	Establishment of the trading market for treasury bonds, and the commencement of government bond transfer operations.
	Planning begins for the establishment of stock exchanges.
	A trading center is established on a trial basis for the Wuhan securities market.
15 March 1989	Funding is completed for the establishment of national non-bank financial institutions, to be responsible for the promotion of securities business and capital market development.
December 1990	Establishment of the Shenzhen Stock Exchange.
1991	Establishment of the first underwriting center for treasury bonds.
	Establishment of the Securities Association.
	Establishment of the first investment funds.
1992	First national offering of corporate stock.
	Establishment of trading market for legal person shares.
	Establishment of the Securities Training Center.
February 1992	First B-shares listed on Shanghai Stock Exchange.
October 1992	Establishment of the State Council Securities Committee (the competent authority) and Securities Regulatory Commission (the regulatory agency), to exercise unified supervision over the stock market in China.
1993	Joint stock companies begin to issue shares to foreign investors.
	Establishment of the Class One securities dealers system on a trial basis.
July 1993	First issuing of H-shares.
November 1993	Establishment of the futures market on a trial basis.
	Futures business is brought within the scope of authority of the China Securities Regulatory Commission.
March 1995	The China Securities Regulatory Commission is formally established as a vice-ministerial level agency coming under the State Council, responsible for the supervision of the securities and futures market.
April 1996	Lifting of restrictions on open market operation.
	Establishment of a unified inter-bank market.
August 1997	Both the Shanghai and Shenzhen stock exchanges are formally placed under the supervision of the China Securities Regulatory Commission (CSRC).
November 1997	The national stock management system is reformed, with the introduction of a vertical hierarchy for local securities management agencies.
	Securities management agencies are now under the supervision of the CSRC rather than the People's Bank of China.

Table 2.1   Continued

18 March 1998	Approval is given for the Industrial and Commercial Bank of China to act as a fund manager, making it the first commercial bank in China to be permitted to undertake fund management business.
23 March 1998	Kai Yuan Securities Investment Fund and Jin Tai Securities Investment Fund are launched on the Shenzhen Stock Exchange and Shanghai Stock Exchange respectively, marking the formal commencement of securities fund operations in China.
April 1998	The State Council Securities Committee and the CSRC are merged, to form a ministry-level agency coming directly under the State Council.
17 April 1998	Following in the footsteps of the Industrial and Commercial Bank of China, the People's Construction Bank of China becomes the second bank in China to be permitted to engage in fund management business.
September 1998	The State Council approves the establishment of the China Securities Regulatory Commission, confirming its status as the regulatory authority for the national securities and futures markets, with 44 local offices.
19 October 1998	The CSRC formally begins to exercise unified supervision over securities and futures markets throughout China.
29 December 1998	The Ninth National People's Congress approves the Securities Law of the People's Republic of China, which comes into effect on July 1, 1999.
27 May 1999	The CSRC promulgates the Regulations Governing the Management of Local Offices of Foreign Securities Institutions.
July 1999	Formal implementation of the Securities Law of the People's Republic of China begins.
October 1999	The CSRC promulgates the Notification Regarding the Quality of Disclosure of Financial Information by Listed Companies.
16 March 2000	The CSRC promulgates the Provisional Regulations Governing the Provision of Guidance for Stock Market Listing, and the Approval Procedures for the Issuing of Securities.
May 2000	The CSRC promulgates the Provisional Regulations Governing the Making of Public Offerings by Listed Companies.
October 2000	The Shenzhen Stock Exchange promulgates the Regulations Governing Trading on the Start-up Board of the Shenzhen Stock Exchange, and the Regulations Governing Listing of Stocks on the Start-up Board of the Shenzhen Stock Exchange.
20 February 2001	The CSRC authorizes the purchase of B-shares by Chinese citizens.

Table 2.1   Continued

7 March 2001	The CSRC issues the Principles Governing the Content and Format of Disclosure of Information by Companies Which Have Made A Public Offering – No. 9: Application Forms for Initial Public Offerings, and the Principles Governing the Content and Format of Disclosure of Information by Companies Which Have Made A Public Offering – No. 12: Legal Opinions and Attorneys' Reports for Public Offerings.
17 March 2001	Formal implementation of the stock issue approval system commences.

Source: Collated from documents produced by the China Securities Regulatory Commission, the Shanghai Stock Exchange, and the Shanghai Securities Report website.

In terms of regional distribution, more listed companies were located in the coastal provinces of eastern China than in the central and western parts of the country. As far as industry distribution is concerned, listed companies falling under the industrial category accounted for 64.8 percent of the total, followed by those falling under the general category, which accounted for 16 percent of the total. Overall, the scale of China's stock market has grown steadily, and the significance of the market should not be underestimated.

The bond market is dominated by government bonds, with more than 98 percent of all government bond trading concentrated on the Shanghai and Shenzhen exchanges, the largest share being on the Shanghai exchange. However, the trading market for government bonds is still very small and continues to be dominated by banks, securities firms and other institutional investors. Participation in government bond buyback transactions is also limited to financial institutions such as banks, trust companies, insurance companies and securities firms. The volume of government bonds issued still accounts for only a very small proportion of GDP; however, since the proportion of GDP accounted for by fiscal revenue is low, the level of dependency on government bonds is relatively high. The majority of bonds issued are medium-term bonds with three to five year terms; but the government bond term structure lacks a balanced distribution, and this tends to increase the principal repayment and interest burden, while providing investors with insufficient choice.

The proportion of non-tradable government bonds has gradually risen, as a result of which the overall liquidity of government bonds has fallen. In addition, the government bond market is fragmented; different types of investors are restricted to trading in different trading markets, which again leads to insufficient liquidity. Like shares, government bonds in China are mainly held by individual investors; however, given the excessively high transaction costs, individual investors participate in buying bonds only in the primary market. Added to this is the fact that individual investors are invariably concerned mainly with the interest and repayment of the principal; their major focus is the direct interest income noted on the bonds.

This concentration of government bonds in the hands of individual investors does not facilitate the undertaking of market operations by the central bank. Since all government bonds issued in China are fixed interest bonds, and since the interest rate on government bonds is higher than the interest rate on bank deposits, an interest burden is created, which increases the difficulty of macro-management of the economy.[1] Furthermore, the primary and secondary markets for government bonds have different interest rate mechanisms, creating difficulties in bond issue which lead to irregularities. In addition, the disparity between government bond interest rates and market interest rates has led to increased speculation on the part of the agencies responsible for bond issue, which has further disrupted the normal operation of the bond market (Li, 1998; Han et al., 1998; Xiao, Yu 1999).

With shares having assumed an increasingly important role, and given that in the future, the bond market functions of the stock exchanges will be largely limited to corporate bond issues and trading, in this chapter the main topic of analysis will be the scale and structure of the stock market. We will be exploring China's stock market from the point of view of types of shares traded, equity structure, investor structure, intermediaries, listed companies, and so on.

2.1 Types of Shares Traded, Equity Structure, Investor Structure and Intermediaries in China's Stock Market

2.1.1 Types of Shares Traded

The shares traded on China's stock market fall mainly into three categories; (i) A-shares (RMB shares, available only to domestic investors); (ii) B-shares (special RMB shares, available only to overseas investors); and (iii) H-shares (companies listed in Hong Kong). A-shares trading has grown dramatically since 1987, and by December 2000, a total of RMB324.213 billion had been raised through the issuing of A-shares (see Table 2.2).

As regards B-shares, since they were first issued in 1992, they have become one of the main instruments through which China is able to secure foreign investment; however, the total amount of money raised has been less than the amounts raised through the issuing of A-shares, H-shares and N-shares (those listed on the New York Stock Exchange). As at December 2000, a total of 114 listed companies had issued B-shares, raising a total of RMB4.926 billion (see Table 2.3).

Table 2.2   A-Share Issues

Year of issue	Total no. of shares issued (billions)	Total amount raised through share issues (RMB billions)
1987	1.000	1.000
1988	2.500	2.500
1989	0.662	0.662
1990	0.428	0.428
1991	0.500	0.500
1992	1.000	5.000
1993	4.259	19.483
1994	1.097	4.962
1995	0.532	2.268
1996	3.829	22.445
1997	10.565	65.506
1998	8.280	44.305
1999	8.311	57.263
2000	11.717	97.891
Total	554.680	324.213

Source: *China Securities and Futures Statistical Yearbook* 2000, p.23; China Securities Regulatory Commission (CSRC) website.

Table 2.3   Foreign Capital Raised through B-Share Issues

	Shenzhen (US$ billion)	Shanghai (US$ billion)	Total (US$ billion)	Total growth compared to previous year(%)
1992	0.0236	0.6770	0.7006	—
1993	0.3268	0.4000	0.7268	3.734
1994	0.0922	0.4630	0.5552	-23.601
1995	0.2810	0.0940	0.3750	-32.465
1996	0.3873	0.1820	0.5693	51.806
1997	0.4885	1.0200	1.5085	165.000
1998	0.1593	0.1158	0.2751	-81.762
1999	0.0262	0.0198	0.0460	-83.270
2000	0.1637	0.0053	0.1690	267.390
Total	1.9486	2.9769	4.9255	—

Source: Chen, Dongsheng (1999), China Securities Regulatory Commission website.

H-shares were first issued in 1993 as another means by which the stock markets could secure foreign capital. By 2000, the total amount of funds secured by the issuing of new shares and allotment shares came to RMB225.226 billion (see Table 2.4). Overall, between 1991 and 2000, China's stock markets raised a total of RMB655.872 billion, of which 72.8 percent was derived from new issues or allotment issues of A-shares issued to domestic investors. The B-shares and H-shares issued to foreign investors accounted for 28 percent of the total amount raised. This shows that in terms of the amount of capital raised, or for that matter, the number of shares issued, the A-share market is the most important element of the Chinese stock market, followed by the H-share market, which has raised more than three times as much as the B-share market.

Table 2.4   Issuing of H- and N-Shares

	1993	1994	1995	1996	1997	1998	1999	2000	Total
Shares issued (billion)	4.041	6.989	1.538	3.177	13.688	1.286	2.305	35.925	68.949
Total amount raised (RMB billion)	6.093	18.873	3.146	8.356	36.000	3.795	4.717	144.246	225.226

Note: The figure for 2000 includes only H-shares.

Source: *China Securities and Futures Statistical Yearbook* 2000, p. 53; China Securities
          Regulatory Commission website.

It is readily apparent that the secondary market for A-shares is livelier; by 1999, the cumulative trading volume for the secondary market for A-shares came to RMB12,234.896 billion, over eighty times (84.89) the cumulative trading volume for B-shares, with the annual average trading volume for A-shares being in excess of RMB1,500 billion (see Table 2.5). By the end of 1999, the total market capitalization for A-shares came to RMB2,616.762 billion, or just 43.79 times the total market capitalization for B-shares (see Table 2.6).

As at 1999, the cumulative trading volume of B-shares in the secondary market came to RMB144.119 billion, with the average annual trading volume being over RMB18 billion (see Table 2.7). By the end of 1999, the total market capitalization for B-shares stood at RMB30.354 billion (see Table 2.8).[2]

Table 2.5   *A-Share Market Trading Volume Statistics (RMB billion)*

	Shenzhen		Shanghai		Total	
	Trading volume	Percentage increase	Trading volume	Percentage increase	Trading volume	Percentage increase
1992	41.744	–	23.272	–	65.016	–
1993	126.087	202.05	230.15	888.96	356.237	447.92
1994	237.635	88.47	562.673	144.48	800.308	124.66
1995	91.595	-61.46	340.263	-39.53	431.858	-46.04
1996	1,203.205	1213.61	902.024	165.10	2,105.229	387.48
1997	1,674.497	39.17	1,355.024	50.22	3,029.521	43.90
1998	1,111.349	-33.63	1,230.423	-9.20	2,341.772	-22.70
1999	1,422.335	27.98	1,682.62	36.75	3,104.955	32.59
Total	5,928.827	–	6,326.449	–	12,234.896	–

Note: The average annual increase was RMB1,738.554 billion; the average annual trading volume was RMB1,529.362 billion.

Source: *China Securities and Futures Statistical Yearbook* 1999, pp. 31–3; *China Securities and Futures Statistical Yearbook* 2000, pp. 54–6.

Table 2.6   *A-Share Market Capitalization Statistics (RMB billion)*

	Shenzhen		Shanghai		Total	
	Market capitalization	Percentage increase	Market capitalization	Percentage increase	Market capitalization	Percentage increase
1992	45.753	–	52.055	–	97.808	–
1993	125.101	173.43	206.766	297.21	331.867	23.930
1994	103.249	-17.47	248.351	20.11	351.603	5.95
1995	87.686	-15.07	243.371	-2.01	331.057	-5.84
1996	413.242	371.27	531.613	118.44	944.855	185.41
1997	812.174	96.54	903.245	69.91	1,715.419	81.55
1998	877.391	8.03	1,052.538	16.53	1,929.929	12.50
1999	1,172.69	33.66	1,444.072	37.20	2,616.762	35.59

Note: The average annual increase was 59.92 percent; the average increase in value was RMB1,174.499 billion; the average annual market capitalization was RMB1,039.913 billion.

Source: *China Securities and Futures Statistical Yearbook* 1999, pp. 31–3; *China Securities and Futures Statistical Yearbook* 2000, pp. 54–6.

Table 2.7   B-Share Market Trading Volume (RMB billion)

	Shenzhen		Shanghai		Total	
	Trading volume	Percentage increase	Trading volume	Percentage increase	Trading volume	Percentage increase
1992	1.663	—	1.445	—	3.108	—
1993	2.579	55.08	7.886	445.74	10.465	236.71
1994	1.620	-37.18	10.835	37.39	12.455	19.01
1995	1.703	5.12	6.083	43.86	7.786	-37.49
1996	18.530	988.08	9.457	55.47	27.987	259.45
1997	21.369	15.32	21.293	125.15	42.662	52.43
1998	4.464	-79.11	8.188	-61.55	12.652	-70.34
1999	13.045	192.23	13.959	70.48	27.004	113.44
Total	64.973	—	79.146	—	144.119	—

Note: The average annual increase was RMB20.144 billion; the average annual trading volume was RMB18.015 billion.

Source: *China Securities and Futures Statistical Yearbook* 1999, pp. 31–3; *China Securities and Futures Statistical Yearbook* 2000, pp. 54–6.

Table 2.8   B-Share Market Capitalization (RMB billion)

	Shenzhen		Shanghai		Total	
	Market capitalization	Percentage increase	Market capitalization	Percentage increase	Market capitalization	Percentage increase
1992	3.220	—	3.785	—	7.005	—
1993	8.431	161.83	12.804	238.28	21.235	203.14
1994	5.798	-31.23	11.659	-8.94	17.457	-17.79
1995	7.175	23.75	9.195	-21.13	16.370	-6.23
1996	23.214	223.54	16.188	76.05	39.402	140.70
1997	18.943	-18.40	18.561	14.66	37.504	-4.82
1998	10.581	-44.14	10.053	-45.84	20.634	-44.98
1999	16.379	54.80	13.975	39.01	30.354	47.11

Note: The average annual increase was 23.3 percent; the average increase in value was RMB26.137 billion; the average annual market capitalization was RMB23.745 billion.

Source: *China Securities and Futures Statistical Yearbook* 1999, pp. 31–3; *China Securities and Futures Statistical Yearbook* 2000, pp. 54–6.

One of the main reasons for the lack of vibrancy in the B-share market is that in their annual reports, those companies which have issued B-shares have to announce not only their net profit according to China's corporate accounting standards and the company's own accounting system, but also the adjusted profit figures according to international accounting standards. Since most B-share investors base their investment decisions on the net profit ratios according to international accounting standards, there is thus a marked disparity between the market price of A-shares and the market price of B-shares (Jiang, 2001).

On 20 February 2001, the China Securities Regulatory Commission (CSRC) announced the opening up of the B-share market to domestic investors, and as a result of the CSRC's policy of allowing residents in China to invest in B-shares, they became the investors' favorite. The aggregate market value of the B-share trading market rose from only RMB50 billion on 19 February 2001 to RMB150 billion by the end of March 2001, while share prices rose significantly. By the end of March 2001, the weighted average price / earnings ratio (PER) for B-shares listed on the Shanghai Stock Exchange was 44.95, while that of the Shenzhen Stock Exchange was 32.52; these figures were, respectively, 19.72 and 19.47 points higher than those for the previous month. By the end of March, 989,500 accounts for investing in B-shares had been opened, 3.6 times the number of accounts at the end of the previous year (Sun and Zhang, 2001).

Equity Structure

Prior to 1992, the cities within which the stock market was being implemented on a trial basis were limited to Shenzhen and Shanghai. Right from the start, the market adopted a strict planned management system, with issue volume management incorporated into the national credit plan and monetary policy. As a result, along with bank loans and bond issue, the scale of stock issues became part of the overall money supply, facilitating the Chinese government's control of society's capital.

The actual management method used to control issue volume after 1993 was through the China Securities Regulatory Commission of the State Council convening a meeting of relevant departments and commissions, to decide on the overall scale of stock issue for that year on the basis of current economic development and the state of the market. Once approval was gained from the State Council, the plan was passed on to the Planning Commission for distribution to individual provinces, autonomous regions, municipalities, planned autonomous cities and relevant government agencies (including ministries, commissions and state enterprises coming directly under the central government).

In 1997, the CSRC announced new regulations governing the issue of new shares, with the implementation of a quota system. In order to encourage the recommendation for listing of large enterprises and key enterprises, within the restrictions of the overall quota, only the number of companies that could make public offerings was limited. However, owing to the numerous failings in quota management, enterprises and local government authorities began to engage in a wide variety of public relations (PR) activities to try to secure their own share of the quota. It has been estimated that, on average, each enterprise has to spend around RMB500,000–RMB3,000,000 on PR to secure listing, which means that for every RMB100 worth of shares listed, RMB0.34–RMB0.98 is spent on PR. Such PR expenditure leads to an increase in rent-seeking activity, which represents a waste of resources. Within this process, weak companies have joined forces with securities firms and intermediary agencies, using falsified financial statements and prospectuses to secure listing, leading to an increase in power for money transactions and numerous cases of corruption (Zhou, 2000).

In light of this situation, on 16 March 2000, the CSRC abolished the quota system, the issue guidelines and other administrative measures, and began moving in the direction of a listing approval system based on the provisions of the Securities Law, with the following features: Firstly, enterprises are selected and recommended by the underwriters, thereby increasing the latter's level of responsibility. Secondly, enterprises can decided on the scale of issue according to their capital needs. Thirdly, as regards a listing review, there is a gradual move towards compulsory disclosure and the implementation of reviews in strict accordance with the requirements of the law, so that the stock market can fulfill its independent review function. Fourthly, the issuing party and the underwriter decide on the issue price together after taking into consideration the state of market demand, so that the issue price genuinely reflects the company's operational status. Fifthly, an issue mechanism has been established whereby both the issuer and the underwriter have to absorb risk (Huang, Yuncheng 2000). On 7 March 2001, the CSRC issued the Principles Governing the Content and Format of Disclosure of Information by Companies which have Made a Public Offering – No. 9: Application Forms for Initial Public Offerings, and the Principles Governing the Content and Format of Disclosure of Information by Companies which have Made a Public Offering – No. 12: Legal Opinions and Attorneys' Reports for Public Offerings. These documents were markedly different from previous regulations, both in terms of their form and content, and on 17 March 2001, formal implementation of the stock issue approval system commenced.

The methods by which stocks are listed and shares issued in China's stock markets violate the market principle. Equity in listed companies is artificially divided into different categories of shares in the same stock – state shares, legal person shares, public shares and internal employee shares – each of which have different rights. For example, holders of state shares can transfer their allotment rights, either in part or whole, to the holders of public shares; holders of state shares can maintain their right to share in the benefits from share allotment, or choose not to participate in share allotment, thereby transferring the risk onto the shoulders of the holders of public shares. By contrast, the holders of public shares can only buy and sell shares on the secondary market.

Table 2.9 provides details of the equity structure of listed companies in China and the changes to that structure. During the period from the end of 1992 to the end of 2000, the equity structure of listed companies was as follows. As a proportion of total shares, state shares tended to fall, but nevertheless remained dominant. The proportion of state shares in the equity structure of listed companies fell from 41.38 percent to 38.9 percent, a decrease of 2.48 percent. The reasons for this decline were: (i) As a result of the fall in central government revenue, China stopped increasing the capitalization of state-owned enterprises; listed companies were constantly implementing capital increments to increase the proportion of public shares, which caused the proportion of state shares to fall; and (ii) Over the last few years there has been a series of cases of state shares being privately transferred to legal persons, which has increased the proportion of legal person shares; however, the reform of state-owned enterprises is still making use of mainly state-owned holding companies, with the government insisting that listed companies must still be subsidiaries of a state-owned holding company. Thus the reform of the state-owned enterprises does not involve wholesale privatization, and state shares therefore continue to play an important role.

As far as founders' stocks are concerned, the proportion of domestic legal person shares has risen from 13.14 percent to 16.94 percent, an increase of 3.8 percent; while the proportion of fund-raising legal person shares has fallen from 9.42 percent to 5.65 percent, a decrease of 3.77 percent. The reasons for this are: (i) Most listed companies have been transformed from state-owned enterprises; listing is usually implemented as part of the restructuring of state-owned enterprises, and the proportion of total capitalization accounted for by the former state-owned enterprise's internal reserve is defined as founder's stock after listing; (ii) Many listed companies are the profitable parts of state-owned enterprises which were spun off, with the state-owned enterprise retaining founder's stock; this has led to a significant increase in the proportion of founder's stock; and (iii) As a result of the general decline in enterprise performance over the last few years, and the restrictions on the circulation of legal person shares, the market for legal person shares is not sufficiently lively, and market prices are unattractively low.

Table 2.9   *Equity Structure of Stocks Listed on China's Stock Markets (Billion shares)*

Share Type	End 1992		End 1997		End 1998		End 1999		End 2000	
	shares	%	shares	%	shares	%	shares	%	shares	%
I. Shares not yet in circulation	4.77	69.25	127.12	65.44	166.485	65.89	200.71	65.02	243.743	64.28
1. Founder's stock	4.04	58.59	107.82	55.50	142.93	56.57	174.71	56.60	216.54	57.11
a. State shares	2.85	41.38	61.23	31.52	86.55	34.25	111.61	36.16	147.51	38.90
b. Domestic legal person shares	0.91	13.14	43.99	22.64	52.81	20.90	59.05	19.13	64.26	16.94
c. Foreign legal person shares	0.28	4.07	2.61	1.34	3.58	1.42	4.05	1.31	4.62	1.22
2. Fund-raising legal person shares	0.65	9.42	13.05	6.72	15.23	6.03	19.01	6.16	21.42	5.65
3. Internal employee shares	0.09	1.23	3.96	2.04	5.17	2.05	3.67	1.19	2.43	0.64
4. Other (transferred allotment)	0.00	0.00	2.29	1.18	3.15	1.25	3.32	1.08	2.46	0.65
II. Shares in circulation	2.118	30.75	67.14	34.56	86.20	34.11	107.97	34.98	135.43	35.72
1. Domestically listed Renminbi shares (A-shares)	1.093	15.87	44.27	22.79	60.80	24.06	81.32	26.34	107.82	28.44
2. Domestically-listed foreign capital shares (B-shares)	1.025	14.88	11.73	6.04	13.40	5.30	14.19	4.60	15.16	4.00
3. Overseas-listed foreign capital shares (H-shares)	0.00	0.00	11.15	5.74	12.00.	4.75	12.45	4.03	12.45	3.28

Note: Each share has a face value of RMB1.00.

Source: *China Securities and Futures Statistical Yearbook* 2000, p.189, China Securities Regulatory Commission website.

There has therefore been a general decrease in mutual-investment between unrelated legal persons, so that the proportion of fund-raising legal person shares has gradually fallen. The proportion of employee shares in unlisted companies rose from 1.23 percent to 2.04 percent, before declining to 0.64 percent. This reflects the way in which, during the process of institutional transformation, enterprises have used employee stock options as a means of improving employee welfare.

With regard to the proportion of total equity accounted for by the various different types of shares, the continual implementation of capital increments to increase the number of public shares, and the private transfer of state shares to legal persons, have caused the proportion of listed company equity accounted for by state shares to fall from 41.38 percent in 1992, to 38.9 percent in 2000. State shares are, however, still the most numerous category of shares. At the same time, because shares that cannot be traded freely, including state shares, account for 60 percent of total equity, company managers do not have to worry that poor management may cause their enterprise's stock price to fall, or that their company will be faced with the threat of being taken over. In other words, holders of public shares cannot 'vote with their feet', and thus, managers are not concerned about the rights of public share shareholders (Xu and Wang, 1999).

Moreover, the regional structure and market structure of the stock exchange system are not determined by market supply and demand, so, speculation is rife. While A-, B- and H-shares can be freely traded, the trading markets for the three categories of share are separate, and in the market for B-shares there is a serious problem with shares being issued at a very low price. As a result, the stock market displays a distinctive form of systemic risk, making it difficult for the market to exercise its major function of the distribution of resources; the stock market is therefore inefficient.

Investor Structure

Most of the investors in China's stock market are individual investors, and most of their funds derive from savings. Taking 1999 as an example, in that year there were approximately 44.81 million stock market investors in China. Among A-share investors, individual members of the general public accounted for 99.59 percent of the total, with institutional investors accounting for 0.4 percent. Among B-share investors, individual members of the general public accounted for 92.53 percent of the total, with institutional investors accounting for 7.47 percent (see Tables 2.10 and 2.11).

The confidence of individual investors tends to be affected by external news and the rise and fall of share prices, since the amount they have available for investment is relatively small and they tend to lack any systematic investment knowledge. They use excessively simple decision-making processes, buying and selling frequently, and thus the fluctuations in China's stock market tend to be large, with considerable speculation and excessive volatility.

Table 2.10   Distribution of A-Share Investors in 1999 (1,000s)

	Whole Country	Shenzhen	Shanghai
Total number of investors	44,617.5	21,895.2	22,722.3
Institutional investors	182.8	107.2	75.6
Individual investors	44,434.7	21,788.0	22,646.7
Number of new accounts	5,690.5	2,884.3	2,806.2
New institutional investors	40.9	20.9	20.0
New individual investors	5,649.6	2,863.4	2,786.2

Source: China Securities and Futures Statistical Yearbook 2000, p.260.

Table 2.11   Distribution of B-Share Investors in 1999 (1,000s)

	Whole Country	Shenzhen	Shanghai
Total number of investors	202.1	113.3	88.8
Institutional investors	15.1	7.5	7.6
Individual investors	187.1	105.8	81.3
Number of new accounts	17.8	6.9	10.9
New institutional investors	1.1	0.5	0.6
New individual investors	16.7	6.4	10.3

Source: China Securities and Futures Statistical Yearbook 2000, p.260.

Nevertheless, the performance of institutional investors is not much better. This is because the vast majority of the various types of securities firms and investment and trust companies not only provide investors with brokerage services, they also engage in dealing operations, thereby destroying market order. Added to this is the fact that the scale of investment funds is usually small, sometimes uneconomically so. With regard to the involvement of contract-type savings institutions in the stock market, in China, contract-type savings institutions such as insurance companies and pension funds are restricted by law from investing in the stock market, which would otherwise increase the number of institutional investors. The general dispersion of pension funds and insurance funds in China is currently very low, accounting for only 3 percent of GDP; this also restricts the potential of contract-type savings funds to serve as institutional investors (Qin and Kong, 1999).

To summarize the above factors, the limited financial assets which the capital markets can make available for members of the public to invest in, and the repeated lowering of interest rates, have encouraged large numbers of investors to turn to the stock market. Moreover, the low return on industrial investment, the weakness of the market, and share price manipulation by listed companies, all serve to cause a rise in speculation in China's stock markets. As Table 2.12 shows, the share turnover rate also provides evidence of the highly speculative nature of the stock markets.

For the purposes of the following analysis, investors are divided into three main categories – individual investors, institutional investors and investment funds.

Table 2.12   Comparison of Share Turnover Rates in Leading Stock Markets (%)

Year	Shanghai	Shenzhen	Taiwan	New York	Tokyo	South Korea	London	Hong Kong	Thailand	Singapore
1992	–	–	161.33	44	19.91	133.42	42.6	53	125.26	12.8
1993	341	213	252.42	53	25.86	186.55	80.5	61	66.19	26.2
1994	787	472	366.11	53	24.93	174.08	77.1	55	64.04	26.7
1995	396	180	227.84	59	26.77	105.11	77.6	38	43.06	17.80
1996	591	902	243.43	62	28.94	102.98	78.6	41	50.91	13.6
1997	326	466	407.32	65.71	32.93	145.56	44.03	90.92	49.56	56.28
1998	297	283	314.06	69.88	34.13	207.00	47.10	61.94	68.86	63.95
1999	315.6	299.61	288.62	74.62	49.37	344.98	56.71	50.60	78.14	75.16
2000	360.4	–	259.16	82.4	58.86	301.56	63.81	62.99	64.91	64.97

Note: The method of calculation for the share turnover rates for Shanghai and Shenzhen was as follows: Share turnover rate = Total number of shares traded in the year/Total number of shares in circulation at the end of the year.

Source: *China Securities and Futures Statistical Yearbook* 1999, p.84; 2000, p.55–6; Taiwan Stock Exchange website.

Individual investors

Individual investors, sometimes referred to as 'general investors', are far greater in number than institutional investors, although in terms of the amount of capital held, prior to 1996 institutional investors held far more than individual investors. Li (1999) undertook detailed analysis of the occupational background, level of education, sex, age structure and capital sources of individual investors in China in 1998. In that year, skilled technicians accounted for the largest single group of individual investors, at 30.3 percent of the total; educators and government employees accounted for

18.1 percent; entrepreneurs and senior managers accounted for 12.1 percent; people working in the service industries and ordinary employees in general enterprises accounted for 17.2 percent (see Figure 2.1). 19.1 percent of investors were unemployed, recent graduates who had not yet found work, housewives or retirees.

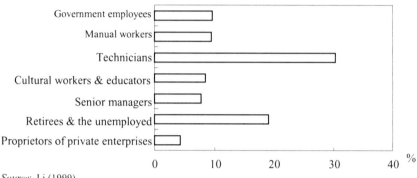

Source: Li (1999).

Figure 2.1   Occupational Background of Investors

As far as the educational level of individual investors is concerned, we can see from Figure 2.2 that the largest group contains those educated to junior college level, accounting for 31.7 percent of the total. The next largest group comprises those educated to university level, accounting for 29 percent of the total. Those educated to high school level account for 25.4 percent of the total, while those educated to junior high school level or below account for only 7.6 percent of the total. With regard to age structure, the largest group of investors is those aged 25–35, accounting for 41.4 percent of the total. The next largest group is those aged 36–50, accounting for 28.9 percent of the total; those aged 51 or over account for 22.9 percent of the total.

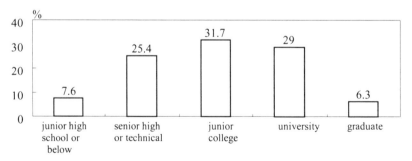

Source: Li (1999).

Figure 2.2   Educational Level of Stock Market Investors

In terms of income structure, we can see from Figure 2.3 that the largest single group comprises those falling into the middle-income segment; 52.60 percent of investors have a monthly income in the range of RMB500 to RMB1,500. Those with a monthly income in the range of RMB1,500–RMB3,000 account for 21.3 percent of the total; and those with a monthly income of RMB3,000 or higher account for 13.2 percent. Investors with a monthly income of under RMB500 account for 12.9 percent.

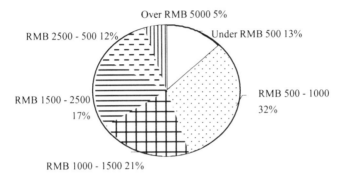

Source: Li (1999).

Figure 2.3   Investors' Monthly Income

Analysis of gender shows that the majority of investors (70.5 percent) are male, with female investors accounting for only 29.5 percent of the total, so clearly the stock market in China is still dominated by men.

Analysis of investors' sources of funds shows that for 72 percent of investors, all of the money invested was their own. 18.6 percent of investors collected money from friends and relatives; 8 percent used some of their own money while also borrowing some; only 1.5 percent of investors relied entirely on borrowed money. The main source of individual investors' funds is thus personal savings.

As regards the amount of money invested in the stock market by individual investors, those investing under RMB5,000 account for 5.2 percent of the total; those investing between RMB5,000 and RMB10,000 account for 11.4 percent of the total; those investing between RMB10,000 and RMB50,000 account for 34.8 percent of the total; those investing between RMB50,000 and RMB100,000 account for 20.7 percent of the total; those investing between RMB100,000 and RMB300,000 account for 17.1 percent of the total; those investing over RMB300,000 account for 10.8 percent of the total. Clearly, the majority of investors invest under RMB100,000 ; these investors account for 72.01 percent of the total (Shao, 2000).

Turning to analysis of investors' profit and loss, average profits fell in 1997, as compared to 1996, while the proportion of investors making a loss increased significantly. 57.6 percent of investors made a profit in 1997, 25.7 percent lower than in 1996, while the proportion of investors making a loss rose to 31.3 percent, higher than in 1996 by 23.4 percent.

Institutional investors

The main institutional investors in China's stock market are securities firms and investment trust companies. Not only do they provide brokerage services for investors, they also engage in buying and selling on their own account, which tends to lead to a loss of market order. Another problem is that the average scale of investment funds is usually quite small, and most of the funds they use for stock market investment derive from their own financial system. As a result, funds obtained through bank loans tend to flow into the stock market, creating the risk of a bubble. On 20 May 1997, the CSRC issued regulations strictly forbidding state-owned enterprises and listed companies from engaging in stock price manipulation; on 6 June 1997, the People's Bank of China issued a Notification Regarding the Prohibition of the Illicit Movement of Bank Funds into the Stock Market. The main aims of these measures were to prohibit listed companies from engaging in stock price manipulation, to prevent bank loan funds from flowing into the stock market and to encourage the de-listing of institutions that violate the regulations. Institutional investors are not the dominant force in the stock market; in 1997, institutional investors accounted for only 0.35 percent of accounts in the Shanghai Stock Exchange, and there was a similar situation at the Shenzhen Stock Exchange. By the first half of 2000, the overall share of accounts held by institutional investors, in the two exchanges combined, had risen to 4.5 percent. Clearly, the proportion of institutional investors in the Chinese stock market is increasing steadily (Yuan and Ho, 2000); however, there is still a lack of economies of scale among institutional investors.

Fund investment

On 14 November 1997, the CSRC promulgated the Provisional Regulations Governing Securities Investment Fund Management. The regulations contained clear stipulations regarding the establishment, floating and transactions of funds, the rights and obligations of trustees, fund managers and fund-holders, and the management methods for investment operations and supervision. By 1999, there were 10 fund management companies in China, along with five trust banks and 22 securities investment funds; with the total amount of funds managed coming to almost RMB50.5 billion.

The total trading volume of securities investment funds in 1999 came to

RMB248.548, representing an annual growth rate of 144.42 percent. The average daily trading volume was RMB660 million, 189.35 percent higher than the previous year, with 54 percent of this trading occurring within the Shanghai Stock Exchange. On the performance of Chinese funds, viewed in terms of net assets per share, this was not particularly impressive for these funds in 1999; around 16 percent of funds had net assets per share of less than RMB1, whilst 36 percent of funds had net assets per share which hovered around RMB1, and only An Xin had net assets per share of over RMB1.5.

Compared with the volume of share trading, the role played by funds seems relatively insignificant. In 1999, the total trading volume of Chinese funds accounted for only 7.93 percent of total stock trading volume (see Table 2.13), and this has affected the stability of the Chinese stock market. A stock market's stability is closely linked to its investor structure. Given the limited knowledge of individual investors, their lack of experience and their restricted access to information, they tend to blindly follow the crowd, buying when the market is rising and selling when it is falling, and as such, their speculative behavior increases the severity of market fluctuations. The development of securities investment funds is beneficial to the stability of the stock market, and helps to improve the investor structure (Hu and Xiang, 1999).

Table 2.13   *Comparison of Fund and Share Trading on the Shanghai and Shenzhen Stock Exchanges (RMB million)*

	Shanghai			Shenzhen		
	Funds	Shares	Funds as percentage of shares (%)	Funds	Shares	Funds as percentage of shares (%)
1995	30,567	310,348	9.85	20,451	93,299	21.92
1996	49,738	911,481	5.46	106,912	1,221,735	8.75
1997	21,953	1,376,318	1.60	58,838	1,695,866	3.47
1998	60,528	1,238,611	4.89	41,161	1,115,814	3.69
1999	136,582	1,696,579	8.05	111,966	1,435,381	7.80

Source: China Securities and Futures Statistical Yearbook 2000, pp. 55–6, 138–9.

2.1.4 Intermediaries

When referring to the stock market, the term 'brokers' includes share dealers, securities firms and investment companies. As at the end of 1999, China had 90 securities firms and 203 investment and trust companies licensed to engage in securities business. Add to this all other financial institutions and companies involved in securities business, and the total number of financial institutions that can be classed as securities brokers comes to approximately 430 (see Table 2.14).

Securities brokerage institutions in China have specific characteristics. Firstly, they are numerous, unevenly distributed on a regional basis, and have a widely varying market share. China has over 430 financial institutions currently involved in securities business, and these institutions have more than 2,400 branches between them; however, there is considerable disparity in the market shares of securities brokers. Of the total number of brokers, in excess of 400, fifty or so large securities firms control 80 percent of all business in the primary and secondary markets, and these securities firms are highly concentrated in both the Special Economic Zones and in the large cities in the coastal regions and Changjiang Valley. Thus, the level of competition among brokers is extremely intense, increasing the frequency of mergers.

Table 2.14   *Chinese Securities and Futures Intermediary Institutions,*
                1994–99

Type of Institution	1994	1995	1996	1997	1998	1999
Stock exchanges	2	2	2	2	2	2
Clearing companies	2	2	2	2	2	2
Securities firms	91	97	94	90	90	90
Securities divisions	2262	NA	2420	2412	2412	2412
Firms of accountants	82	102	105	105	107	106
Law offices	179	217	322	317	286	304
Asset appraisal companies	97	115	116	116	116	116
Securities rating agencies	2	2	2	2	2	2
Futures exchanges	14	14	14	14	3	3
Futures brokerages	NA	NA	329	294	278	213

Source: China Securities and Futures Statistical Yearbook 2000, p. 301.

Secondly, there is fierce competition, low efficiency and weak market order. There are a large number of securities firms in China with their main areas of business including the provision of guidance for companies wishing to list on the primary market, underwriting and share brokerage and dealing operations in the secondary market. In recent years, new areas of business such as the establishment of securities investment funds, fund management companies, mergers and acquisitions, and so on, have become more important. In 1998, there were 120 listed companies either merging with, or taking over, 277 state enterprises, with the total amount involved exceeding RMB100 billion (Xu, 1999); for example, in 1997, Nan Fang Securities served as financial consultants for Hunan Provincial Government for the reorganization and use of state-owned assets and the reorganization and stock market listing of state-owned enterprises; as such, they were involved in regional economic development planning and operations. Guang Fa Securities was commissioned to manage state-owned assets amounting to many tens of billions of RMB for the Hunan Province Light Industry Bureau (Chen and Zhou, 1999). However, in the primary market, owing to the limits on the number of companies that may be listed and the high level of similarity in underwriting business, supply and demand in the underwriting market is seriously out of balance. The underwriting market has become very much a buyer's market, and almost all business in this sector is monopolized by the 20 leading securities firms.[3] Furthermore, in the secondary market securities brokerage business relies on contacts to secure clients, creating a warped form of competition. The larger securities firms, such as Hua Xia Securities, Guo Tai Securities, Shen Yin Wan Guo Securities, and so on, will exploit their monopoly in underwriting business to secure issue fees, while the smaller securities firms are forced to include profits from share price manipulation on the secondary market in their annual operating plans. In other words, because of the large number of securities firms, the small volume of underwriting business, and the fact that the products offered by the different firms are highly uniform with low profits, competition between securities firms is fierce, resulting in low efficiency and weak market order.

Thirdly, securities firms generally have low capitalization. This means that they have a weak base for expanding their capitalization, and their ability to withstand risk is also low. High capital density is normally a characteristic of securities firms; however, the total current assets of China's 90 securities firms come to only around RMB205.5 billion, with total capitalization amounting to approximately RMB19.755 billion. This means that on average, each securities firm has capital of only around RMB219 million, and on a nationwide scale, the average capital of securities firms is only RMB20 million–RMB30 million. Even the largest firm, Shen Yin Wan Guo, has capitalization of only RMB136 million.

All securities and futures intermediary companies in China are characterized by low capitalization. In 1997, of all securities firms in China, only 12 percent had capitalization of RMB400 million or higher; 58 percent had capitalization of between RMB100 million and RMB300 million, and 23 percent had capitalization of under RMB100 million. The vast majority of securities firms thus had capitalization of under RMB300 million (see Table 2.15). Once allowance has been made for basic operating needs, very little of this money is left. At the end of 1997, the funding sources for Chinese securities firms were as shown in Table 2.16. In accordance with the Securities Law which came into effect on July 1, 1997, the practice of using investors' deposits for unapproved purposes will be restricted; securities firms will then required to meet their operating needs mainly from rollover and buyback, thus creating a huge demand for funds (Chen, Qiumin 1999).

Table 2.15   Capitalization   of   Securities   and   Futures   Intermediary Companies in China, 1997 (enterprise)

	Shanghai Stock Exchange	Shenzhen Stock Exchange	Whole country
Under RMB100 million	82	89	171
RMB100–200 million	166	141	307
RMB200–300 million	64	63	127
RMB300–400 million	19	32	51
RMB400 million or over	52	37	89
Total	383	362	745

Source: *China Securities and Futures Statistical Yearbook* 1998, p. 182.

Table 2.16   Funding Source Structure of Chinese Securities Firms

	Amount (RMB million)	%
Owner equity	31 704	14.71
Investors' deposits	112 825	52.20
Rollover and buyback	18 557	8.58
Loans from ordinary citizens and institutions	52 466	24.36
Total	215 552	100.00

Source: Chen, Qiumin(1999).

The small scale of operation of Chinese securities firms and the low level of concentration in the industry, as well as their low level of capitalization, has been an obstacle to their expansion and long-term development, and has also reduced their ability to withstand risk. Added to this is an unbalanced situation with regard to market share. In the primary market, the strict restrictions imposed by the government on lead underwriters' capitalization allows the large firms to monopolize the market, with small and medium securities firms being at a disadvantage; the ten largest securities firms currently have a combined market share of over 60 percent. The degree of concentration in the secondary market is not as high as in the primary market, but even here the ten largest firms have a combined market share of 30–40 percent (Jiang, Shuncai 1999).

Furthermore, the competition in the primary and secondary markets is not properly regulated. As a result, the allocation of resources and competitiveness of securities firms are not in conformity with the needs of China's rapid economic development and the reform of state-owned enterprises. There has consequently been a growing trend towards mergers amongst securities firms, to enable them to compete with the big firms. This began with the merger between Shenzhen's Chang Cheng Securities and Hainan's Hui Tong Securities in late 1995 and early 1996; this was followed by the mergers between Shen Yin of Shanghai and Wan Guo, between Beijing Securities and Cai Zheng Securities of Beijing, and between Guo Tai Securities and Jun An Securities. The reform of state-owned enterprises in China requires mergers and the adoption of the joint stock system to ensure that resources are allocated with maximum efficiency; this will provide securities firms with potential business opportunities. During this process, given the diversification of equity transactions, only large securities firms, with their enhanced scale of operation and extensive resources, will be able to provide the financial consultancy and investment consultancy functions needed.

With the opening up of China's economy and the deepening of financial reform, as well as China's accession to the WTO, the opening up of the stock market and the securities business to international capital is inevitable. As China's securities firms will be forced to compete with transnational securities firms such as Merrill Lynch and Morgan Stanley, given the pressure of surviving in a buyer's market, their small scale of operations and low overall competitiveness, these firms will be forced to merge and form large securities groups if they are to be able to cope with this institution transformation.

2.2   Regional Distribution and Industry Structure of Listed Companies

China's regional development policy with respect to institutional transformation is a lopsided strategy of first developing the coastal regions of eastern China. This has affected the regional distribution of listed companies (Lin, 1999; Qu and Zhao, 1999). As can be seen from Table 2.17, during the period from 1 January 1996 to 30 June 1998, of all the companies listed on the Shanghai and Shenzhen stock exchanges, 252 (53.2 percent of the total) were based in the eastern region, whilst 221 (46.8 percent of the total) were based in the middle and western regions. This was mainly because, during the process of institutional transformation, the coastal eastern region was the first to be opened up, receiving preferential treatment to attract foreign capital and technology, foreign trade, and so on. As a result, companies based in the eastern region account for a higher proportion of the listed companies; however, as more emphasis has come to be placed on the development of the western region, the proportion of companies located in the eastern region that are listed on the Shenzhen and Shanghai stock exchanges has fallen, while the proportion located in the middle and western regions has risen.

An analysis of the locations registered by newly listed companies over the period 1 January 1996 to 30 June 1998, reveals the following results (see Table 2.18). First of all, in terms of the greatest number of listed companies, the provinces and autonomous regions are ranked as follows: Guangdong (including Shenzhen) (36 companies), Liaoning (33), Sichuan (33), Shandong (30), Hubei (30), Jiangsu (27), Beijing (24), Zhejiang (21), Fujian (21), Shanghai (20), Hunan (18), Hebei (16), and Jilin (15). All of these provinces and regions are located in coastal regions or along the Changjiang River; they began switching over to a market economy relatively early, had better economic infrastructure to start with, and had stronger enterprise management and investment management capabilities.

Secondly, again from the number of listed companies in each region, one can see that the provinces and cities that have developed most rapidly are: Beijing, Tibet, Shanxi, Inner Mongolia, Hebei, Guizhou and Hunan. Those that have developed the slowest are Shanghai and Guangdong, since they already had many listed companies. We can see from this that the regions in which new listings are concentrated fall into three categories, the first of which contains the major heavy industry centers where listing is promoted by the various government ministries. The second category comprises the remote regions, and regions populated largely by minority peoples, where funds are lacking. The third category consists of the leading energy producers and old industrial areas. Within their respective provinces, the enterprises listed are often long-established companies which are large in scale, have had

Table 2.17 *Regional Distribution of Companies Listed on the Shanghai and Shenzhen Stock Exchanges (enterprises)*

		Shanghai		Shenzhen		Total	
		No.	%	No.	%	No.	%
31/12/95	Eastern region	145	78.8	91	71.7	236	75.9
	Middle region	19	10.3	13	10.2	32	10.3
	Western region	20	10.9	23	18.1	43	13.8
	Total	184	100.0	127	100.0	311	100.0
30/06/96	Eastern region	161	74.2	102	68.4	263	71.9
	Middle region	29	13.4	18	12.1	47	12.8
	Western region	27	12.4	29	19.5	56	15.3
	Total	217	100.0	149	100.0	366	100.0
31/12/96	Eastern region	200	69.7	140	61.7	340	66.1
	Middle region	45	15.7	47	20.7	92	17.9
	Western region	42	14.6	40	17.6	82	16.0
	Total	287	100.0	227	100.0	514	100.0
30/06/97	Eastern region	231	67.4	186	59.6	417	63.7
	Middle region	56	16.3	71	22.8	127	19.4
	Western region	56	16.3	55	17.6	111	16.9
	Total	343	100.0	312	100.0	655	100.0
31/12/97	Eastern region	246	66.1	207	59.5	453	62.9
	Middle region	61	16.4	80	23.0	141	19.6
	Western region	65	17.5	61	17.5	126	17.5
	Total	372	100.0	348	100.0	720	100.0
30/06/98	Eastern region	266	65.8	222	58.4	488	62.2
	Middle region	69	17.1	84	22.1	153	19.5
	Western region	69	17.1	74	19.5	143	18.3
	Total	404	100.0	380	100.0	784	100.0

Note: The eastern region includes 12 provinces, municipalities and autonomous regions – Beijing, Tianjin, Shanghai, Hebei, Liaoning, Shandong, Jiangsu, Fujian, Guangdong, Guangxi, Hainan and Zhejiang. The middle region includes nine provinces, municipalities and autonomous regions – Heilongjiang, Jilin, Inner Mongolia, Shanxi, Henan, Anhui, Jiangxi, Hubei and Hunan. The western Region includes 10 provinces, municipalities and autonomous regions – Shaanxi, Gansu, Ningxia, Xinjiang, Sichuan, Chongqing, Yunnan, Qinghai, Tibet and Guizhou.

Source: Qu and Zhao (1999).

Table 2.18　　Number of Companies Newly Listed on the Shanghai and Shenzhen Stock Exchanges from Each Province, Municipality and Autonomous Region

Province	Shanghai	Shenzhen	Total	Province	Shanghai	Shenzhen	Total
Liaoning	11	22	33	Henan	5	5	10
Sichuan	12	21	33	Jiangxi	4	6	10
Shandong	15	15	30	Xinjiang	8	2	10
Hubei	14	16	30	Chongqing	5	5	10
Jiangsu	16	11	27	Anhui	3	6	9
Beijing	13	11	24	Hainan	3	6	9
Guangdong	2	20	22	Inner Mongolia	4	5	9
Fujian	10	11	21	Shanxi	2	6	8
Zhejiang	19	2	21	Gansu	4	4	8
Shanghai	20	0	20	Tianjin	5	3	8
Hunan	5	13	18	Guangxi	1	6	7
Hebei	6	10	16	Yunnan	4	3	7
Jilin	5	10	15	Guizhou	3	3	6
Shenzhen	0	14	14	Qinghai	3	2	5
Shaanxi	6	6	12	Ningxia	2	3	5
Heilongjiang	8	4	12	Tibet	2	2	4

Source: Qu and Zhao (1999).

a considerable amounts of capital invested in them, and exercise considerable influence. Examples include Bengang Steel Plate, Zhangze Electric Power and Jiangxi Cement. Their reorganization and stock exchange listing is in conformity with the government's industrial policy emphasizing the cultivation of the energy, basic industries and agricultural sectors.

In this section, in order to analyze the production structure of listed companies, we divide all companies listed between 1 January 1996 and 30 June 1998 into five categories – industrial, commercial, general, public utilities and real estate (see Table 2.19).

During the period 1 January 1996 to 30 June 1998, on average, industrial companies accounted for 65.2 percent of new listing on the Shanghai and Shenzhen stock exchanges. Industrial companies find it easier to improve their technology and introduce high-tech, high value added products; thus they possess good development potential. Given China's policy of fostering the development of knowledge-based high-tech industry, it is easier for companies in this sector to secure listing than it is for companies in other sectors.

Table 2.19   *A Comparison of Listed Companies in the Five Main Industry Sectors (enterprises)*

| | 1996 | | | | 1997 | | | | 1998 | |
| | Jan. – June | | July – Dec. | | Jan. – June | | July – Dec. | | Jan. – June | |
	No.	%	No.	%	No.	%	No.	%	No.	%
Industrial	33	60.0	86	58.1	95	66.9	44	67.7	46	71.8
General	11	20.0	36	24.3	28	19.7	11	16.9	12	18.8
Commercial	7	12.7	16	10.2	12	8.5	7	10.8	1	1.6
Utilities	3	5.5	10	6.8	7	4.9	3	4.6	5	7.8
Real estate	1	1.8	0	0.0	0	0.0	0	0.0	0	0.0
Total	55	100.0	148	100.0	142	100.0	65	100.0	64	100.0

Source: Qu and Zhao (1999).

As far as public utilities companies are concerned, as this sector accounts for a relatively small number of industries, during the five time periods covered in this analysis, the number of companies listed was relatively low. However, this sector saw the most rapid rate of increase in the number of companies being listed. The main reasons for this situation were first of all, that this sector benefited from supportive government policies, and secondly, as a result of the government's monetary and fiscal policy, the monopolies and economies of scale that have been created through the establishment of basic infrastructure have enabled public utilities companies to maintain stable revenue; this provides them with a much better foundation with respect to meeting the requirements for listing.

The commercial sector is rapidly approaching saturation point, and in recent years controls have been placed on the number of companies in this sector that have been allowed to list. The main reasons for this are as follows. Firstly, the government's guidelines regarding listing application review clearly stipulate that restrictions are to be placed on listing by companies in the distribution and finance industries. This leads directly to a reduction in the proportion of listed companies in the commercial sector. Secondly, competition in the commercial sector has been extremely fierce over the last few years, and average profits have fallen. Another factor is the impact of the Asian financial crisis on China's economy; as state-owned enterprises have been laying off employees, this has led to a reduction in income growth for both urban and rural residents and a consequent fall in purchasing power; which results in a fall in the profitability of commercial enterprises.

In terms of capitalization, 41.2 percent of listed companies in China have capitalization of between RMB100 million and RMB200 million; 22.95 percent have capitalization of less than RMB100 million, and 17.05 percent have capitalization of between RMB200 million and RMB300 million. These three groups combined account for 81.29 percent of all listed companies; however, the unreasonable equity structure of listed companies creates a situation in which it is difficult for listed companies to implement cross-industry, inter-regional mergers, which would otherwise help improve the allocation of resources.

Finally, as regards the listing of companies in the financial sector, on 27 November 2000, Minsheng Bank made a public offering of A-shares on the Shanghai Stock Exchange worth RMB350 million, becoming the third bank in China to secure listing. However, the number of financial enterprises that have secured listing is still low. So far, only seven financial enterprises have listed – Shenzhen Development Bank, Shanghai Pudong Development Bank, Minsheng Bank, Shaanxi National Investment, Ai Jian Ltd., Hong Yuan Trust and An Shan Trust. Other commercial banks, such as Zhao Shang, Guang Da, Hua Xia, Jiao Tong, Zhong Xin and Fujian Development Bank have already submitted applications for listing. This means that those banks which secure listing in 2001 will mostly be small and medium-sized banks; the big four state-owned commercial banks are not yet considering stock market listing (Yang et al., 2001).

Although the number of companies within the financial sector which have secured listing is limited, accounting for only 0.65 percent of all listed companies, they still occupy an important place in the stock market. Their total capitalization and total assets respectively account for 1.85 percent and 10.93 percent of the market total. Their average earnings per share are RMB0.3478, 70.49 percent higher than the average for the Shanghai and Shenzhen stock markets; their return on net assets is 13.89 percent, 68.98 percent higher than the average for the two markets as a whole. As regards the regional distribution of the seven financial enterprises which have secured listing so far, most of Shenzhen Development Bank's branches are in Shenzhen City, Guangdong Province and a few other major cities; most of Shanghai Pudong Development Bank's branches are in Shanghai City, the Changjiang valley and a few other major cities. The other four enterprises (three trust companies and one quasi-trust company) are all even more restricted in the distribution of their branches. This kind of geographical distribution is not beneficial as far as the long-term development of listed companies in the financial sector is concerned.

2.3 Conclusions

Overall, the characteristics and risks of the Chinese stock market can be summarized under a number of principal headings. Firstly, the structure and method for listing in the Chinese stock market violates the market principle. At the same time, the regional structure of the trading system and the market structure are not based on market supply and demand. Although A-shares, B-shares and H-shares can all be freely traded, the trading markets for the three types of share are kept separate. There is too much speculation, and in the B-share market there is a serious problem with shares being issued at excessively low valuation. In consequence, the stock market displays a unique form of systemic risk, which makes it difficult for it to fulfill its function in the allocation of resources; and as a result, the overall efficiency of the market is poor.

Secondly, different categories of share in the same company have different rights. Equity in the same company is artificially divided into state shares, legal person shares, public shares and internal (employee) shares, all with different rights. For example, holders of state shares can transfer the subscription rights (either in part or in whole) to holders of public shares. Holders of state shares thus have the option of sharing in the profits from investment or, instead of this, not subscribing and passing on the risk of investment to the holders of public shares. In contrast, holders of public shares can only buy and sell shares on the secondary market.

Thirdly, the proportion of non-transferable shares is extremely high. As a result of listed companies' constantly implementing capital increments, and the fact that state shares are often privately transferred to corporations, the proportion of listed company equity accounted for by state shares has fallen from 41.38 percent in 1992 to 38.9 percent in 2000; nevertheless, state shares are still the dominant category of share. As non-transferable shares, including state shares, account for 60 percent of all shares, enterprise managers do not have to worry about the possibility that poor management could lead to a fall in share price with the company becoming liable to a takeover. In other words, since shareholders cannot 'vote with their feet', managers do not have to be concerned about their rights.

Fourthly, the stability of the stock market is closely linked to investor structure. The majority of investors in China are individual investors. Owing to their limited knowledge, lack of experience and restricted access to information, individual investors tend to blindly follow the herd, leading to increased speculation, and much more severe market fluctuations.

Furthermore, the financial risk in China's stock market derives from the listing quota system in the primary market,[4] and the practice of planned price issue.[5] The abuse of listing shares at an artificially low price is intended to eliminate risk from the primary market, but actually leads to an imbalance in supply and demand in the primary market, causing disruption to normal economic activity and the financial order. The huge profits that can be made in the primary market encourage securities firms to obtain short-term loans from banks, at far higher than the normal borrowing rate, in order to subscribe to shares, engaging in ultra-short term arbitrage, speculation and price manipulation. As a result, capital flow into non-productive sectors is created and consequently, a 'bubble' economy is formed.

There is also lack of clarity with respect to property rights, which represents another major cause of risk in the Chinese stock market. The failure to clearly regulate property rights relationships destroys one of the basic principles of market operation (Tam, 1991), and leads to an increase in speculation in the secondary market, the creation of a 'bubble', and a marked reduction in the value of investments.

Finally, the large number of securities companies, the small volume of underwriting business available, the lack of variety in products, and the low profit margins all result in fierce competition between securities firms, leading to low efficiency and disorder. This is one of the main sources of risk in China's stock market. The allocation of resources among securities firms and their overall competitiveness is not in accordance with the needs created by the rapid development of the Chinese economy and the promotion of state-owned enterprises reform. Securities firms tend to have small scales of operation, with a low level of concentration in the industry; in addition, securities firms generally have low capitalization. This creates an obstacle to capital formation and long-term development, and reduces securities firms' ability to withstand risk, while increasing the level of risk in the stock market.

Notes

1. In the 1990s, China entered a peak period for bond repayment and the government was forced to issue new bonds every year to cover the repayment of old bonds. As a result, the scale of government bond issue snowballed and the financial burden on the central government increased steadily. The amount of interest that had to be paid on government bonds in 1995 was RMB 86.9 billion, in 1996 the amount due was RMB 130 billion, and by 1997, this had risen to RMB 195.9 billion.
2. Xu (2000) found through empirical verification that, as far as the Shanghai B-share market is concerned, there is no cause and effect relationship between trading volume and price fluctuation. Sun and Tong (2000) found that foreign investors were particularly concerned about macroeconomic variables in China and the impact of exchange rate risk on share prices.
3. Taking 1998 as an example, a total of 222 new companies were listed on the Shanghai and Shenzhen stock exchanges, with a total of RMB84 billion being raised. More than 50 securities companies participated in underwriting operations, and although the average value of underwriting business per securities company was only RMB1.68 billion, the 20 largest firms had a market share of 71.89 percent (Xu, 1999).
4. Although stocks also have to conform to listing standards, listing still occurs within a planned quota.
5. The price at which new stocks are listed in the primary market is not the anticipated market price; it is a price far lower than the market price set by the regulatory authorities.

3. Operational Efficiency and Regulatory System of the Chinese Stock Market

3.1 Analysis of Stock Market Efficiency

The efficiency of a stock market includes operational efficiency and pricing efficiency. The term 'operational efficiency' refers to whether the cost of the transaction service provided to investors during the transaction process is the lowest available; that is to say, whether the transaction efficiency of the stock market is capable of completing stock transactions for the party wishing to conduct a transaction in the shortest possible time and at the lowest possible cost, thus reflecting the organization and service functions of the stock market. In addition, transaction times and transaction expenses affect the liquidity of a stock market. If transaction times are long, or expenses are high, or both, this will reduce the liquidity of stock in the market, and will affect the judgments which investors make when adapting their investments according to market information. The term 'pricing efficiency' refers to whether the pricing of stock fully reflects all relevant information. What one is concerned with here is whether prices are fully disclosed and evenly distributed, so that every investor receives information of equivalent quantity and value during the same period of time (Fama, 1970, 1991). However, if securities prices are subjected to manipulation, or if relevant information is not fully disclosed, or both, then the stock market will misdirect the flow of funds.[1] This will not be beneficial to the regulation of the stock market or to the allocation of funds.

We further investigate the state of development of the stock market in China from the point of view of the level of securitization and the frequency with which shares change hands. First of all, as far as securitization is concerned, we can use market capitalization as a proportion of GDP to calculate the level of securitization. The combined total market capitalization (for A-shares) on the Shanghai and Shenzhen stock exchanges was RMB1,929.929 billion in 1998 and RMB2,616.762 in 1999. Comparison with the GDP figures for these two years, reveals a level of securitization of 24.52 percent in 1998 and 31.82 percent in 1999. In comparison with the 1992 figure of 3.93 percent, this clearly represents a high rate of growth (see

Table 3.1). It is still some way behind the 54 percent level of the advanced
nations, but is considerably higher than the 15 percent average of the
developing nations. However, these figures are based on the market price of
the total equity of listed companies, including non-transferable state shares
and corporate shares; they therefore do not give an entirely accurate picture
of the level of securitization in China.

*Table 3.1   Total Market Capitalization as a Proportion of GDP for Leading
Stock Markets (%)*

Year	China	Taiwan	New York	Tokyo	South Korea	London	Hong Kong	Thailand	Singapore
1992	3.93	47.15	64.60	62.43	34.8	90.2	171.80	60.13*	281.7
1993	10.20	86.70	69.40	67.88	42.1	126.3	331.90	68.24*	523.2
1994	7.92	102.90	64.13	76.67	50.4	117.0	205.66	93.58	446.5
1995	5.96	71.87	82.80	68.97	40.1	125.6	216.27	88.68	173.3
1996	14.52	100.62	95.60	64.92	29.3	149.5	290.32	54.40	159.4
1997	23.44	119.20	109.90	53.44	9.5	159.8	241.52	22.94	148.4
1998	24.52	96.24	120.7	64.74	35.7	165.6	206.61	30.9	107.4
1999	31.82	127.06	123.6	105.18	75.3	201.1	383.46	46.00	227.1

Note: * indicates that the figure represents total market capitalization as a proportion of GNP.

Source: China Securities and Futures Statistical Yearbook 2000, p.24, Securities Statistics
Compendium 1998, p.671, Taiwan Stock Exchange website.

Looking at trading volume as a proportion of GDP, we see that over the
years 1995 to 1999, the respective figures were 7.52 percent, 31.7 percent,
41.09 percent, 29.6 percent and 38.17 percent. The figure for 1992 was only
2.56 percent, demonstrating how the stock market has gradually come to life
since that year. Since 1996, the figure for trading volume as a proportion of
GDP has surpassed the 24 percent level of the advanced nations, and is
considerably higher than the 9 percent average for the developing nations.

The rate at which shares change hands in the stock market demonstrates
the highly speculative character of China's stock market (see Table 2.12 for
details). The reason for the level of speculation during the 1996 to 1997
period was that the range of financial assets available for China's citizens to
invest in was too limited. Added to this were the repeated reductions in bank
interest rates, which caused investors to shift their funds into the stock market,
while at the same time corporate profits were low, which encouraged
enterprises to use their funds for stock market price manipulation. As a result,

the level of speculation increased markedly (Jiang, Weijun 1999).

There is a need to establish a competitive environment in order to improve the level of efficiency of the stock market; the restriction of competition may hinder the raising of market efficiency. However, it can be seen from the above analysis that in many respects, the operations of China's stock market still show signs of the command economy system; for example, the issuing of new shares and price-setting are not determined by the underwriters and listing company in accordance with market conditions, instead, quota for the issuing of new shares is set and divided up according to a plan, and the timing of share issues is decided by the government. In other words, right from its establishment, it is hard for a listed company to avoid administrative interference.

Administrative allocation replaces market selection to create classic planned economy controls. This makes the quota for new share issues a scarce resource, and the additional value over par at which shares are issued becomes the rent in a rent-seeking activity. When small companies are listed, they are particularly prone to stock price manipulation, which has a negative impact on the stock market's function of regulating capital flows. In addition, because price setting for share issues is subject to administrative interference, prices are often set too low, creating more room for price manipulation and increasing the level of risk in the secondary market, thus encouraging stock market fluctuations (Zhang, 2000). The market trading system includes the settlement and clearance system (the system which controls the amount by which share prices rise and fall), the trading cost system and the matching system; these are the fundamental systems underlying stock market operation. Once the trading system has been established and put into practice, a reasonable level of stability needs to be maintained if the market is to operate efficiently.

In June 1990, the Shenzhen Stock Exchange began charging stamp tax on share transactions; the party selling the shares was required to pay stamp tax at a rate of 0.6 percent of the total transaction price. Soon afterwards, stamp tax was also imposed on share purchasers. Thereafter, although the tax rate changed several times, stamp tax continued to be imposed on both seller and buyer. In May 1997, in response to the excessive level of speculation in the stock market at that time, the stamp tax rate was raised from 0.3 percent to 0.5 percent, but was later lowered to 0.4 percent in 1998 in order to stimulate the market's development. Furthermore, in order to stimulate the stock market, the Ministry of Finance announced on 16 November 2001 that the rate at which stamp tax is charged will be reduced. For A-shares, the stamp tax rate will be reduced from 0.4 percent to 0.2 percent; for B-shares, it will be reduced from 0.3 percent to 0.2 percent (*Renmin Ribao*, 16 November 2001).

If one looks at the current level of transaction costs in China's stock market, commissions account for approximately 3.5–4 percent, while stamp tax accounts for 0.2 percent, neither of which are particularly high figures. However, adjustment of the stamp tax rate is constantly being used to implement changes in the trading system. If the market is depressed, the restrictions on daily price fluctuations are lifted, with a change from T+1 to T+0, and the stamp tax rate is reduced, in order to revitalize the market. When the market is overheating, price fluctuation restrictions are re-imposed, with a change from T+0 to T+1, and the stamp tax rate is raised, in order to discourage excessive speculation (Hu, 1999). On 20 November 2001, the China Securities Regulatory Commission gave its approval for the Trading Regulations of the Shanghai and Shenzhen Stock Exchanges to come into effect on 1 December 2001. Under these new Trading Regulations, the method of trading in B-shares will be adjusted to bring it into line with the method used with A-shares; that is to say, the current T+0 method will be replaced with the T+1 method. Changes in the trading system affect share liquidity and risk, and have a major impact on market operations.

In addition, stamp tax has the following inherent flaws, which tend to affect market operation: (i) Stamp tax is assessed only on transactions involving listed shares; there are no provisions for imposing stamp tax on unlisted shares, listed corporate shares, listed and unlisted corporate bonds and investment funds, and so on; (ii) The 0.2 percent rate, at which stamp tax is assessed on both buyer and seller, is significantly higher than the rate in other countries. Not only does the imposition of stamp tax on both buyer and seller increase the buyer's costs, thereby acting as an obstacle to liquidity, but it also fails to achieve the goal of using taxation as leverage to control speculation; and (iii) With a single tax rate, the tax cannot be flexibly adjusted in line with changes in the market. This is not conducive to the encouragement of long-term investment, nor does it help to deter short-term share price manipulation (Zeng and Mei, 2000).

As far as the settlement system is concerned, at present both the Shanghai and Shenzhen stock exchanges have their own independent settlement systems. The vast amounts of share registration data involved are divided into two different systems that are unconnected, thus preventing the sharing of resources. This duplication of both system establishment and operation results in a situation whereby accounts from one exchange cannot be used for the other; thus, those investors and securities firms wishing to participate in both exchanges have to open two separate accounts, representing a waste of resources. Not only is this unbeneficial to the trading and settlement activities of investors and securities firms, it also reduces the efficiency of fund use and affects stock market operation (Yu, Yimin 2000).

On 14 February 2000, the People's Bank of China (PBC) and the China

Securities Regulatory Commission (CSRC) promulgated the Regulations Governing the Pledging of Securities by Securities Firms. These regulations allowed those securities firms that conformed to the specified qualifications to use securities and fund certificates as collateral to obtain loans from banks. While this should help to improve the efficiency of fund use, sound risk management will be a prerequisite. That is to say, before issuing a loan, the banks should undertake rigorous auditing of the operational performance of the companies whose shares the securities firm is using as collateral. The bank should also implement ongoing monitoring of the relationship between the market value of the pledged securities and the size of the loan. If the ratio of the market value of the pledged securities to the size of the loan is too low, it is likely to result in heavy selling on a large scale, which will increase the risk of fluctuation in share prices, and will have an adverse affect on the normal operation of the stock market (Chen and Wu, 2000).

Finally, as far as financing risk disclosure is concerned, although the information disclosure system in China's stock markets is being constantly improved and has made significant progress, it still has many deficiencies. For example: (i) The timing of information disclosure is excessively concentrated, which tends to exacerbate market fluctuations. As China's accounting year is based on the calendar year, almost all listed companies issue their financial statements at the same time, causing the market to rise and fall heavily; (ii) Listed companies still have to report their production and operations status to the regulatory authorities and statistical authorities. This makes it easy for information to leak out, in violation of the principle that the disclosure of information should be open, fair and prompt; and (iii) Disclosure is inadequate, and tends to be characterized by long delays. This is particularly true with regard to annual reports; as a rule, more than half of all listed companies delay publication of their annual report until the last 15 days. This means that the information is less up-to-date, and tends to result in leaks, enabling a minority of persons to engage in insider dealing (Cao, 1998).

The factors affecting stock prices are all reflected in the form of information. There is still some room for improvement in China's stock markets in terms of the accuracy, timeliness and openness of disclosure. In addition, China's media need to disclose information fully, promptly and comprehensively, rather than serving merely as a propaganda tool. Only then can public opinion exercise its supervisory function, thereby assisting the development of the stock market (Wang, 2000). Taking 1998 as an example, as Table 3.2 shows, listed companies' total profits available for dividends were insufficient to cover investors' transaction costs; this gives some idea of the level of market efficiency.

Fama (1970) divided stock market efficiency into three categories – the weak form, the semi-strong form and the strong form. In a market with the weak form of market efficiency, prices incorporate all historical information; in a market with the semi-strong form of efficiency, prices reflect not only historical information but also all information that has been made available to the public. In a market with the strong form of market efficiency, prices reflect not only the factors noted above, but also all information known to insiders.

Table 3.2   Listed Companies in China – Profits Available for Dividends and Expenses, 1995–98 (RMB billion)

Item	1995	1996	1997	1998
Listed companies' profits available for dividends	31.920	33.405	35.0679	34.3287
Total stamp duty payable on securities	1.614	8.533	12.2890	22.5750
Total investor commission expenditure	1.412	7.466	10.7530	19.7530

Source: Chen, Yehua (2000).

In the literature, empirical studies of the Chinese stock markets using the efficient market hypothesis include that of Yu (1994), who conducted an empirical test of the efficient markets hypothesis for the combined index of the Shanghai and Shenzhen stock markets over the period 29 April 1990 to 28 April 1994, and found that the Shanghai and Shenzhen stock markets did not display weak market efficiency. Song and Jin (1995) divided the period since the establishment of the Shanghai Stock Exchange into two periods, with the second stage extending from January 1993 to October 1994. They undertook quantitative analysis of the weekly rate of return for 29 stocks and found that for this period the Shanghai Stock Exchange passed the weak market efficiency test. Mookerjee and Yu (1995) noted that although the Shanghai and Shenzhen stock markets were developing rapidly, they were still in the early stages of development. As a result of the excessively small scale of operation, problems with the supply of shares, inadequate professionalism, lack of the necessary hardware and an insufficiently comprehensive legal framework, the stock market was not efficient.

Liu, Song and Romilly (1997) took the stock prices for the Shanghai and Shenzhen stock markets over the period 21 May 1992 to 18 December 1995 as their sample. They used the Dickey-Fuller test to determine whether each market was efficient, and used the Johanson cointegration test and the Granger causality test to investigate the relationship between the Shanghai stock market and Shenzhen stock markets. In terms of the individual stock markets, they found that there was a random wandering process, and that individually, the two markets were efficient; however, the results of the cointegration test and Granger causality test showed that there was a causal relationship between the Shanghai and Shenzhen stock markets, and that the two markets were not efficient. Li, Lin and Li (1997) analyzed the stock index movements in the Shanghai and Shenzhen stock markets over the period 1 January 1994 to 31 August 1995, using the GARCH model to conduct empirical testing of the market fluctuations. Their results showed that there had been significant changes in the fluctuation structure of the Shanghai and Shenzhen stock markets, implying that the stock markets were inefficient. The fundamental reason behind China's stock market inefficiency is the weakness of the competition mechanism, which leads to imperfect competition and rent-seeking activity.

3.2 The Stock Market Regulation System

Violations of trading rules, a phenomenon that tends to accompany institutional transformation, occurs frequently in China's stock market; since 1993, there have been more than 100 cases of listed companies and an equal number of cases of financial institutions and securities firms having had penalties imposed upon them by the CSRC or other relevant agencies. Violations of trading rules have thus become endemic. Typical examples include, in 1996, the Zhang Jiajie Travel Agency, which bought and sold shares in violation of trading regulations both before and after an announcement of share transfer by the board; again in 1996, Hainan's Minyuan Xiandai Agricultural Development Company (Qiong Minyuan) and Hong Guang Enterprises made falsified profit reports; and in 1999, Daqing Alliance was found to have falsified its listing application documents. These violations exposed the regulatory problems affecting China's stock market (Cai, 1999).

Fundamentally speaking, the legal framework, regulations and supervisory system established for China's stock market in the early stages of its development were not sufficiently comprehensive. Prior to the establishment of the CSRC in October 1992, the main regulatory organs for the stock market were the People's Bank of China, its regional branches and local government authorities (see Figure 3.1).

The regulatory system of China's stock market is based on the considerations of overall control which are dominant in a centrally planned economy. The local authorities in Shenzhen and Shanghai established stock market leadership teams in order to strengthen the management of the stock market, with these teams also being responsible for planning stock market development and for formulating policies and regulations relating to stock market management and development.

Source: Chen (1997).

*Figure 3.1   The Regulatory System in the Early Stages of China's Stock
              Market Development*

In the regulatory system established in the early period of the development
of the market, a hierarchical relationship existed between the headquarters of
the People's Bank of China and its branches, while the relationship between
the local government stock market leadership teams and the branches of the
People's Bank of China was one based on coordination. This stock market
regulation system, based on the operation of the People's Bank of China, the
National Commission on Institutional Reform, local government authorities
and the local branches of the People's Bank of China, resulted in a situation
where stock market regulation was affected by many abuses.

According to Chen (1997), the main problems with such a system were: (i)
The People's Bank of China lacked the power to make decisions
independently. In order to be listed, a company's application to become a
joint stock company had to be first approved by the local institutional reform
committee before the application for listing itself could be reviewed. This
increased the complexity of the administrative process, led to delays in listing
and made it difficult for the People's Bank of China to plan the development
of the stock market; (ii) Since local government authorities were in a position
to affect stock market development, administrative interference tended to
replace marketized management, which affected the regulation and
development of the stock market; (iii) A primary consideration of local
government authorities was the advancement of their own self-interest. In
order to promote local economic development, each region competed to
increase the number of listed companies within its own region, which
hindered the development of the Shanghai and Shenzhen stock exchanges as

a national market; and (iv) The legal framework was unsound, too many different government departments were involved, and there were too many stock market management agencies organized in too complex a manner. The various agencies involved included the Securities Committee of the State Council, the Securities Regulatory Commission, the People's Bank of China, the State Development Planning Commission, the National Commission on Institutional Reform, the Ministry of Finance, and relevant departments at all levels of local government. Conflicts occurred between these agencies with respect to regulations and policy objectives, which reduced the efficiency of securities regulation.

In October 1992, the State Council formally established the State Council Securities Committee and the Securities Regulatory Commission to serve as regulatory authorities for the national stock market, in order to strengthen the overall management of the stock market, integrating the regulations and policies relating to shares, corporate bonds, treasury bonds, and so on, so as to protect the rights of the investor and to ensure that the stock market could develop in a healthy manner. On 17 December of that same year, the State Council promulgated the Notification Regarding Further Strengthening of Overall Securities Market Regulation, confirming the status and responsibilities of the State Council Securities Committee, the Securities Regulatory Commission, local government authorities, the People's Bank of China, the Ministry of Finance, the State Development Planning Commission and other agencies with respect to securities regulation (see Figure 3.2).

A committee system was adopted for the organization of the State Council Securities Committee with each of the State Council's 14 ministries and bureaus being represented by either a minister or a bureau chief. The Committee established an Office, under the State Council's Secretariat, with responsibility for day-to-day administration.

The responsibilities of the State Council Securities Committee were as follows:

(i) Responsibility for the formulation of draft laws and regulations relating to the stock market.
(ii) Formulation of policies and rules relating to the stock market.
(iii) Responsibility for drawing up plans and proposing recommendations for the development of the stock market.
(iv) Provision of guidance, coordination, supervision and inspection of the work performed by relevant agencies with respect to the stock market.
(v) Responsibility for undertaking overall supervision of the Securities Regulatory Commission.

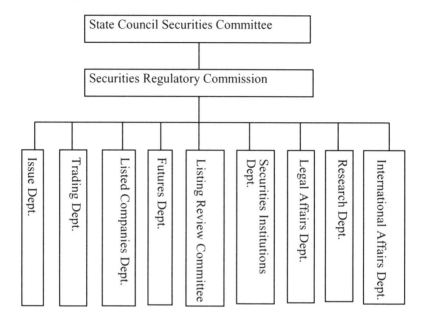

Source: Chen (1997).

Figure 3.2   The Transformation of China's Stock Market Regulatory System, 1992–98

In 1998, the State Council Securities Committee was abolished and the responsibility for formulating policies and regulations was transferred to the Securities Regulatory Commission. This created a regulatory system which involving a combination of government supervision and self-regulation, comprising the Securities Regulatory Commission, subsequently renamed the China Securities Regulatory Commission (CSRC), the local securities regulation agencies, industry self-regulation agencies and the stock exchanges (Zhao and Guo, 1998). The China Securities Regulatory Commission (CSRC) is the executive agency for securities regulation, originally coming under the State Council Securities Committee. It comprises experts with professional knowledge and practical experience in the field of securities, and functions as the industry regulator. The responsibilities of the CSRC are as follows:

(i)   Formulation of management regulations for the stock market as authorized by the State Council Securities Committee.
(ii)   Regulation of securities institutions with respect to the undertaking of

securities business, and particularly proprietary dealing.

(iii) Regulation of the issuing and trading of marketable securities, and of companies that have made a public offering, in accordance with the requirements of the law.

(iv) Regulation of overseas listing by domestic companies.

(v) Collaboration with other relevant departments on the production of securities statistics, in order to study and analyze market trends and to provide the State Council Securities Committee with timely reports and suggestions.

Several departments have been established under the CSRC, covering areas such as the Issue Department, Trading Department, Listed Companies Department, Securities Institutions Department, Legal Affairs Department, Research Department, International Affairs Department and Futures Department. These departments are responsible for implementing CSRC policy. Also coming under the CSRC is a relatively independent Listing Review Committee, formed from outside experts and relevant CSRC personnel, which is responsible for reviewing the prospectuses issued by applicants to make initial public offerings and fund issue prospectuses (Chen, 1997).

After a ten-year exploratory period in stock market management, the regulatory authorities in China have finally come to appreciate the importance of regulation, i.e. the need to provide market participants with an environment based on fair transactions and equal access to information. The emphasis in market regulation has shifted away from controlling risk towards disclosing risk; as a result, regulation is entering a new stage of development. Beginning in the second half of 2000, the CSRC began to issue numerous new policies with regard to stock market regulation. The main thrust in these new policies was as follows:

Fairness
There is a huge price differential between China's primary and secondary market which results in a considerable amount of unfairness in the issuing of new shares by listed companies. Funds and the so-called 'strategic investors', are able to participate in the original share allocation almost unconditionally, which distorts the principle of fairness in the stock market. In response to repeated appeals from small and medium investors, the CSRC promulgated the Notification Regarding Problems Concerning the Allocation of New Shares to Investors in the Secondary Market and the Notification Regarding Further Improvement of the Method of Share Issue. These notifications further expanded the scope of application of online issue and combined allocation to corporations with regard to ordinary investors, allowing issuing

companies to choose the most appropriate method of issue in accordance with market conditions and their own circumstances. The CSRC also promulgated the Notification Regarding the Regulation of Securities Investment Fund Subscription to New Shares, which stipulated that when new shares were issued no separate allocation of shares would be made to funds; in this way, small and medium investors are placed on an almost equal footing with funds. The CSRC also promulgated the Guidelines for Share Issue Using Allocation to Corporate Bodies, which restricted the proportion of shares that could be allocated to corporations.

From review and control to the maintenance of market order

The main emphasis of regulation of the stock market has been switched from review and control to the maintenance of market order. In the past, most of the CSRC's energy was expended on the review of listing and financial institution operations; insufficient importance was attached to the regulation of market order, and the methods used were too slow and therefore unable to meet the needs of market development. In 2000, the CSRC promulgated the CSRC Procedures for the Approval of Securities Issue, which involved a shift over from a review system to an approval system in the primary market; with the elimination of quota management, the right to make decisions on company listing and share issue was now transferred to the market.[2] As more shares were issued and the market became more marketized, the main focus in regulatory work came to be placed on maintaining market order, and the main focus in maintaining market order was in the regulation of the behavior of listed companies, securities investment funds and securities firms.

Transparency

In mid-2000, the CSRC issued the Provisional Guidelines for the Making of Public Offerings by Listed Companies, the Notification Regarding the Retaining of Auditing Agencies by Joint Stock Companies Planning to Issue Shares, and the Regulations Governing Disclosure by Companies Making Public Offerings — Nos. 1–6. In addition, a system was introduced requiring that legal opinions submitted by companies applying for listing must be confirmed before listing. The emphasis in all these regulations was on disclosure during the issue and listing process. Beginning in 2001, a requirement for listed companies to issue quarterly financial statements is to be implemented, initially applying only to particular treatment (PT) and special treatment (ST)[3] companies, but which will eventually apply to all listed companies; the aim here is to improve the system of disclosure by listed companies. On 30 November 2001, the China Securities Regulatory Commission announced the Revised Implementation Regulations for the Temporary Suspension of Listing and Permanent De-listing of Companies

Which Are Making a Loss; these Regulations will come into effect on 1 January 2002. Under the new de-listing regulations, the China Securities Regulatory Commission authorizes the stock exchanges to make decisions regarding temporary suspension of listing, restoration of listing and permanent de-listing in accordance with the law. The abolition of the PT system demonstrates that the de-listing system is becoming more market-oriented.

Greater responsibility for front-line regulators
The responsibilities of front-line regulators in stock exchanges and other institutions will be increased, thereby improving regulatory efficiency. Appropriate division of labor will be used to place the emphasis in regulatory work on systemic regulation and on the monitoring and punishment of major legal and regulatory violations.

Higher efficiency and order
The CSRC has promulgated the Provisional Method for the Provision of Guidance for Share Issue and Listing and the Supplementary Notification Regarding the Regulation of Share Underwriting by Securities Institutions. It thus use the listing guidance system to regulate the behavior of companies applying for listing. The establishment of regulations for underwriter reputation-building should improve the level of efficiency in listing application reporting and act as a stimulus for underwriters.

The systematization of regulatory methods
A real-time monitoring system has been established for the stock market, with the formulation of Regulations Governing Inspection of Securities Firms and Regulations Governing Inspection of Listed Companies. An electronic monitoring system for securities institutions has also been introduced to oversee the whole process of securities firm brokerage operations and trading operations, and a separate system has been established for holding discussions with the senior managers of securities firms and the chairmen of listed companies (Hou, 2000; Fei et al., 2001b; *Renmin Ribao*, 3 April 2001).

Listed companies, securities institutions and institutional investors (mainly funds), have felt the strongest impact of these regulatory developments. Companies' financing activities will become further marketized, with a strengthening of disclosure, and the new regulations will have a significant impact on those listed companies violating market regulations. For securities firms, the systematization of company management will be further heightened, competition for underwriting business will become much more fierce and significant adjustments will need to be made to brokerage business development strategy. The scale of asset management and investment banking revenue will also increase.

For institutional investors, as the disclosure system is improved, the implementation of the system for discussion with the senior managers of listed companies and securities firms, the raising of the efficiency of front-line regulators, the prohibition on introducing loan funds into the stock market and the imposition of severe punishments for violation of market regulations, will inevitably lead to investor behavior being effectively regulated. As a result, the profits that institutional investors and listed companies are able to make from price manipulation, insider trading and other abuses will be reduced (Fei et al., 2001c).

Prior to any exploration of the problems affecting the regulation of China's stock market, we must first of all familiarize ourselves with the chief characteristics of the regulatory system that has been introduced since the institutional transformation began. The main characteristics of the regulatory system used in the Chinese stock market are as follows.

China's non-unified stock market and its non-comprehensive legal framework

The establishment of the State Council Securities Committee and the Securities Regulatory Commission in October 1992 helped to strengthen the regulatory function. In 1993, the State Council promulgated the Provisional Regulations Governing the Management of Share Issue and Trading, which served as the legal basis for securities issue and trading prior to the implementation of the Securities Law. The Company Law was subsequently promulgated (coming into effect on 19 December 1993) to regulate company behavior, along with the Provisional Regulations Governing the Management of Share Issue and Trading, the Notification Prohibiting Securities Fraud, the Provisional Regulations for the Management of Stock Exchanges, the Notification Regarding the Strict Prohibition of the Use of Overdrafts in Securities Issue, and so on. However, most of these Provisional Regulations fall under the category of administrative measures, whereas share trading is a market activity, which cannot be managed properly using administrative regulation; one has to rely on the law and on economic measures to make the necessary adjustments and undertake the necessary supervision, with effective legal sanctions being of particularly importance (Chen, 1998b).

In 1993, with the promulgation of the Accounting Law and Registered Accountants Law, the CSRC and Ministry of Finance began to implement a permit system with respect to firms of accountants and registered accountants as regards securities business. In 1996, the Revised Regulations for the Management of Stock Exchanges were promulgated, authorizing local securities regulation agencies to exercise some regulatory functions. In order to promote proper regulation of listing, the government promulgated the

Regulations Governing the Undertaking of Underwriting Business by Securities Institutions, in an effort to clean up the securities institutions and keep banking and securities business separate, reiterating the prohibition on stock price manipulation. In March 1997, the CSRC promulgated the Provisional Regulations Governing the Restriction of Access to Securities Markets, with the revised Criminal Code (which came into effect in 1997) incorporating provisions relating to securities crime (Yao and Sun, 1997; Yang and Shih, 1999).

The Securities Law eventually came into effect on 1 July 1999, with the main purposes being to improve the efficiency of market operation, to maintain order in market transactions and to ensure that the rights of investors are protected. The Securities Law is the fundamental law governing the regulation of the securities business, and it has helped to clarify the legality, or otherwise, of various forms of investment behavior, as well as stipulating the powers of the market regulators. The contents of the Securities Law are analyzed below (Xu, 1998; Zhang, Kaiping 1999).

a. Stock market regulation is highly centralized and unified. The legal framework for the stock market covers the whole process from share issue to share trading, with regulation to be performed by the securities regulation and management agencies. There is also a high level of coordination between the Securities Law and Company Law, Criminal Law and Administrative Law. This high level of unification in stock market regulation overcomes the problem of the lack of statutory basis for regulation that existed in the past and eliminates the problems of having multiple regulators and local protectionism, whilst ensuring the quality of listed companies.
b. In the securities issue system, there has been a change from a review system to an approval system.
c. With regard to the openness of securities issue and trading, the compulsory disclosure system provided for by the Securities Law implies that sufficient information must be made available to investors regarding listed companies' financial and operational status if they are to be able to make rational judgements with regard to share value. In this way, investors can have confidence in the market while at the same time capital costs will be reduced, improving the overall efficiency of resource allocation in society.
d. A stock market risk prevention mechanism has been established with a high degree of transparency. Table 3.3 lists the various articles in the Securities Law relating to risk prevention. This kind of risk prevention mechanism can effectively prevent market manipulation by issuing companies, securities firms, other intermediary institutions and investors, ensuring that share prices are based on operational performance.

Table 3.3   Risk Prevention Mechanisms Provided for by the Securities Law

Object of regulation	Contents	Securities Law Article
i. Issuing companies	Issuing and listing standards	Article 11
	Temporary or permanent de-listing	Article 49
ii. Securities firms	Separation of securities business from the banking, trust and insurance industries	Article 6
	Separation of integrated securities firms from brokerage-type securities firms	Article 119
	Minimum capitalization requirements	Article 121
	Separation of proprietary trading and brokerage activities	Article 122
	Prohibition of the provision of financing and securities loans to customers	Article 141
	Prohibition of cross-trading	Article 35
	Balance sheet requirements	Article 124
	Risk reserve system	Article 128
iii. Other intermediary institutions	Establishment of risk funds by stock exchanges and registered companies	Articles 111 and 154
	Prohibition of the transmission of false information	Article 72
iv. Banks and state-owned or state-controlled enterprises	Prohibition of the illegal introduction of bank funds into the stock market	Article 133
	Prohibition of price manipulation of the shares of listed companies by state-owned and state-controlled enterprises	Article 76

Source: Zhang, Kaiping (1999).

e. There has been a strengthening of the system of the legal responsibility provided for by the Securities Law, which not only lays down the legal responsibilities of market participants, but also specifies the responsibilities of the regulatory agencies. There has been a shift away from the simple public law responsibility (administrative and criminal liability) of the past, towards placing equal emphasis on civil and public liability. In particular, under the provisions of Article 115, 'Those persons violating transaction regulations shall be required to bear civil liability', the principle of giving priority to civil liability is adhered to.

f. Following the rapid development of the 1990s, there are now a considerable number of securities firms in China, with approximately 90 institutions in the country engaged solely in securities business, along with over 300 institutions combining securities business with other activities, through a combined total of over 2,400 branches. However, as a result of the failure to establish the necessary legal and regulatory restrictions, the development of the securities business has been somewhat chaotic. As things stand at present, the securities industry in China is characterized by the following features: a large number of securities firms, highly concentrated in certain geographical areas, with excessively small scale of operations, low capitalization, uniformity of business activities, lack of regulation, high operating costs, poor manpower quality, and disorderly competition.

There are also frequent violations of laws and regulations by securities firms. Article 6 of the Securities Law stipulates that 'operation and management of the securities business shall be kept separate from that of the banking industry, trust industry and insurance industry; securities companies shall be established separately from banks, trust companies and insurance companies'. At present, the separation of the securities industry from the banking industry has more or less been maintained; however, trust companies and insurance companies are still involved in securities business on a large scale; these companies' securities business operations account for over 60 percent of all securities business nationwide. Article 6 also clearly stipulates that securities business must be kept separate from trust and insurance business; the securities operations established by trust companies and insurance companies will therefore need to be spun off from their parent companies, after which reorganization and mergers will be necessary.

g. Article 119 of the Securities Law stipulates that 'the state shall implement the separation of securities firms into integrated securities firms and brokerage-type securities firms. The China Securities Regulatory Commission of the State Council shall issue operating permits according to which category the firm falls into'. In addition, Articles 121 and 122 stipulate that the minimum capitalization requirement for the registration of integrated securities firms shall be RMB500 million, while the minimum capitalization requirement for the registration of brokerage-type securities firms shall be RMB50 million. Articles 129 and 130 clearly stipulate the scope of business activities for the different categories of securities firms: 'integrated securities firms may engage in the following types of securities business: (i) securities brokerage business; (ii) securities dealing business; (iii) underwriting business; and (iv) other types of securities business approved by the China Securities Regulatory Commission of the State Council' while 'brokerage-type securities firms may only engage in securities brokerage business'. These articles provide the necessary systemic arrangements for the specialization of securities firms in China (He and Zhu, 1999).

Although Company Law already contained many articles relating to stock market management, and although the fundamental law for the regulation of the stock market – the Securities Law – came into effect in July 1999, there is insufficient dovetailing between the Securities Law and existing laws and regulations such as Company Law, Criminal Law, the Law of Administrative Litigation, and the Provisional Regulations Governing Futures Trading; for example, there are some contradictions between the Securities Law and Company Law. There is thus a need for the revision of the relevant laws and for the formulation of ancillary legislation to fill in the gaps left by the Securities Law and other laws and regulations, reducing the gray areas and creating a comprehensive legal framework to regulate the operation of the stock market.

The ineffectiveness of self-regulation
In countries and regions with a developed stock market, self-regulation plays an indispensable role in market regulation. What is meant by 'self-regulation' is a situation in which securities institutions establish their own organization to undertake self-management within the scope permitted by law, including the regulation and management of market activity, management of market participants, mediation in the event of disputes and assuming responsibility for ensuring that participants' rights are protected. At present, the self-regulatory organizations in China can be divided into three levels; (i) The China Securities Association (established in 1991), which is a registered independent corporate body. It is formed from financial and other institutions involved in securities business, including securities firms, the stock exchanges, intermediary institutions, and so on; (ii) The stock exchange. At present, there are only two stock exchanges, the Shanghai Stock Exchange and Shenzhen Stock Exchange; and (iii) The internal management of

securities institutions and listed companies, including securities firms, joint stock corporations and intermediary institutions (firms of accountants, law firms, asset appraisal agencies, and the like), which can strengthen the self-regulation of the securities business and maintain trading order (Liu and Hu, 2000). Of these three self-regulatory levels, the most important agency in the stock market at the present time is the second level, the Shanghai and Shenzhen stock exchanges.

Securities firms often violate laws and regulations, use customers' funds for their own profit, engage in tax evasion, and manipulate the media to mislead the public (Zheng, 1999). As a result, the self-regulatory function of China's stock market is not yet functioning properly, and securities institutions have failed to help the China Securities Association to implement self-regulation.

Direct government involvement in economic activity

China is in the process of being transformed from a traditional command economy to a market economy and administrative interference in economic activity is still very common. The government is responsible for reviewing enterprises' applications to convert themselves into joint stock companies, for deciding on the number and scale of initial public offerings that may be made and for reviewing enterprises' share issue, listing and trading activities. Within these areas, government control is still very strong.

Stock market regulation by various government agencies

The balance of power between different agencies is uneven, resulting in unnecessary friction and wastage, which in turn affects the efficiency of market regulation. Starting in the second half of 1998, authority over the various securities regulation agencies in different parts of China began to be transferred to the CSRC, in order to facilitate the implementation of vertical leadership, and to establish a centralized, unified securities regulatory system for the stock market. This should help to reduce improper administrative interference by government agencies and local interests. With the implementation of the Securities Law on 1 July 1999, the Securities Law and other relevant laws and regulations have come to form the legal framework for China's stock market; however, the establishment of the regulatory system and legal framework should not be taken to mean that securities regulation can operate effectively; the key factor is the way in which the system operates.

The question of whether or not the stock market can be effectively regulated during the course of institutional transformation in China is strongly influenced by the following factors: (i) Whether or not the government is (directly or indirectly) a controlling shareholder in state-owned enterprises, i.e. whether the government is at the same time the market regulator and a market participant, which would tend to encourage the government to intervene directly in the market through administrative measures, thereby creating obstacles to the establishment of the rule of law; (ii) There has yet to be an overall change to the government-centered attitude which stock market regulators have developed over a period of many years. Furthermore, the quality of regulation is not high and regulators lack experience; (iii) There has been no thorough clarification of the relationship between the CSRC, its local branches and local government authorities; and (iv) State shares, which account for 60 percent of all shares, cannot be traded freely. This is an important factor affecting the efficient operation of the regulatory system and the legal framework (Southwest Financial and Economic University Project Team, 1999).

Inadequate regulations governing disclosure by listed companies

By comparison with the stock markets of the advanced Western nations, the regulations governing disclosure by listed companies in China are still inadequate. The State Council, Securities Committee and CSRC have promulgated a series of administrative and accounting principles relating to the disclosure of information, including the Provisional Regulations Governing the Management of Share Issue and Trading, the Provisional Implementation Regulations Governing Disclosure by Companies Which Have Made a Public Offering, the Provisional Regulations Governing the Prevention of Securities Fraud, the Provisional Regulations Governing Share Issue Prospectus Contents and Format, the Provisional Regulations Governing Annual Report Contents and Format, the Provisional Regulations Governing the Contents and Format of Interim Financial Statements, the Principles Governing the Contents and Format of Disclosure by Companies Which Have Made a Public Offering, the Principles of Corporate Accounting – Matters Occurring After the Balance Sheet Date, Principles of Corporate Accounting – Accounting Policy, Alteration of Estimates and Correction of Errors, and Principles of Corporate Accounting – Associate Corporations and Disclosure of Transactions Among Associates. However, disclosure by listed companies has still not been comprehensively implemented. The actual state of companies' operations is often not fully reported; for example, some companies will often window dress their financial data; some will include all subscription interest directly in the reserve fund; whilst others violate the CSRC's regulations regarding the use of account-type balance sheets, using instead a report-type balance sheet. Another problem is that disclosure by listed companies is not comprehensive; for example, companies tend not to give sufficient details of capital use, revenue from major investments and transactions with associates. There are often problems with respect to the timing of disclosure by listed companies; for example, companies may disclose information in advance, or delay disclosing information about events that have already taken place.

To summarize, there is room for further improvement in the accuracy, objectivity, quality and regulation of disclosure in China (Yao and Sun, 1997). At the same time, if the regulators can strengthen the regulation of disclosure by listed companies, this will help make disclosure more systematic, and will improve the regulation of listed companies (Chen, Ge 1999b; Song, 1999). In other words, owing to mismatch in the quality of the participants in China's stock market, there is a need for the establishment of a powerful securities appraisal institution, along with the formation of a securities rating system and the division of shares into different classes, so as to ensure that investors' rights are protected.

Notes

1. As Chow et al. (1999) pointed out, although the Shanghai stock market developed relatively late, its market pricing behavior is the same as those of the Hong Kong or New York stock markets.
2. This came into effect in March 2001.
3. ST companies are those that have made a loss for two years in a row; PT companies are those that have made a loss for at least three years in a row.

4. Operational Performance of Listed Companies

4.1 The Relationship Between the Stock Market and the Reform of State-Owned Enterprises

During the course of China's institutional transformation, the reform of state-owned enterprises (SOEs) has moved from giving enterprises greater autonomy to enterprise system innovation, a process that can be divided into the following stages. The first stage, from December 1978 to June 1980, was a trial period in which the amount of autonomy granted to enterprises was increased. During the second stage, from June 1980 to 1982, the responsibility system was implemented on a trial basis, followed by the third stage, from 1983 to 1987, which saw the replacement of profit delivery with tax payment, and a deepening of enterprise reform. The fourth stage, from April 1987 to December 1991, saw the across-the-board implementation of the contracting system, and alteration of enterprise management methods, and in the current fifth stage, from 1992 onwards, the management mechanism has been changed, with the establishment of a modern enterprise system. 1995 was the point at which establishment of modern companies began on a trial basis.

By the end of the 1990s, the majority of state-owned enterprises had been reorganized as companies (including limited liability companies) and joint stock companies; however, the problem of poor enterprise performance in China continued as a direct result of the public ownership of property rights (China Macroeconomic Issues Project Team, 1998). These problems stemming from the public ownership of property rights can be summarized as follows (Mao, 1998) : (i) In the vast majority of state-owned enterprises ownership is unclear and responsibilities and rights have not been clarified; (ii) A high debt burden is a malady shared by almost all SOEs, thus it is difficult for SOEs themselves to deal with the problem of large-scale over-manning; (iii) SOEs have to bear responsibility for a large proportion of social welfare provision, which should be the responsibility of society and of the government. SOEs have limited access to financing channels, which makes it difficult for them to compete effectively; and (iv) SOEs lack autonomy with respect to their investment activities, which makes it difficult for them to develop independent capital management.

Without full corporate property rights and the right to utilize their capital independently, SOEs are unable to reorganize themselves in accordance with the principles of capital market supply and demand, thus they are forced to rely almost entirely upon banks for their funding needs; the number of enterprises that are able to benefit from direct financing is extremely limited. As Table 4.1 shows, through analyses of the financing structure of Chinese enterprises, it becomes apparent that the proportion of enterprises using direct financing is very low; as virtually all enterprises rely mainly upon indirect financing.

Table 4.1　*Financing Structure of Chinese Enterprises (%)*

	1989	1990	1991	1992	1993	1994	1995	1996
Direct financing	3.37	2.35	3.24	6.27	5.82	4.29	3.59	3.53
Indirect financing	96.93	97.65	96.96	93.73	94.18	95.71	96.41	96.47

Source:　Liu and Yuan (1999).

The rebirth and development of China's stock market was closely linked with the reform of state-owned enterprises. As the stock market began to develop in the mid-1980s, it so happened that the reform of the urban economy was also starting to get underway in 1984/85. In the reform of the urban economy, the main focus was on granting greater autonomy to SOEs and implementing the responsibility system. Under these circumstances, SOEs began to raise capital, and the first shares developed from the capital raising function. As the volume of shares issued increased, the first stock exchanges (the securities trading centers) began to be established.

At the same time, the development of the capital markets, and particularly the stock market, impacted on the reform of the SOEs in a number of ways (Wang, Yi 1999; Wang and Yuan, 1999): (i) The government was promoting the reform of the enterprise ownership structure and internal management structure. Through the capital markets, and particularly the stock market, SOEs could become listed and obtain direct financing, thereby increasing their owned capital. Mergers and acquisitions among enterprises made ownership more liquid and allowed it to be reorganized, making it possible for SOEs to reorganize their bad debts, and thereby reducing the bank's non-performing loan burden and altering the situation whereby SOEs had low owned capital ratios and high debt ratios. The first step in the restructuring of the SOEs had to be a reorganization of debt, through measures such as the 'replacement of loans by investment' (converting bank loans to investment by the state) and 'replacement of debt by equity'[1] (switching over from enterprise debt to bank equity). By using the capital markets to securitize

SOEs' debts and assets, it was possible to change the SOEs' unitary ownership structure, switching over to a more diversified range of ownership forms, thereby benefiting the development of a modern enterprise ownership and management mechanism; (ii) An effective capital flow mechanism was provided for the reform of the SOEs; (iii) Acquisitions and other forms of asset reorganization were promoted; (iv) The development of the capital markets encouraged the selection of competitive managers for state-owned assets. The stock market is an important means for achieving economic growth and direct financing through the stock market can become an important means of investment. Through the raising of funds on the stock market, the managers of SOEs can be placed under pressure from shareholders, creditors, and the market; in other words, listed company managers are forced to make the maximization of profit their main objective, encouraging them to proactively improve their management practices and the efficiency of capital utilization, thereby promoting the ongoing development of the company, giving shareholders a satisfactory return on their investment and ensuring that bondholders receive both payment of interest and repayment of the principal in a timely manner; (v) The adoption of the corporate governance system among SOEs was promoted. The listing of and issuing of shares by SOEs has to be conducted in accordance with the provisions of Company Law and the Provisional Regulations Governing the Management of Share Issue and Trading. In the course of the reform of SOEs, the assets of SOEs have to undergo appraisal by an asset appraisal agency, as well as undergoing review by a firm of accountants and a law firm, in order to promote the clarification of ownership rights; (vi) The development of the stock markets has encouraged greater transparency in enterprise management and encouraged the preservation and growth of state-owned assets. During the process of listing and thereafter, SOEs are subject to supervision by investors, intermediary agencies, the media, the relevant government agencies and the stock exchanges. They are required to issue both regular and occasional financial statements, as well as being required to disclose other important information likely to affect the company's operations. Compulsory disclosure, coupled with supervision by the public, and regulation in accordance with the requirements of the law, has significantly increased the level of transparency among SOEs. Any mistake on the part of a listed company is likely to have an effect on the company's share price and any violation of government regulations is likely to be discovered and made public at any time, which could result in serious loss to the listed company in question. This has helped to solve the problems of soft budget and poor management that have plagued SOEs for so long; and (vii) Over the period from 1991 to the end of 2000, listed companies in China raised a total of over RMB655.872 billion on both the domestic and overseas stock markets. This has improved the asset structure and financial status of listed SOEs. Beginning in early 2000, the government embarked on the reorganization of SOEs in several industries, including petroleum,[2] communications,[3] railways and electric power, establishing a regulated company system to bring about the reform of the SOEs. The reorganized SOEs were listed on domestic and overseas stock markets, establishing the effective corporate governance that would be necessary to turn these SOEs into real enterprises.

To summarize, not only can the development of the stock market help to expand the financing channels available to enterprises,[4] it can also change enterprises' ownership structure and internal governance structure. An enterprise's governance structure is a set of incentive and restrictive mechanisms, predicated on the assumption that shareholders and managers are separate entities, which are intended to reduce agency costs and to ensure that investors receive a proper return on their investment; however, there are still many weaknesses in the governance structure of China's SOEs. As far as incentive mechanisms are concerned, despite twenty years of reform, there has been no significant improvement in the incentive mechanisms of SOEs. Imitation by SOEs of the systems of punishment and reward used in private enterprises is affected by two major difficulties. The first is that it is difficult to find a suitable benchmark that can be applied to state-owned enterprises with different starting points and different policy burdens. The second is lack of faith with regard to incentives and undertakings; the SOEs' restrictive mechanisms could be described as a mixture of administrative interference and insider control.[5] This has resulted in a situation where enterprise management is divorced from the interests of the owners. It is thus insufficient to rely on the development of the stock market as a means of directing the course of SOEs reform; this has to be combined with other measures aimed at improving the governance structure of SOEs and the creation of an environment favorable to privatization if the cause of SOE reform is to produce genuine benefit (Wu and Zhao, 2000).

4.2 Exploration of the Relationship Between the Stock Market and Economic Development

4.2.1 Review of the Literature and Model Establishment

There is still considerable debate in economic theory as to whether the financial system affects economic growth; no consensus has yet been established on this point. Schumpeter (1934) felt that a sound banking system allowed entrepreneurs to secure their much-needed funds, was beneficial to technological innovation and thereby helped to boost economic growth.

Robinson (1979) took the view that non-financial enterprises led the financial sector. Lucas (1988) also suggested that economists had overemphasized the role played by the financial sector in economic growth. Levine (1997) used the function approach to analyze the relationship between the financial system and economic growth, finding that the rise of financial markets helped to reduce transaction costs and the cost of collecting information, made transactions in goods and labor more convenient, encouraged saving, provided supervision of company managers, helped to ensure efficient allocation of resources and helped to spread risk, thereby promoting capital accumulation and economic growth.

As regards the relationship between the stock market and economic growth, Greenwood and Smith (1997) claim that the development of the stock market helps to reduce the cost of capital accumulation, thereby facilitating the upgrading of production technology. Levine (1991) felt that liquidity in the stock market was beneficial to economic growth, and that to be profitable, investment requires the provision of long-term funding; however, savers tend to shy away from long-term lending. The liquidity of the stock market makes it easy for savers to convert their securities into cash, while at the same time companies are able to secure funds through direct financing from the stock market. Kyle (1984) and Holmstrom and Tirole (1993) claimed that the liquidity of the stock market increased the incentive for investors to obtain information about the company, thereby increasing the level of oversight of companies. Obstfeld (1994) noted that the internationalization of the stock market helped to spread risk, improve the efficiency of resource allocation and promote economic growth. Beck et al. (2000) suggested that sound financial intermediaries could help to improve the allocation of resources and raise total factor productivity, thereby helping to increase long-term economic growth. Among those adopting a different view of whether the rise of the stock market was beneficial to economic development, Mayer (1988) felt that even a large stock market was unimportant as far as corporate financing is concerned. Stiglitz (1985, 1994) claimed that the liquidity of the stock market did not provide investors with greater incentives to obtain information about companies, and did not therefore improve corporate management. According to Devereux and Smith (1994), the internationalization of the stock market will increase risk, and the savings rate would therefore decline, bringing down with it economic growth.

Jin and Yu (1998) looked at the movements in the Shanghai and Shenzhen stock price indices over the period from January 1993 to August 1996, carrying out empirical testing and looking at the relationship between the business cycle and inflation. The results of their regression analyses showed that on average, the Shanghai and Shenzhen stock indices anticipated changes in the business cycle eight months in advance and that inflation had a negative impact on the stock market.

Zhao (1999) analyzed the Shanghai stock index over the period from January 1993 to March 1998, conducting empirical testing of the relationship between inflation, income and share prices, and discovered that there was a significant positive correlation between share prices and unanticipated income, along with a significant negative correlation between share prices and anticipated income. There was also a significant negative correlation between share prices and inflation.

Dan (1999) looked at quarterly data for financial development and economic growth in China between 1993 and 1998 and conducted empirical testing of the relationship between the two. He came to the conclusion that the development of financial intermediary institutions in China could stimulate economic growth, but that the impact of the stock market on economic growth was limited.

Zhao (1999) used only Shanghai share price data as his sample; he did not include data for the Shenzhen Stock Exchange. As a result, his data cannot reflect the full picture of the relationship between the stock market and economic growth in China. There is thus a need for more rigorous empirical analysis of the relationship between the stock market and economic development.

Given that in theory the stock market can promote economic growth by improving the operational performance of listed companies, for the purposes of this study we have used five financial indicators for listed companies – profitability, liquidity, stability, management performance and growth – to explore the development of the stock market in China, including regional and industry variation. We have gone on from this to use the Chi-square method to investigate whether there is a relationship between the types of share issued and the region in which the company is listed; we have also used multivariate analysis to study the impact of stock market listing on listed companies' operational performance, to verify the impact of the stock market on economic development in China during the period of institutional transformation.

The variables used are taken from listed companies financial ratios. After standardization, these were used to calculate the five indices, which in turn were used as the basis for empirical analysis. Variable design is explained below:

Standardization of financial ratios

Given that the measurement standards used for financial ratios vary, in order to ensure that the same basis of comparison is used for all indices, the ratios were standardized using the formula:

$$Z_{i,t} = (X_{i,t} - \bar{X_i}) / STD(Y_i)$$

that is to say, the original variable had the average value subtracted and was then divided by the standard variation. After standardization, what the ratios represent is value based on the average level for listed companies; good or bad performance is thus relative.

Profitability indicator (F_1)

The profitability indicator is obtained by averaging earnings per share $(Z_1=EPS)$, return on net assets $(Z_2=ROE)$ and return on total assets $(Z_3=ROA)$ after standardization. Thus:

$$F_1 = (Z_1 + Z_2 + Z_3) / 3$$

where return on net assets = net profit / shareholders' equity at the end of the year; and return on total assets = net profit after tax / total assets at the end of the year.

Liquidity indicator (F_2)

The liquidity indicator is obtained by averaging the quick ratio (Z_4) and current ratio (Z_5) after standardization. Thus:

$$F_2 = (Z_4 + Z_5) / 2$$

where quick ratio = (current assets – inventory) / current liabilities; and current ratio = current assets / current liabilities.

Stability indicator (F_3)

The stability indicator is the debt ratio (Z_6) after standardization. Thus:

$$F_2 = Z_6$$

where debt ratio = total liabilities / total assets.

Management performance indicator (F_4)

The management performance indicator is obtained by averaging total asset turnover (Z_7) and shareholder equity turnover (Z_8) after standardization. Thus:

$$F_4 = (Z_7 + Z_8) / 2$$

where total asset turnover = operating revenue / total assets; and shareholder equity turnover = operating revenue / shareholder equity.

Growth indicator (F_5)
The growth indicator is obtained by averaging the growth rate for the operating revenue from core business (Z_9), the net profit growth rate (Z_{10}), the shareholder equity growth rate (Z_{11}) and the total assets growth rate (Z_{12}) after standardization. Thus:

$$F_5 = (Z_9 + Z_{10} + Z_{11} + Z_{12}) / 4$$

where growth rate for the operating revenue from core business = (end of period operating revenue from operating revenue from core business – beginning of period operating revenue from operating revenue from core business) / beginning of period operating revenue from operating revenue from core business; net profit growth rate = (end of period net profit – beginning of period net profit) / beginning of period net profit; shareholder equity growth rate = (end of period shareholder equity – beginning of period shareholder equity) / beginning of period shareholder equity; and total assets growth rate = (end of period total assets – beginning of period total assets) / beginning of period total assets.

4.2.2 Description of Sample and Empirical Methods

Listed companies' interim financial reports for 1999 were used, providing data covering the period from mid-1995 to mid-1999. The sample included 884 companies (including both A-shares and B-shares); 437 of the companies were listed on the Shanghai Stock Market, and 447 were listed on the Shenzhen Stock Market.

As regards industry classification, the Shanghai stock market divides all listed companies into five categories – industrial, commercial, real estate, public utilities and general. The Shenzhen stock market divides all listed companies into six categories – industrial, commercial, financial, real estate, public utilities and general. This classification is unsatisfactory, partly because the two stock exchanges use different classification systems, and partly because the classification is not sufficiently precise. If the industry data produced by the Shanghai and Shenzhen stock markets is used, not only is the classification imprecise, but the disparity between the number of enterprises in each category is too great. To facilitate comparison, for the purposes of this study all listed companies were divided into 21 industries: agriculture, forestry and fisheries; mining; food, textiles and garments;

printing and papermaking; metals and metal products; chemical industry; pharmaceuticals; construction materials; machinery; electronics and electrical appliances; precision instruments; vehicles; miscellaneous; public utilities; transportation; finance; real estate and construction; travel and hotels; commercial; trade; and information (see Table 4.2).

The data collected covered the period 1995 to 1999, a period during which both the Asian financial crisis and the economic recovery of 1999 occurred. It would therefore be inappropriate to compare the data for different years. In addition, as regards the comparison of financial indicators between listed companies, as a reasonable level of comprehension has already been achieved with respect to listed companies financial statements, the main emphasis in the following analysis will be on the comparison of industry performance in each year and on industry performance within the sample as a whole.

The industries to which the listed companies belonged were divided into four categories. Category One included those industries where the 1999 average value for a given financial indicator was not only higher than the average for all listed companies for that indicator, but was also higher than the average value for all listed companies for that indicator over the period 1995 to 1999. Category Two included those industries where, for a given indicator, while the 1999 average value was not higher than the average for all listed companies for that indicator, it was nevertheless higher than the average value for listed companies for that indicator over the period 1995 to 1999. Category Three included those industries where the 1999 average value for an indicator was higher than the average value for all listed companies for that indicator, but was lower than the average value for listed companies for that indicator over the period 1995 to 1999. Category Four included those industries where the 1999 average value for a given financial indicator was lower than the average for all listed companies for that indicator, and was also lower than the average value for all listed companies for that indicator over the period 1995 to 1999. Those industries in Category One were industries that performed better than industry as a whole during the period under observation; those industries in Categories Two and Three were industries that displayed second-class performance during the period under observation; and those industries in Category Four were industries which performed worse than industry as a whole, during the period under observation.

Table 4.2   Sample Data Industry Categories

Industry category	Original category	Industry category	Original category
Agriculture	Agriculture	Vehicles	Bicycles
	Forestry		Motorcycles
	Fisheries		Auto accessories
	Livestock		Auto manufacturing
Mining	Mining		Shipbuilding
Food, textiles & garments	Food		Aircraft manufacturing
	Textiles		
	Garments	Miscellaneous	Pens
Printing and papermaking	Printing		Toys
	Paper industry		Jewelry
Chemical industry	Chemicals		Sports
	Artificial fiber		Industrial
	Paints	Transportation	Warehousing
Pharmaceuticals	Pharmaceuticals		Transportation
	Biotechnology		Containers
Construction materials	Glass	Finance	Finance
	Construction materials	Commerce	Commerce
	Cement		Rental
Metals and metal products	Iron and steel		Packaging
	Metallurgy		General
Machinery	Agricultural machinery	Foreign trade	Trade
	Machinery	Real estate and construction	Materials
	Milling machines & materials		Highway construction
	Textile machinery		Basic construction
Electronics and electrical appliances	Electromechanical		Ceramics
	Electronic appliances		Harbor construction
	Wire and cable	Public utilities	Industrial districts
	Refrigeration equipment		Real estate
	Home appliances		Public utilities
Information	Computers		Energy
	Communications		Water supply
Precision instruments	Instruments and meters		Building contractors
	Medical instruments		
Travel and hotels	Travel		
	Hotels		
	Brewing		

The Chi-square method was used to determine whether there was a significant disparity between the types of share issued by listed companies and the regional distribution. The null hypothesis was that there would be no significant disparity between the types of share issued by listed companies and the regional distribution.

In order to determine the impact of listing on listed companies' operational performance, we used analysis of variance (ANOVA) and the Least Squares Means (LSM) value to discover whether there was any significant disparity in the operational performance of listed companies classified by type of share issue, region, or period of operation. The null hypothesis was that a listed company's operational performance would not change after stock market listing.

4.2.3 Empirical Results and Analysis – Financial Indicators

Profitability indicator analysis

The analysis in this section is based largely on the profitability indicator (F_1) for listed companies. Over the period 1995 to 1999, the profitability performance of approximately 50 percent of industries was better than overall industry performance during the same period. Examining the situation for different stock exchanges, we can see that, over the same period, the average profitability performance for companies listed on the Shanghai and Shenzhen stock exchanges was roughly the same; however, profitability for companies listed on the Shenzhen Stock Exchange was more widely distributed. If we look at the situation for different types of shares, we can see that over the same period, the average profitability for A-share listed companies was better than for B-share listed companies, but that profitability for A-share listed companies was more widely distributed.

An examination of the profitability for different industries reveals that miscellaneous, public utilities, information, chemicals, mining and machinery displayed good profitability, placing them in Category One, referred to above. Their average profitability index value for 1999 was not only higher than the average value for all listed companies for 1999, it was also higher than the average value for all listed companies over the period 1995 to 1999. Those industries displaying second-class performance during the period under consideration, or in other words, those falling into Category Two, included precision instruments, travel and hotels, and construction materials. Category Three included metals and metal products, printing and papermaking, and food, textiles and garments. Electronics and electrical appliances, agriculture, commerce, real estate and construction, pharmaceuticals, vehicles, finance, transportation and trade all fell into Category Four, displaying worse performance than the average for all listed companies during the period under consideration (see Figure 4.1 for details).

Liquidity indicator analysis

The analysis in this section is based on the liquidity indicator (F_2) for listed companies. Over the period 1995 to 1999, approximately 40 percent of industries displayed liquidity better than the average for all industries. Looking at the situation in different stock exchanges, we can see that during this period, the average liquidity performance on the Shenzhen Stock Exchange was better than that on the Shanghai Stock Exchange; however, the liquidity performance of companies listed on the Shenzhen Stock Exchange was more widely distributed. As regards the situation for different types of shares, during the same period, A-share listed companies displayed better average liquidity than B-share listed companies, although the liquidity performance of A-share listed companies was also more widely dispersed.

Viewed in terms of industry sectors, trade, precision instruments, mining, information, travel and hotels, public utilities and chemicals all displayed good liquidity performance, falling into the Category One, referred to above; their average value for the liquidity indicator in 1999 was not only better than the average value for all listed companies in 1999, it was also higher than the average value for all listed companies over the period 1995 to 1999. Those industries displaying second-class performance during the period under consideration included, in Category Two, transportation and real estate and construction, and in Category Three, miscellaneous, machinery, printing and papermaking, and vehicles. Agriculture, construction materials, pharmaceuticals, commerce, metals and metal products, electronics and electrical appliances, food, textiles and garments, and finance all fell into Category Four, with worse performance than industry as a whole during the period under consideration (see Figure 4.2 for details).

Stability indicator analysis

The analysis in this section is based on the stability indicator (F_3) for listed companies. Over the period 1995 to 1999, although 80 percent of industries displayed better stability performance than industry as a whole, overall the level of financial risk among China's listed companies is still quite high. Comparing the different stock exchanges, we see that during the same period, on average, companies listed on the Shenzhen Stock Exchange displayed better stability performance than those listed on the Shanghai Stock Exchange, and that the stability performance of companies listed on the Shanghai Stock Exchange was more widely dispersed. As far as different types of shares are concerned, during the same period the average stability performance of B-shares was better than that of A-shares, while the stability performance of A-shares was more widely dispersed than that of B-shares.

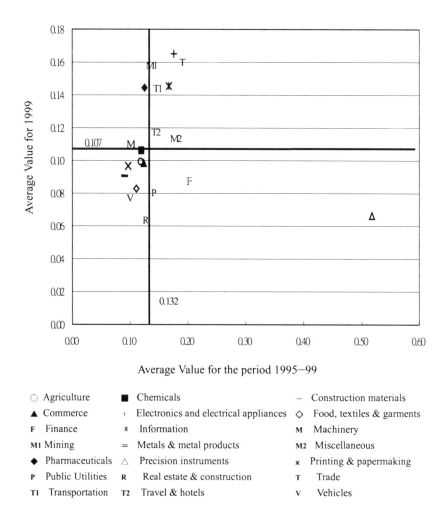

Figure 4.1   Profitability Indicator (F₁) – Industry Distribution

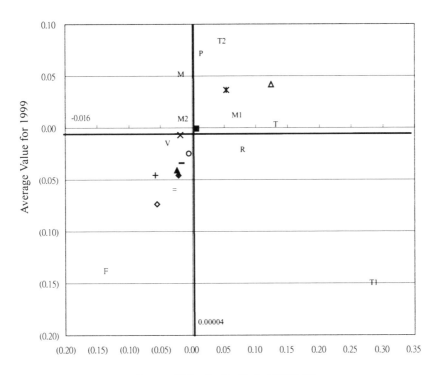

Figure 4.2   Liquidity Indicator (F2) – Industry Distribution

Viewed in terms of industry sectors, we can see that electronics and electrical appliances, agriculture, vehicles, information, real estate and construction, commerce and trade all displayed relatively good stability performance, falling into Category One; the average value of the stability indicator for listed companies in these industries was not only higher than the average value for all listed companies in 1999, it was also higher than the average value for all listed companies over the period 1995 to 1999. Industries displaying second-class stability performance during the period under consideration included, in Category Two, printing and papermaking, machinery, chemicals, metals and metal products, construction materials, mining, miscellaneous, precision instruments, food, textiles and garments, public utilities, and pharmaceuticals, and in Category Three, finance and transportation. Travel and hotels fell into Category Four, with worse stability performance than industry as a whole during the period under consideration (see Figure 4.3 for details).

Management performance indicator analysis
The analysis in this section is based on the management performance indicator (F_4). Over the period 1995 to 1999, although around 60 percent of industries displayed management performance better than that of industry as a whole, the overall management performance of listed companies in China was not good. If we look at the situation for different stock exchanges, we can see that over the same period companies listed on the Shanghai Stock Exchange displayed better average management performance than those listed on the Shenzhen Stock Exchange, but that companies listed on the Shanghai Stock Exchange had more widely dispersed management performance. As regards the situation for different types of shares, during the same period, A-share listed companies displayed better average management performance than B-share listed companies; however, A-share listed companies also had more widely dispersed management performance than B-share listed companies.

Turning to the comparison of different industries, food, textiles and garments, electronics and electrical appliances and mining all had good management performance, coming under Category One; not only was the average value for the management performance indicator of companies in these industries in 1999 higher than the average value for all listed companies in 1999, it was also higher than the average value for all listed companies over the period 1995 to 1999.

Those industries which displayed second-class performance during the period under consideration included, in Category Two, trade, travel and hotels, chemicals, machinery, printing and papermaking, transportation, metals and metal products, vehicles and agriculture, and in Category Three,

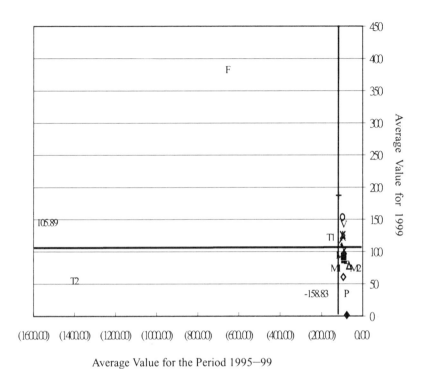

Average Value for the Period 1995–99

○	Agriculture	■	Chemicals	—	Construction materials
▲	Commerce	┼	Electronics and electrical appliances	◇	Food, textiles & garments
F	Finance	*	Information	M	Machinery
M1	Mining	=	Metals & metal products	M2	Miscellaneous
◆	Pharmaceuticals	△	Precision instruments	x	Printing & papermaking
P	Public Utilities	R	Real estate & construction	T	Trade
T1	Transportation	T2	Travel & hotels	V	Vehicles

Figure 4.3   Stability Indicator (F₃) – Industry Distribution

construction materials and commerce. Those industries falling into Category Four included information, precision instruments, pharmaceuticals, public utilities, real estate and construction, finance and miscellaneous; during the period under consideration, the listed companies in these industries demonstrated poorer management performance than industry as a whole (see Figure 4.4 for details).

Growth indicator analysis

The analysis in this section is based on the growth indicator (F_5) for listed companies. Although 50 percent of industries displayed growth performance better than that of industry as a whole during the period 1995 to 1999, the overall growth rate for listed companies in China is not high. If we look at the situation for different stock exchanges, we can see that over the same period, the average growth performance of companies listed on the Shanghai Stock Exchange was better than that of companies listed on the Shenzhen Stock Exchange, and that companies listed on the Shenzhen Stock Exchange also had more widely dispersed growth performance. With regard to different types of shares, over the same period, A-share listed companies displayed better average growth performance than B-share listed companies, but A-share listed companies also had more widely dispersed growth performance. Comparing different industries, we see that real estate and construction, precision instruments, electronics and electrical appliances, chemicals and printing and papermaking all had relatively good growth performance, falling within the abovementioned Category One. The industries displaying second-class growth performance during the period under consideration included, in Category Two, agriculture, commerce, information, food, textiles and garments, public utilities and miscellaneous, and in Category Three, pharmaceuticals and machinery, trade, construction materials, transportation, finance, metals and metal products, travel and hotels, vehicles and mining all fell into Category Four, with poorer growth performance than industry as a whole during the period under consideration (see Figure 4.5 for details).

4.2.4 Empirical Results and Analysis – The Overall Operational Performance of Listed Companies

In the above analysis we looked at the operational performance of listed companies in terms of five individual financial indicators – profitability, liquidity, stability, management performance, and growth. We now turn to the overall analysis of the performance of China's listed companies.

With regard to the analysis of overall industry operating revenue and profitability, Li (1999) suggested that operating revenue growth rate from core

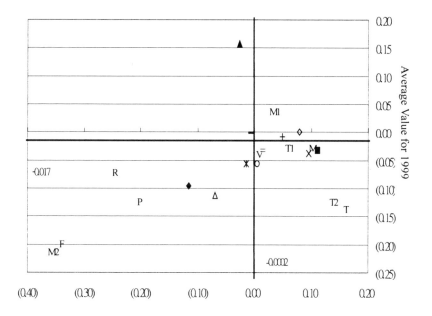

Average Value for the Period 1995–99

○	Agriculture	■	Chemicals	–	Construction materials
▲	Commerce	+	Electronics and electrical appliances	◇	Food, textiles & garments
F	Finance	*	Information	M	Machinery
M1	Mining	=	Metals & metal products	M2	Miscellaneous
◆	Pharmaceuticals	∧	Precision instruments	x	Printing & papermaking
P	Public Utilities	R	Real estate & construction	T	Trade
T1	Transportation	T2	Travel & hotels	V	Vehicles

Figure 4.4   Management Performance Indicator (F_4) – Industry Distribution

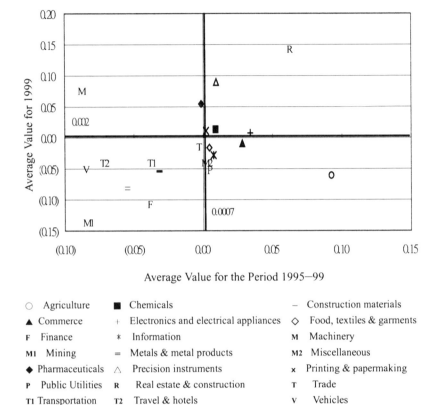

Figure 4.5   Growth Indicator (F_5) – Industry Distribution

business activities and return on equity were the indicators most representative of a listed company's operating revenue and profitability. The industry's growth rate in operating revenue from core business is taken as the horizontal axis, with return on equity as the vertical axis, and the relevant values from the Shanghai and Shenzhen stock exchanges are then plotted on the graph. The average value for all companies listed on the two exchanges is taken as the demarcation point, and all industries divided into four categories – industries with high growth and high profits (the first quadrant on the graph), industries with low growth but high profits (the second quadrant), industries with high growth but low profits (the fourth quadrant), and industries with low growth and low profits (the third quadrant). Those industries with high growth and high profits have the highest overall revenue and profitability; those industries with low growth and low profits have the lowest overall revenue and profitability; those industries with high growth and low profits or low growth and high profits lie between the two (see Figure 4.6 and Figure 4.7).

(1) Industries with high growth and high profitability
This category includes public utilities and trade. Their chief characteristics are that they have a large potential market and good development potential.

(2) Industries with low growth and high profitability
This category includes transportation, pharmaceuticals, agriculture, and mining. These industries have stable market prices, and while they do experience temporary slumps, overall they are stable, mature industries with high profitability.

(3) Industries with high growth and low profitability
On the Shanghai Stock Exchange, this category includes precision instruments, information, electronics and electrical appliances, the chemical industry, commerce, and miscellaneous, a total of six industries. On the Shenzhen Stock Exchange, it includes food, textiles and garments, pharmaceuticals, printing and papermaking, machinery and information, a total of five industries. The chief characteristic of these industries is that competition within the industry is extremely fierce. Although overall demand is still increasing, the rate at which the supply is increasing is far higher than the rate of demand. As a result, price-cutting competition is causing earnings to fall and there is market polarization in the performance of companies within the industry; however, the prospects for the industry as a whole are still good, and there is considerable potential for development in the medium and long term.

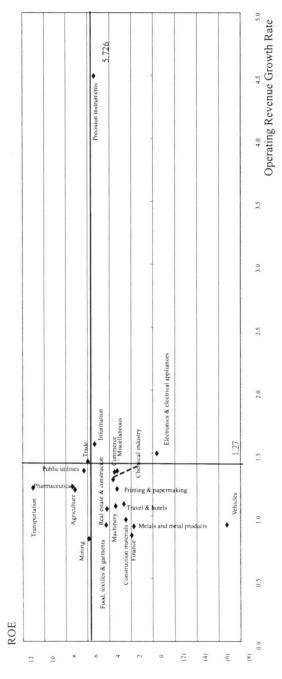

Figure 4.6 Distribution of ROE and Operating Revenue Growth Rate for Companies Listed on the Shanghai Stock Exchange – By Industry

96

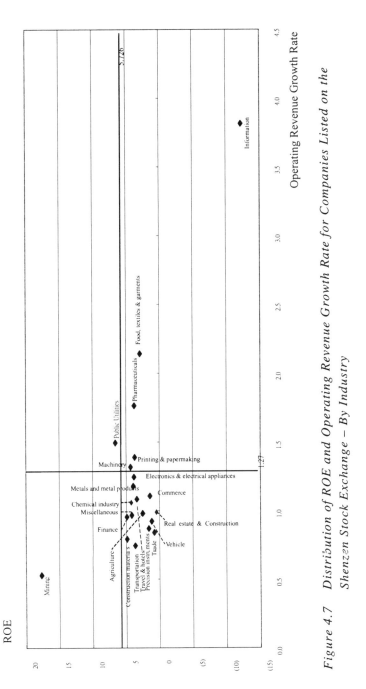

Figure 4.7 Distribution of ROE and Operating Revenue Growth Rate for Companies Listed on the Shenzen Stock Exchange – By Industry

97

(4) Industries with low growth and low profits

On the Shanghai Stock Exchange this category includes real estate and construction, travel and hotels, construction materials, metals and metal products, finance, vehicles, machinery, food, textiles and garments, and printing and papermaking, a total of nine industries. On the Shenzhen Stock Exchange, it includes real estate and construction, travel and hotels, construction materials, metals and metal products, finance, vehicles, electronics and electrical appliances, the chemical industry, commerce, miscellaneous, agriculture, forestry and fisheries, precision instruments, trade, and transportation, a total of 14 industries. The main characteristic of these industries is that many of them are primary industries. In recent years, the price of raw materials and energy in China has risen, but the price of finished products has fallen. As a result, the market has contracted, competition has become much fiercer, and overall industry performance has fallen.

4.2.5 The Impact of Listing on Listed Companies

In the preceding section, we undertook structural analysis of the financial indicators of listed companies in China; however, further analysis is required to determine whether stock market listing actually has a positive impact on companies' performance. In order to gain an understanding of whether there is any relationship between companies issuing A-shares or B-shares, and the region in which they list (Shanghai or Shenzhen), prior to undertaking the ANOVA test, we apply the Chi-square method to profitability, liquidity, stability, management performance and growth, in order to test whether there is any significant disparity between type of share issued and regional distribution. The results show that there is a significant correlation between whether a listed company issues A-shares or B-shares and the region of listing (Shanghai or Shenzhen) (see Table 4.3).

We then go on to look at the data for listed companies in the year of listing and the following three years, using the ANOVA test and the LSM value, and applying them to profitability, liquidity, stability, management performance and growth, in order to test whether there is any significant disparity in the operational performance of listed companies according to type of share, region of listing, or period of operation.[6] There are a total of four null hypotheses for the ANOVA test: The first hypothesis is that there is no significant disparity between the operational performance indicators of A-share listed companies and B-share listed companies. The second hypothesis is that there is no significant disparity between the operational performance indicators of companies listed on the Shanghai Stock Exchange and those listed on the Shenzhen Stock Exchange. The third hypothesis is that there is no significant disparity between the operational performances of listed companies during different periods of operation. The fourth hypothesis is that there is no interaction between types of shares, region of listing and period of operation.

Table 4.3   Chi-square Test Table

Indicator	DF	Value	Pr > F
F_1 Chi-square	1	5.759	0.016*
Likelihood ratio Chi-square	1	5.712	0.017*
F_2 Chi-square	1	5.83	0.016*
Likelihood ratio Chi-square	1	5.781	0.016*
F_3 Chi-square	1	5.83	0.016*
Likelihood ratio Chi-square	1	5.781	0.016*
F_4 Chi-square	1	5.83	0.016*
Likelihood ratio Chi-square	1	5.781	0.016*
F_5 Chi-square	1	41.553	0.001*
Likelihood ratio Chi-square	1	45.073	0.001*

Note: * indicates that the null hypothesis is rejected with a 5 percent level of significance.

The results of the ANOVA test show that, for listed companies in China, there is a significant improvement in profitability (F_1), liquidity (F_2) and management performance (F_4) after stock market listing, and that the main source of disparity is period of operation; in other words, the greater the period of time that has elapsed since listing, the greater the difference that can be observed in listed companies' profitability (F_1), liquidity (F_2) and management performance (F_4). Secondly, once companies are listed, their performance will vary only according to the types of shares and the region of listing, not according to the amount of time that has elapsed since listing. Furthermore, interaction between types of shares, region of listing and period of operation can be observed for profitability (F_1), liquidity (F_2), management performance (F_4) and growth (F_5) (see Table 4.4). There are two sets of null hypotheses for the ANOVA/LSM testing. One is that there is no significant disparity in operational indicators between the Shanghai and Shenzhen stock exchanges; the other is that there is no significant disparity in operational indicators between A-shares and B-shares.

Table 4.4   ANOVA Testing of the Impact of Stock Market Listing on Listed Companies' Operational Performance

Operational characteristic indicator		Type ISS	Mean square	F value	Pr > f
Profitability (F_1)	Type of share	0.705	0.705	1.39	0.239
	Region	0.004	0.004	0.01	0.928
	Period of operation	13.421	4.473	8.80	0.001*
	Interaction	14.13	2.83	5.56	0.0001*
Liquidity ($F2$)	Type of share	0.291	0.291	1.21	0.271
	Region	0.094	0.094	0.39	0.53
	Period of operation	3.775	1.258	5.25	0.001*
	Interaction	4.161	0.832	3.47	0.004*
Stability ($F3$)	Type of share	575531	575531	0.03	0.854
	Region	19164837	19164837	1.13	0.287
	Period of operation	45498609	15166203	0.90	0.442
	Interaction	65238978	13047795	0.77	0.57
Management	Type of share	1.043	1.043	1.39	0.239
performance ($F4$)	Region	4.508	4.508	5.99	0.015*
	Period of operation	6.948	2.315	3.08	0.027*
	Interaction	12.498	2.499	3.32	0.005*
Growth (F_5)	Type of share	1.182	1.182	2.82	0.094**
	Region	1.321	1.321	3.15	0.076**
	Period of operation	1.8667	0.622	1.48	0.218
	Interaction	4.371	0.874	2.08	0.065**

Note: * indicates that the null hypothesis is rejected with a 5 percent level of significance.
          ** indicates that the null hypothesis is rejected with a 10 percent level of significance.

We can see from Table 4.5 that while the Shanghai Stock Exchange displays significantly better performance than the Shenzhen Stock Exchange with respect to management performance and growth, there is no significant difference between the two stock exchanges with respect to profitability, liquidity and stability. Going on to compare different types of shares, we can see that while A-share listed companies display better growth performance than B-share listed companies, there is no significant difference between different types of shares for other operational characteristics.

Table 4.5   *ANOVA / LSM Testing of the Impact of Stock Market Listing on Listed Companies' Operational Performance*

Operational characteristic indicators	Shanghai LSM value	Shenzhen LSM value	Pr>|T|	A-share LSM value	B-share LSM value	Pr>|T|
Profitability (F_1)	0.06	0.08	0.68	0.08	-0.06	0.18
Liquidity (F_2)	0.04	0.02	0.45	0.03	-0.04	0.25
Stability (F_3)	-291.81	78.31	0.30	-182.07	-74.48	0.84
Management performance (F_4)	0.08	-0.03	0.011*	0.03	-0.11	0.22
Growth (F_5)	0.10	0.03	0.07**	0.06	-0.17	0.096**

Notes: Ho : LSM1=LSM2.
    *   indicates that the null hypothesis is rejected with a 5 percent level of significance.
    ** indicates that the null hypothesis is rejected with a 10 percent level of significance.

If the financial indicators for listed companies before and after stock market listing are grouped in sets of two years, as shown in Figures 4.8 to 4.15, then a number of observations can be made from these figures.

As regards the core business operating revenue growth rate, regardless of whether the company is listed on the Shanghai Stock Exchange or Shenzhen Stock Exchange, the distribution of the core business operating revenue growth rate for the year of listing and the following three years all lie below a line drawn at a 45° angle, showing that core business operating revenue growth tends to decline sharply after listing; there is a clear disparity here with the annual statistics reported at the time of listing.

With regard to net profit growth rate, regardless of whether a company was listed on the Shanghai Stock Exchange or the Shenzhen Stock Exchange, the distribution of the net profit growth rate for the year of listing and the following three years tends to lie below a line drawn at a 45° angle, showing that net profit growth tends to decline sharply after listing; there is a clear disparity here with the annual statistics reported at the time of listing.

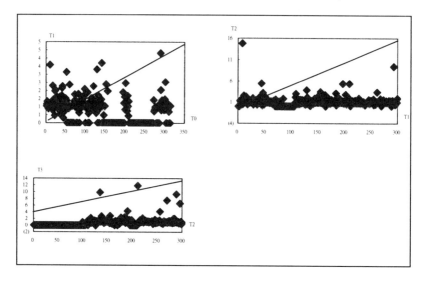

Figure 4.8   Distribution of the Operating Revenue from the Core Business for Listed Companies Before and After Stock Market Listing on the Shanghai Stock Exchange

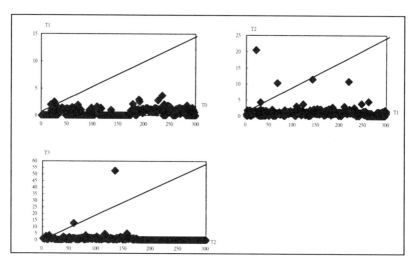

Figure 4.9   Distribution of the Operating Revenue from the Core Business for Listed Companies Before and After Stock Market Listing on the Shenzhen Stock Exchange

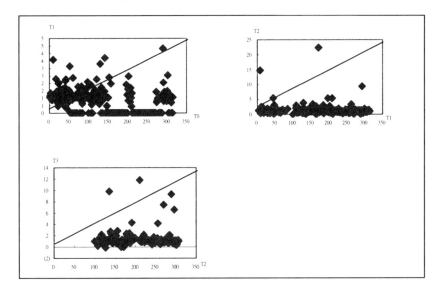

Figure 4.10 Distribution of Net Profit Growth Rate for Listed Companies Before and After Stock Market Listing on the Shanghai Stock Exchange

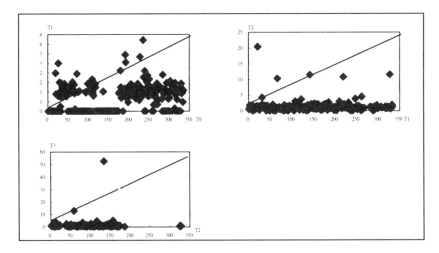

Figure 4.11 Distribution of Net Profit Growth Rate for Listed Companies Before and After Stock Market Listing on the Shenzhen Stock Exchange

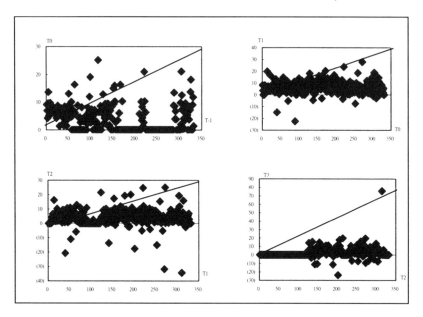

Figure 4.12   Distribution of ROE for Listed Companies Before and After Stock Market Listing on the Shanghai Stock Exchange

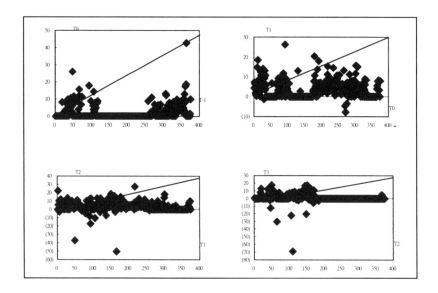

Figure 4.13   Distribution of ROE for Listed Companies Before and After Stock Market Listing on the Shenzhen Stock Exchange

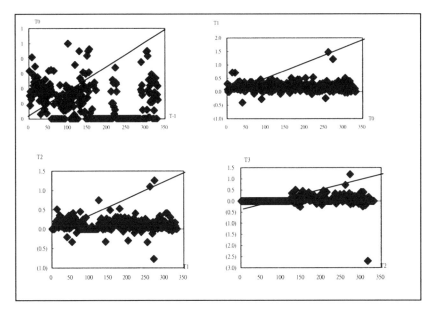

Figure 4.14   Distribution of EPS for Listed Companies Before and After Stock Market Listing on the Shanghai Stock Exchange

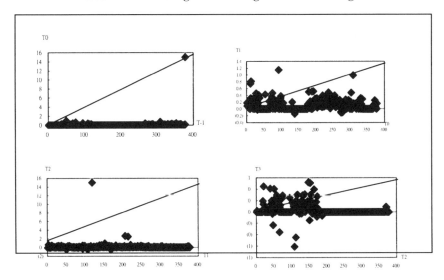

Figure 4.15   Distribution of EPS for Listed Companies Before and After Stock Market Listing on the Shenzhen Stock Exchange

In terms of return on equity, regardless of whether a company was listed on the Shanghai Stock Exchange or the Shenzhen Stock Exchange, the distribution of return on equity for the year of listing and the following three years all lie below a line drawn at a 45° angle, showing that return on equity tends to fall sharply after listing; there is a clear disparity here with the financial statements submitted at the time of listing.

As regards earnings per share, regardless of whether a company was listed on the Shanghai Stock Exchange or the Shenzhen Stock Exchange, the distribution of earnings per share for the year of listing and the following three years all tend to lie below a line drawn at a 45° angle, showing that earnings per share tends to fall sharply after listing; in the case of companies listed on the Shanghai Stock Exchange, there was a clear disparity with the financial statements submitted at the time of listing, while for companies listed on the Shenzhen Stock Exchange this was not the case, and some improvement could be seen in the tendency for earnings per share to fall.

To summarize, the above analysis shows that for enterprises in China stock market listing does not have any very marked benefits with respect to their operational performance, and in fact, operational performance tends to worsen. One of the reasons for this is that in order to implement the initial public offering and secure stock market listing, companies tend to submit inflated figures in the financial statements they are required to provide; the real situation starts to gradually unfold only after the company has secured listing. In addition, the state still retains a majority shareholding in most listed state-owned enterprises in China. The fundamental character of these enterprises has not changed, and the influence of the original state-owned enterprise systems and structures has not been erased. In particular, the government still appoints, or interferes in the appointment of, senior managers for some companies; there are frequent examples of the company chairman or president being appointed by the government authorities. In their governance structure, therefore, many listed companies retain an agency relationship within the company, rather than a property ownership relationship. At best, governance in these companies is a mixture of political interest and economic interest. What is more, the control which holders of 'state shares' exercise over the company tends to be weak in economic terms but strong in political terms. As a result, in their role as 'agents', the managers tend to be opportunistic with respect to political matters and to be affected by moral hazard with respect to economic matters.

Furthermore, owing to the dual identity of the manager/agent, the mechanism for encouragement and sanction by the company's managers cannot lead to the maximization of benefit for the company. There are also other serious problems, such as the fact that internal control of company personnel is not kept within reasonable limits (Li and Huang, 1999). In other words, the inherent defects of the governance structure of the Chinese company lead to poor operational performance (He and Liu, 2000; Wu and Zhao, 2000). For example, it is unclear how much control ownership of 'state shares' confers, there is too much insider trading, the responsibilities of the board of directors are not sufficiently well defined, there is too much administrative interference, there are too many problems of internal control, and so on. As a result, although working capital may have increased after listing, there has been no corresponding improvement in operational management. Consequently, the improvement in the company's operational performance as a result of listing is not that dramatic. Of course, operational performance is also affected by other factors not directly related to the company itself, such as the business cycle, the government's industrial policy, and developments in related industries; as such, the Asian financial crisis and the weakening of demand in China which occurred during the period covered by the sample may be another explanatory reason for the sudden drop in financial indicators.

4.3 Conclusions

Regardless of whether we look at the individual financial indicators of profitability, liquidity, stability, management performance and growth, or at a combination of these indicators, the only industries in China which display good performance are public utilities, transportation and finance; that is to say, China's 'sunrise' industries. The overall performance of other industries is noticeably poor and low growth rates are a particularly widespread problem. Owing to weak domestic demand and excess of supply over demand, competition within industries has become increasingly fierce, and profit margins have been squeezed. In reality, in many industries the majority of enterprises have already lost their financing ability, making it difficult to achieve further development. In other words, companies have accepted lower profits as the price for increasing operating revenue or market share, thereby affecting their financing capability.

With regard to companies' operational performance after stock market listing, viewed in terms of the region of listing, we can see that, for the management performance and growth indicators, the performance of companies listed on the Shanghai Stock Exchange is noticeably superior to that of those companies listed on the Shenzhen Stock Exchange. If one compares the situation with respect to different types of shares, it is clear that the growth performance of A-share listed companies is superior to that of B-share listed companies. As far as changes in the financial indicators are concerned, while there are changes in profitability (F_1), liquidity (F_2) and management performance (F_4) according to the length of time that a company has been listed, such changes are not noticeable for the other indicators. Furthermore, the growth-type indicators have a tendency to fall over time, suggesting that stock market listing is not markedly beneficial for a company's overall operational performance and that in fact, operational performance tends to worsen. One of the reasons for this is that when applying for listing, companies tend to inflate their performance, with the true situation being gradually revealed over a period of several years after listing. Another reason may be the impact of poor corporate governance in Chinese companies; examples include the lack of clarity regarding the control of state shares, the prevalence of cross-transactions, the fact that the functions of the board of directors are not properly regulated, excessive administrative interference, problems with internal controls. Although operating capital has increased after listing, there is no corresponding increase in management capability, and consequently listing does not lead to any real marked improvement in the company's operational performance. Of course, the fact that the Asian financial crisis and the downturn in domestic demand in China occurred during the period covered by the sample would also have contributed to the sharp fall in financial indicators.

Notes

1. An example is the RMB680 million debt conversion agreement signed on 16 November 1999 by the Hua Rong, Xin Da and Dong Fang asset management companies, the State Development Bank and the Anshan Steel Group. On 30 December 1999, the Zhongguo Hua Rong, Xin Da, Dong Fang and Chang Cheng asset management companies signed a RMB850 million debt conversion agreement with the State Development Bank, Shou Gang Ltd., Dongfeng Autos and Hengyang Steel Pipes of Hunan, whereby the asset management companies became the leading shareholders, helping the enterprises in question to restructure.
2. China Petroleum and Natural Gas made an initial public offering in March 2000 on the Hong Kong and New York stock exchanges in the form of H-shares and American Depository Receipts (ADR) respectively. After this initial public offering (IPO), the stake held in China Petroleum and Natural Gas by its parent company, CNPC, was reduced to 90 percent (Wu, 2001).
3. In June 2000, following reorganization, Zhong Lian Tong implemented an initial public offering on the Hong Kong and New York stock exchanges in the form of 'Red Chip' shares and ADR respectively. The total amount raised was US$6.278 billion, making this the largest IPO in Asia ever outside Japan. Following this IPO, the state's share in the company was reduced to 80 percent (Wu, 2001).
4. The benefits are however limited. Over the period 1960–89, the amount of financing which enterprises worldwide secured from the stock market accounted for only a relatively small proportion of total financing. The financing which Japanese companies obtain from the stock market every year (including corporate bonds and shares) accounts for around 5 percent of their total financing, and rarely exceeds 10 percent. In the USA, stock market financing accounts for around 10 percent of total financing, and hardly ever exceeds 20 percent; in Germany it does not exceed 5 percent, and is usually around 2–3 percent; in the UK it is usually around 5 percent, 10 percent at most (Lin, 2001).
5. For example, the Zhongguo Yituo Group of Henan Province succeeded in raising RMB1.6

billion on the stock market in 1997, but owing to errors in the Group's expansion plans, a considerable part of this sum was wasted.
6. Period of operation refers to classification of operational performance of listed companies according to the first, second or third year after listing.

5. The Impact of China's WTO Accession on the Stock Market

5.1 Analysis of the Level of Openness of the Stock Market

Once China gains accession into the World Trade Organization (WTO), the opening up of the stock market will have to be implemented in accordance with a set of principles that all signatory nations are required to abide by, including the principles of most favored nation (MFN) treatment, transparency, equal treatment with local citizens, market opening, more opportunities for participation by developing nations, and so on, as well as the principle of gradual liberalization. The impact on the stock market from the Agreement on Trade in Services is that all the signatory nations must be opened up to all other signatory nations. Unless clearly specified otherwise in the list of obligations, no signatory nation may restrict foreign capital from moving into their own securities market; this includes placing restrictions on the maximum shareholding in a company by foreigners, or placing restrictions on individual or cumulative foreign investment. However, the way in which China's stock markets have developed differs considerably from the requirements of the WTO Agreement on Trade in Services and the new Agreement on Trade in Financial Services. The most significant effects of WTO entry on China's stock markets will be as follows (Liu and Cui, 2000):

The internationalization of China's stock market
First of all, China's stock market is still relatively small, making it difficult for it to play any meaningful role in stimulating economic growth and also making it vulnerable to the impact of international capital. However, if China wishes to fully enjoy the benefits of WTO membership, and be granted most favored nation status by other signatory nations, then China's stock market will have to be gradually internationalized, to become an integral part of the global market.

The impact of foreign securities investment on the capital structure and supply and demand status of China's stock market should not be underestimated. Fundamentally speaking, overseas securities investment and relatively free inflow of foreign capital could cause the secondary market to grow, leading to expanding market scale and more complex investor composition. Given the current weakness in China's financial system, the need for improved financial supervision and particularly the lack of effective methods for managing or preventing the impact of speculative international capital on China's financial markets, market risk is bound to increase, thus market supply and demand and price trends will be increasingly influenced by the fluctuations in international markets.

Competition from foreign enterprises

The vast majority of China's listed companies would find it hard to compete with the enterprises of the developed nations in terms of management, production technology, product quality, after-sales service or economies of scale, and there is also a particular need for more regulation in the areas of enterprise accounting, credit rating and the disclosure of information. Once China has joined the WTO, foreign enterprises will be able to secure the same treatment as domestic enterprises, while at the same time, the amount of protection that Chinese listed companies receive from the government is bound to decline, with the subsidies they currently receive gradually being eliminated. Faced with fierce competition from overseas companies, listed companies will face new challenges in terms of raw materials, products, technology, capital, production and management methods, product marketing and the need to conform to international production standards and international practice regarding product exchange. This is bound to lead to changes in listed companies' operational status, which in turn will alter the stock market environment and the economy as a whole. This will affect the stability and development of the stock market, causing the performance of listed companies to fall, and share prices to fall with them.

Competition from foreign securities firms after WTO accession

Once China is within the WTO, foreign securities agencies will gradually start to enter the Chinese securities market and as a result, Chinese domestic securities agencies will start to feel the impact of foreign competition. Although China's stock market will not be opened up completely straight away, foreign securities agencies will gradually be able to secure a share of the market. According to the agreement reached between China and the USA, once China has joined the WTO, a small number of joint venture enterprises will be allowed to engage in fund management, with a maximum foreign shareholding of up to 33 percent, to be increased to 49 percent within three years. Joint venture firms will also be permitted to engage in securities issue and in foreign-currency denominated securities transactions, with a maximum foreign shareholding of up to 33 percent. As foreign securities firms start to move into the China market, in addition to the expected competition with local firms for talented staff, a 'sales war' can also be expected to break out.

The main areas of competition between foreign securities firms and local firms will include the following: (i) Foreign firms will be able to use their wide variety of services, flexible service methods and first-rate service quality to secure market share in those business areas offering low risk, low costs and high profits, such as information provision, household financial planning, corporate merger and reorganization, financial consultancy, and so on; (ii) They will be able to make use of their advanced hardware and other advantages to secure brokerage business in the secondary market; (iii) They will be able to make use of their flexible management mechanisms and other advantages to take away underwriting business from the local firms in the primary market. By contrast, all Chinese securities firms have similar business structure. They are limited to engaging in underwriting business in the primary market and brokerage and dealing business in the secondary market; and they have had little involvement in other business areas such as mergers and acquisitions, project financing, asset management, or information provision. Foreign firms will thus be able to rapidly increase their sales in these areas, obtaining first-mover advantage.

The composition of Chinese investors

The majority of stock market investors in China are individual investors with limited capital. There is too much speculation and too little real investment. The number of institutional investors is limited and management standards need to be improved. Once China has gained WTO accession, speculative international capital will move into China's stock market through a variety of channels, creating disorder and seeking to secure high profits. The risks faced by Chinese investors will increase, and the risks that have been building up over an extended period will explode.

Separation of the banking and securities industries

The banking and securities industries are kept distinctly separate in China. Foreign securities firms, which are permitted to engage in banking business, have a significant advantage over Chinese firms, whether in terms of funding sources or spreading of risk. Foreign securities firms can make use of a wide range of funding channels, including the issuing of shares and bonds, bank loans, bill financing and securities financing. By contrast, the range of financing channels available to Chinese securities firms is very limited; they cannot issue shares or bonds, nor can they secure loans from banks. As the treatment of foreign banks improves and the restrictions placed on them are reduced, unfair competition and inequality will develop between Chinese securities companies and foreign banks.

Structural inequality

China's securities companies are in significantly better shape than the country's four main state-owned commercial banks, both in terms of their structure and the extent to which their operations follow market principles; however, as a result of the high proportion of their shares held by the state, it is difficult for them to become genuine corporate institutions. This means that the securities companies will find themselves at a structural disadvantage in competition with the profit-centered foreign banks.

(1) Inequality of scope of operations

The various segments of China's financial sector are kept separate from one another, and the banking, securities and insurance industries are each separately administered. This separation of management is well suited to conditions in China, insofar as it helps to control financial risk; however, from an international standpoint, spurred on by financial liberalization, collective operation has already become a global trend in banking sector development. Those foreign banks that have already established branches in China are all leading international banks, combining the functions of commercial banks, investment banks, securities firms and insurance companies, and China's securities companies are simply in no position to compete with them. In contrast to China's securities firms, the multi-operations of foreign universal banks provide an even bigger advantage in that they can link up with the money markets and capital markets to implement various types of efficient investment portfolios. Not only does this help to significantly reduce costs, it also gives them greater autonomy when it comes to securing and using funds; their funds are able to flow freely between the money markets and capital markets. For China's securities firms, on the other hand, financing channels have always been one of the main factors obstructing their development.

(2) Inequality of taxation

On the surface, foreign financial institutions and China's securities companies are in the same situation in this respect, since the income tax rate is the same for both of them; however, in reality, like many other foreign companies, foreign banks enjoy special privileges, and their actual income tax rate is 15 percent. In comparison, not only do China's securities firms have to pay income tax at a rate of 33 percent, they are also the ideal candidate to be called upon by government ministries for assistance in funding, fee collection and tax payment arrangements for special tasks, which means that Chinese securities firms lack competitive advantage.

5.1.1 Current Penetration by Foreign Companies into the Chinese Stock Market

China's A-share market exists basically for medium-sized and large state-owned enterprises (SOEs) to convert themselves and raise funds; it has been opened up to foreigners to only a very limited extent. The listing quota system also constitutes a major obstacle to foreign companies and joint ventures wishing to list on the stock market in China. However, this has not stopped foreign companies from trying to move into the Chinese stock market. Some of the listed companies on the Shanghai and Shenzhen stock exchanges developed from joint venture firms; in other cases, foreign shareholders undertook share transfer or strategic investment. Some examples include: (i) Ford participated in B-share subscription and sale, becoming the second largest shareholder in Jiangling Autos; (ii) South Korea's Samsung Kang Ning used equity transfer to become the second largest shareholder in Sai Ge Samsung; (iii) Beifang Ltd. has become the first listed company in the A-share market to have a joint venture company as its promoter; (iv) France's Saint–Gobain Group used two Hong Kong companies to secure a 42.16 percent share in Fu Yao Glass; the two companies in question were San Yi Development, Fu Yao Glass's largest shareholder (with 63.4135 million shares, accounting for 24.89 percent of the total) and Hong Qiao (with 43.9942 million shares, accounting for 17.27 percent of the total); (v) Hainan Air's largest, eighth largest and ninth largest shareholders are all foreign companies – American Aviation Ltd., Naito Securities Co., Ltd. and Wardley James Capel Far East Ltd.; (vi) Shenyang Development is an H-share company approved by the China Securities Regulatory Commission (CSRC). Its shareholders include foreign strategic investors, with foreign shareholders having two seats on the board. A subsidiary of Shenyang Development in the water business is also run by foreign shareholders (Chen, Zhengrong 2001).

The CSRC has now eliminated the quota restrictions, and the administrative review system has been replaced by an approval system. This means that, in future, all foreign companies operating in China will receive the same treatment as domestic firms. The first move in this direction is to allow foreign firms to underwrite A-shares,[1] establish joint venture funds and issue A-shares both inside China and overseas (*Shanghai Securities Report*, 19 April 2001). Once China has joined the WTO, the upper limit on foreign shareholding will be raised to 33 percent and the restrictions on the establishment of joint venture funds in the A-share market should be lifted.

China is also considering introducing the Qualified Foreign Institutional Investor (QFII) system to encourage foreign institutional investors to invest in the Chinese stock market; if this does come about, the investment channels available to foreign companies and joint venture fund companies will become significantly broader; for example, companies would be able to participate in pension fund and social insurance fund management. At the same time, in order to meet the challenge that WTO accession will bring, Chinese securities firms are starting to engage in international collaboration to improve their competitiveness. Recent examples of collaboration between Chinese and foreign securities firms include the takeover of Shen Yin Wan Guo Securities by the Guang Ta Group, and the tie-ups between Dalu Huaxia Securities and Beijing Securities, Guang Fa Securities and Guangdong Securities, Nanfang Fund Management and Hongkong and Shanghai Investment Management, Fu Guo Fund Management and Canada's Bank of Montreal, Southern Securities and Commerzbank, and Yin He Securities and the UK's Shellord Group. In addition, Dresdner Bank has signed a technical collaboration agreement with Guotai Junan Securities, and Hong Kong's Jardine Matheson aims to invest directly in a joint venture once conditions are favorable. One of the main objectives of foreign companies in collaborating with Chinese securities firms is to be able to engage in open-end fund management. The Bank of Montreal has indicated that it will be providing Fukuo Fund Management with advice on how to launch open-end funds, and that in the future it hopes to be allowed to establish a joint venture fund management company; Yin He Securities and the Shellord Group have similar plans (*Zhong Jing Wang*, 26 April 2001; *Economic Daily News*, 5 July 2000 and 20 January 2001).

The methods whereby foreign institutional investors can enter the Chinese stock market are as follows. They can: purchase B-shares either in China or overseas; establish a fund management company in collaboration with a Chinese firm to manage closed-end funds in China; establish a fund management company in collaboration with a Chinese firm to manage open-end funds; establish a joint venture fund management company to manage open-end funds in China; and establish an investment fund through private subscription by foreign investors. Foreign institutional investors are also allowed to purchase Chinese treasury bonds and corporate bonds to establish foreign-owned fund management companies to manage both closed-end funds and open-end funds in China, to purchase Chinese currency market funds, to subscribe to Chinese securities on the primary market and to purchase shares on the secondary market. The probable scale of the different forms of investment is shown in Table 5.1. China finally became a member of the World Trade Organization (WTO) on 11 December 2001; the agreements made by China to secure accession will come into effect on 1 January 2002.

Table 5.1   Estimates of the Scale of Foreign Involvement in the A-Share Market in China (RMB billion)

Forms of foreign investment	Estimated scale of involvement
Purchase of B-shares inside China or overseas by foreign institutional investors	13.189 (already implemented)
Establishment of fund management companies in collaboration with Chinese firms to manage closed-end funds in China	3
Establishment of joint-venture fund management companies to manage closed-end funds in China	3
Purchase of investment funds in China by foreign institutional investors	10
Establishment of fund management companies in collaboration with Chinese firms to manage open-end funds in China	5
Establishment of joint-venture fund management companies to manage open-end funds in China	15
Establishment of investment funds through private subscription by foreign investors	20
Purchase of Chinese treasury bonds by foreign institutional investors	2
Purchase of Chinese corporate bonds by foreign institutional investors	5
Establishment of foreign-owned fund management companies to manage closed-end funds in China	5
Establishment of foreign-owned fund management companies to manage open-end funds in China	5
Purchase of Chinese currency market funds by foreign investors	5
Subscription to Chinese shares on the primary market by foreign investors	5
Purchase of Chinese shares on the secondary market by foreign institutional investors	20

Source: Yuan et al. (2001).

5.2 The Impact of WTO Accession on Listed Companies

Faced with the varying demands of the countries with which it needed to conduct WTO pre-accession negotiations, China announced the following basic negotiating principles: (i) In accordance with the principle of maintaining a balance between obligations and rights, China is willing to accept only those obligations appropriate to its current level of economic development; (ii) Bilateral and multilateral negotiations should be conducted on the foundations established in the Uruguay Round; (iii) China insists on joining the WTO with developing nation status.

The USA was therefore asked by China to grant unconditional most-favored nation status in accordance with Section Four of GATT and the 'Authorization Clause' agreed on in the Tokyo Round. In order to secure WTO accession as soon as possible, in November 1995, China began to reduce its tariffs step by step. Tariffs were reduced from the original 43 percent to 17 percent, and a promise was made that by 2005 they would be reduced to the average level for the developing nations (10 percent). China has also begun opening up the financial, insurance, marine transport and travel sectors on a trial basis.[2]

So far, China has completed pre-accession negotiations and signed bilateral agreements with 35 WTO members, including the USA, Japan, South Korea, Australia and Canada. Given that the bilateral negotiations between the USA and China are clearly indicative, and bearing in mind the application of the non-discrimination principle, studying the contents of the bilateral negotiations between China and the USA should help to clarify the extent to which China's markets will be opened up (see Tables 5.2 to 5.4).

In the following section, the contents of the Sino-American negotiations have been collated, in order to gain a clearer understanding of how China's markets will ultimately be opened up. Overall, the key points of the Sino-American negotiations were as described under the following sub section headings.

Commodity trade negotiations

The USA insisted that should China reduce its tariffs on agricultural products, requesting that the average tariff rate be reduced to 17 percent by 2004; the tariff rate for primary products from the USA was to be reduced even further, to 14.5 percent. At the same time, the USA requested that import quotas should be eliminated along with a reduction in the level of involvement of state-owned trading companies trading in key products, with a tariff quota system being adopted for particularly sensitive sectors.

Table 5.2   Sino-American Bilateral Agreement – Agricultural Markets

Tariff reductions	
1. Average tariff rate for agricultural products to be reduced to 17%.	
2. Average tariff rate for US primary products to be reduced to 14.5%.	
3. All tariff reductions to be implemented by 2004; no tariff increases to be permitted after that date.	
	Tariff rate
Soya beans (reduction to be implemented immediately after WTO accession)	3% (with no import quotas)
Oats	9%
Meat (to be implemented by 2004)	
Beef	45% → 12%
Pork	20% → 12%
Chicken	20% → 10%
Fruit (to be implemented by 2004)	
Oranges	40% → 12%
Grapes	40% → 13%
Apples	30% → 10%
Almonds	30% → 10%
Wines and spirits (70% tariff reduction)	65% → 20%
Milk products (to be implemented by 2004)	
Cheese	50% → 12%
Ice cream	45% → 19%

China is required to abolish import quotas, reduce the involvement of state-owned trading companies in key products and adopt a tariff quota system for particularly sensitive sectors.*

1. After China joins the WTO, the total tariff quota system amount shall exceed current import levels.
2. China to guarantee that private importers will be allowed to participate in the initial stage of import quota allocation. If SOEs are not able to purchase the full amount of their quota, the remainder shall be allocated to private companies.

Table 5.2   Continued

	Quota	Percentage to be allocated to private sector
Soya beans (tariff rate quota system to be abolished by 2006)	1.7 million tons → 3.3 million tons (2005) (tariff rate: 9%)	50%→ 90%
Wheat	7.3 million tons → 9.3 million tons	10% (SOE quotas that are not fully used can be reallocated in the latter part of the year)
Corn	4.5 million tons → 7.2 million tons	25% → 40% (2004 – SOE quotas that are not fully used can be reallocated in the latter part of the year)
Rice	2.5 million tons → 5.3 million tons (almost half of which is to comprise intermediate grade and unpolished rice)	50%
Cotton	743,000 tons → 894,000 tons	67%
Oats	No quota	

Tariff quota system to be applied to wool, sugar, palm oil and rapeseed oil.

Sanitary and phyto-sanitary (SPS) restrictions

China to sign bilateral agreements for wheat, oranges and meat, and to abolish inappropriate SPS restrictions on wheat, oranges and meat.

Meat	China to accept the Food and Drug Administration's safety certification system for meat exports, and to open up its pork, beef and poultry markets to US imports.
Oranges	China to open its market for tangerines, Cantonese oranges and other oranges to US imports (estimated annual trade volume, US$1.2 billion)
Wheat	China to abolish restrictions on the importation of wheat from the northwestern states affected by TCK disease.

Abolition of export subsidies

This applies mainly to subsidies for wheat, other grains, cotton, rice, meat, milk products and sugar.

Note: * The 'tariff quota system' refers to the system whereby a low tariff (usually 1–3 percent) is applied to imports within the quota, and a high tariff is applied to imports in excess of the quota.

Source: Collated for this study.

Table 5.3   Sino-American   Bilateral   Agreement   –   Industrial   Product
Markets

Trading rights and distribution [a]
1. China agreed to allow American companies to import and export freely, and to distribute and sell their products in China.
2. The above permission was to apply to the chemical fertilizer, crude oil, petroleum processing, timber and paper industries.
3. Implementation was to take place in stages over a period of three years.

Across-the-board reduction of tariffs for industrial products
1. The average tariff rate was to be reduced from 24.6% to 9.44%.
2. For certain American products, the tariff rate was to be further reduced to 7.1%.
3. Tariffs would not be brought back up again; i.e., China did not reserve the right to raise tariffs significantly again in the future.
4. Implementation was to take place in stages, with two-thirds of tariff reductions to take place by 2003. With a limited number of exceptions, all remaining tariff reductions were to be completed by 2005.

Areas to be given preferential treatment for tariff reduction	
High technology	1. Tariff reduction for high technology was to be implemented in accordance with the Information Technology Agreement (ITA).
	2. Tariff to be reduced to zero for semiconductors, computers, computer peripherals, electronic communication equipment and other IT products (the current tariff rate for this category of products is 13.3%).
	3. Implementation to take place in stages, with the majority of the reductions to be completed by 2003; extension until 2005 was permitted for some exceptions.
Autos[b]	The tariff on autos was to be reduced from the present rate of 80 – 100% to 25% by 2006, with a proportional reduction each year.
	The tariff on auto components was to be reduced to an average of 10%.
Products conforming to APEC voluntary liberalization provisions	Tariffs on the following products and services were to be reduced: Forestry products; Environmental protection products and services; Energy and energy facilities; Chemical products; Fish products; Toys; Precious stones and jewelry; Medical equipment and scientific instruments.

Table 5.3   Continued

Areas to be given preferential treatment for tariff reduction	
Forestry products	Timber (12% - 18% → 5% - 7.5%); paper (15% - 25% → 5% - 7.5%); there is to be a transitional period of two years for key US products.
Chemical products	1. China has accepted most of the articles of the Tariff Agreement for Chemical Products. 2. Tariffs to be reduced to 5.5% – 6.5% for 70% of chemical products, and to 0% for some products. 3. The tariff on soda ash is to be reduced to 5.5%. 4. The tariffs on cosmetics, pharmaceuticals, motion pictures and some plastics products are also to be reduced.
Fish products	The tariffs for the major US products are to be reduced to 10%.
Spirits	61% → 10%
Textiles	1. The quota on Chinese textiles was to be abolished by 2005. 2. China agreed that the USA could maintain the special defensive mechanism with respect to sudden increases in the importation of Chinese textiles until the end of 2008.

Ancillary and other non-tariff measures

1. Quotas are to be abolished for the products of most concern to the USA (such as some chemical fertilizers and fiber-optic cable).
2. All quotas to be abolished by 2002 (2005 at the latest).
3. The average quota is to be increased by 5% each year, in order to guarantee market opening and reduce the impact of quantity restrictions.
4. Quotas for automobiles were to be completely eliminated by 2005. During the transitional period, the base quota was to be set at US$6 billion, with an annual increase of 15% and eventually total elimination.
5. The US is to be allowed to retain its current anti-dumping appraisal method, whereby China is treated as a 'non-market economy,' for 15 years.
6. The US is to be allowed to retain its 'Special Defensive Regulations' for dealing with sudden rises in imports, for 12 years.

Notes: a The term 'trading rights' is used to refer to import and export rights; the term 'distribution' is used to refer to wholesale, retail, maintenance, repair and transportation.
b China agreed that the minimum level be set at 30 percent.

Source: Collated for this study.

Table 5.4   Sino-American Bilateral Agreement – Service Sector

Market opening

1. China agreed to accept the Multilateral Service Agreement for basic telecommunications and financial services.
2. China undertook to maintain the current level of market openness for American service providers (including distribution services, financial services, professional services and other service providers).
3. China agreed to abolish all restrictions on distribution services (including wholesale, retail, maintenance and repair, transportation etc.) within three years.
4. China agreed to provide distribution rights for chemical fertilizers, raw materials and petroleum products within five years.
5. China agreed to gradually lift the restrictions on ancillary distribution services[a] over a period of 3 to 4 years. US service providers would be permitted to set up wholly-owned subsidiaries.

Telecommunications industry[b]

1. China agreed to implement regulatory principles for encouraging competition – pricing based on cost, interconnection rights, and an independent regulatory authority.
2. China agreed to accept technology-neutral projects, whereby foreign companies are allowed to use whatever technology they wish to provide telecommunications service.
3. At the time of joining the WTO, the Beijing, Shanghai and Guangzhou telecommunications corridors will be opened up. In the future, all geographical restrictions will gradually be eliminated, and in 2003 the opening up of the entire telecommunications services sector will begin. However, for the following industries liberalization will not be completed for the periods specified: paging and added-value services – 3 years; mobile phone service – 5 years; domestic fixed-line service and closed user groups – 6 years.
4. Foreign companies will be allowed to hold a 49% share in pager and added-value services companies (including Internet and satellite technology companies) established as a Sino-US joint venture; commencing two years after China has joined the WTO, foreign companies will be allowed to hold a 50% share in such joint ventures. For basic telecommunications services, the maximum foreign share will be 49%.

Banking industry

1. The scope of operation permitted to foreign banks will be gradually expanded. Once China has joined the WTO, US banks will immediately be permitted to provide foreign customers with all types of foreign exchange services; one year after accession, US banks will be allowed to provide foreign exchange services to Chinese customers. Sino-American joint venture banks will immediately be permitted to engage in financial services activities (RMB services and retail financial services). Foreign banks will be given permission to engage in RMB services within two years of accession, and will be allowed to provide retail financial services within five years of accession.
2. Geographical restrictions will be lifted (to an appropriate extent).
3. Quantity restrictions will be lifted (to an appropriate extent).
4. Non-bank financial institutions will be permitted to engage in auto loan business.

Table 5.4   Continued

Securities
1. A limited number of joint venture enterprises will be permitted to engage in fund management business, enjoying the same treatment as Chinese fund management companies. When the permitted scope of operation of China's securities industry is enlarged, joint venture securities firms will be given the same treatment as Chinese securities firms.
2. Joint venture securities firms will be permitted to underwrite the issuing of Chinese securities, and will be permitted to underwrite and trade securities denominated in foreign currencies, including both bonds and shares.
3. For joint venture securities firms involved in fund management, the maximum foreign share will initially be set at 33%, rising to 49% after three years. For joint venture securities firms involved in underwriting, the maximum foreign share will be set at 33%.

Insurance industry
1. Licenses will be awarded in accordance with the principle of caution; the number of licenses awarded will not be restricted on the basis of economic considerations, nor will quantity restrictions be imposed.
2. Foreign property and accident insurance companies: Once China has joined the WTO, foreign property and accident insurance companies will immediately be allowed to operate throughout the country; the geographical restrictions on licenses will be abolished five years after China joins the WTO.
3. The key US interest groups will be allowed to begin operating in key cities in China within 2 – 3 years.
4. The permitted scope of operation of foreign insurance companies will be expanded in stages over a period of five years, to include group, health and endowment insurance.
5. Life insurance companies: Life insurance companies will be permitted to hold a majority share in joint venture companies (when China joins the WTO, a 50% share will be permitted; this will gradually be increased to 51% within one year). The joint venture requirements and the restrictions on the number of branches will be abolished, and foreign insurance companies will be allowed to choose their own joint venture partners.
6. Non-life insurance companies: Non-life insurance companies will be permitted to hold a majority share in joint venture companies (when China joins the WTO, a 51% share will be permitted immediately; within two years after accession, foreign non-life insurance companies will be permitted to establish wholly-owned subsidiaries.

Professional services
1. Foreigners will be permitted to hold a majority share in the following types of business – accounting, tax collection, management consultancy, firms of architects, engineering, urban planning, medical and dentistry, computer-related services etc. (law firms will be excluded).
2. For accounting firms, the compulsory localization requirements will be eliminated. Accounting firms will be permitted to register freely, and will enjoy the same treatment as Chinese firms with respect to permit issue. The approval procedures will be made more transparent.

Table 5.4   Continued

Audiovisual products
1. Audio and video tapes: Foreign companies will be permitted to hold up to a 49% share in companies engaged in the retail sale of audio and video tapes.
2. Motion pictures: The number of foreign motion pictures allowed to be imported each year will be increased to not less than 40, of which a share in the profits will be permitted for 20.
3. Movie theaters: Within three years, foreign companies will be permitted to hold a majority share in companies engaged in the construction, renovation, owning and management of movie theaters.
Travel and hotels
1. Hotels: Foreign companies will be permitted to enter the hotel business. At the time of accession, foreign companies will be permitted to hold a majority share; wholly-owned hotels will be permitted within three years.
2. Travel services: Foreign companies will be permitted to provide the full range of travel agency services: Foreign travel agencies will be allowed to operate in major tourist centers, and in Beijing, Shanghai, Guangzhou and Xian.

Notes: a Ancillary distribution services include express delivery, rental, express air shipment, shipping, storage and warehousing, advertising, technical appraisal and analysis, and packaging services.
   b The main points of contention in the Sino-American negotiations were as follows: The USA wanted foreign companies to be allowed up to a 50 percent share in Chinese telecommunications companies, whereas China would only agree to a maximum share of 35 percent; China was only willing to allow foreign companies to lease the use of existing telecommunications networks, rather than constructing new ones.

Source: Collated for this study.

The USA also asked for export subsidies to be abolished and raised objections to China's restrictions placed upon the importation of wheat from the northwestern states affected by TCK disease, and on oranges and meat products, insisting that scientifically based health standards be applied. China claimed that although the production costs for its agricultural products were low, their quality was also low, and it therefore remained conservative with regard to opening up its agricultural markets, particularly with regard to the state monopoly on wheat, corn, rice, cotton, sugar, cooking oil and chemical fertilizers.[3]

As far as industrial products are concerned, China accepted the USA anti-dumping appraisal method based on treating China as a 'non-market economy' and special defensive measures against a sudden increase in imports; the USA will be able to retain the former for 15 years, and the latter for 12 years. At the same time, China will permit American companies to import and export freely and to sell their goods in China. Import quota restrictions will be gradually eliminated and by 2005 the average tariff rate will have been reduced to 9.44 percent; for certain USA products the rate is to be reduced further, to 7.1 percent. In addition, special provisions were made in respect of areas in which the USA has a special interest, for example, requiring China to participate in several existing international zero-tariff agreements such as Information Technology Agreement (ITA), and individual sectors such as autos, timber and timber products, chemical products, fisheries products, and some other products and sectors. With regard to textile quotas, China agreed to a delay in the lifting of USA quotas on textile imports from China until 2005, and also agreed to allow the USA to retain a special defensive mechanism against any sudden rise in Chinese textile imports until the end of 2008.[4]

Negotiations on trade in services

As regards the opening up of the banking, insurance, telecommunications and other service sectors, in order to open up the China market, the USA asked China to accept the fundamental multilateral agreements for telecommunications and financial services. For American service suppliers (including distribution service, financial services, professional services and other service providers), all markets that had already been opened would be kept open, and all existing operational activities protected. Restrictions on distribution services (including wholesale, retail, maintenance and transportation) would be abolished in stages over a period of three years. Distribution rights would be made available for sensitive and protected products such as chemical fertilizers, raw materials and petrochemical products, within five years. In addition, the restrictions on ancillary distribution services would be gradually lifted over a period of 3 to 4 years, and USA service providers would be allowed to establish wholly-owned subsidiaries.

Within the banking and insurance industries, all geographical restrictions, business scope restrictions and majority ownership restrictions would be eliminated step by step. The main provisions with respect to the opening up of the securities market were as follows: (i) Joint-venture fund management companies would be allowed to engage in fund management business, enjoying the same treatment as Chinese fund management companies; (ii) As Chinese securities firms expand their scope of business, joint-venture securities firms would receive equal treatment; and (iii) Joint-venture securities firms in which the foreign partner is the minority shareholder would be allowed to engage in the underwriting of Chinese securities, as well as underwriting and trading of securities denominated in foreign currency (bonds and shares). Taking into consideration the current state of China's industry development, China refused to give ground regarding the question of telecommunications sector holding companies and the opening up of A-shares to foreign investment.[5]

Investment and technology transfer

On investment and technology transfer, the USA insisted that after China joins the WTO, it must immediately start to abide by Trade Related Investment Measures (TRIMs), without benefiting from the grace period allowed to other developing countries. The USA also insisted that China cancel all demands in respect of trade and foreign currency equalization and localization, and that China implement all intellectual property right protection relating to the WTO, along with all trade-related laws and regulations relating to technology and technology transfer. China, for its part, insisted that it be allowed to join the WTO with developing nation status, so that it could benefit from the 'Authorization Clause' provided for by Section Four of the GATT and by the Tokyo Round.

5.2.1 The Impact of WTO Accession on Chinese Industry

One important issue facing China upon WTO accession is the impact of market opening on the development of its industries. The impact will be felt particularly heavily by the telecommunications, commerce, financial, insurance and securities industries. In the following section, we consider the effect of accession on the country's primary, manufacturing and service industries.

The impact upon China's primary industry

Gaining WTO accession will lead to an overall increase in the output and exports of China's pastoral farming sector; however, the impact will be relatively limited as this industry has a low level of export-orientation. Added to this, the shortage of agricultural resources in China, the small scale of production, the weakness of basic infrastructure, the low overall productivity level and low labor productivity, and the restrictions on the development of agricultural technology, mean that accession will lead to a rapid reduction in the proportion of China's GDP accounted for by its primary industry. Large numbers of people currently employed in agriculture will move into other sectors, and the output of those agricultural sectors protected by quotas will fall.

Fortunately for China, it joins the WTO with the status of a developing nation, which allows it to maintain import restrictions for ten years after accession. In addition, the actual level of protection afforded to Chinese agriculture is far lower than the nominal level; joining the WTO will merely reduce the disparity between the nominal level of protection and the actual level of protection. Furthermore, China currently imports very little rice; an increase in imports will thus not have a significant impact on China's own rice production. Overall, therefore, the short term impact of WTO accession on agriculture will not be all that significant. However, as far as grains, cotton and milk products are concerned, as these products have already lost trade competitiveness, the impact from accession will be greater. Soybeans and soybean products will also come under heavy pressure from American imports. As regards other cash crops such as vegetable oils, sugar, fruit (with the exception of oranges, where there will be a crisis), vegetables, etc., and aquatic products and meat (excluding beef), WTO accession will provide increased room for development. At the same time, the high level of interference in the price of agricultural products through the use of subsidies means that fundamental changes will be needed after accession; the impact on the price system for agricultural products in China will thus be quite significant.[6]

The impact upon China's manufacturing industry

There is considerable variation in the technical level and productivity of China's manufacturing industries; consequently, the impact of WTO accession will vary. The overall effect on China's manufacturing sector will be: (i) Light industry and textile products (such as garments, travel goods, sporting goods and toys), as well as export-oriented agricultural firms and electromechanical products using simple technology, will be able to increase their level of exports. (ii) The impact will be greater on the high-tech industries which are just starting to develop (such as the aerospace, car manufacturing, transportation and telecommunications sectors) than on traditional industries; (iii) The capital- and technology-intensive industries will be more heavily affected than labor-intensive industries; (iv) Those industries whose development has been characterized by duplication and poor planning will be more heavily affected than those industries which have developed in accordance with market demand; and (v) The environmental protection industry will find itself entering a golden age.

Overall, given the high level of competition from foreign products, those enterprises with poor technology, products that are not saleable over the long-term, or poor management, or which have been making a loss for many years and have no chance of a turn for the better, as well as those enterprises affected by duplication and poor economies of scale, will find themselves facing bankruptcy and closure once they have lost financial and loan support from local government and central government ministries.[7]

(1) The textiles industry

China's textiles industry is affected by various problems, including low production efficiency, poor product quality, a lack of competition, inappropriate product mix and production equipment, out-dated technology, and so on. Once China gains WTO accession, those industries and enterprises that have only just started to develop, or which have low competitiveness, will find themselves facing a serious threat. However, the provision for gradual trading system implementation allowed for by the Multilateral Fiber Agreement will be a great help in terms of improving the international competitiveness of China's textile products (including knitted fabric, cotton and hemp textiles and silk products) as well as its clothing industry. In other words, the textile and clothing industries will have greater opportunities for development. However, as tariffs are lowered further, the more backward parts of the textile sector, such as the chemical fiber materials industry, woolen textiles, the cotton material industry, printing and dyeing and the textiles machinery industry, will find themselves facing a greater challenge. To summarize, in comparison with China's other industries, the industries in this sector have relatively high competitiveness; there would therefore seem to be little need for China to adopt protective measures with regard to these industries.[8]

(2) Light industry

China's light industry is affected by problems of industry structure, particularly in the sense that industry structure has not kept pace with the changes in the consumption structure. With China inside the WTO, its light industry will face the challenge presented by substantial quantities of imported goods. In particular, certain industries will be more seriously affected than those manufacturing labor intensive products, traditional products, and products where development is appropriately balanced. These include industries manufacturing capital- and technology-intensive products; new technologies, new industries and new products where development started late and where they are only just starting to get off the ground, and those industries and products with serious problems of duplication and misguided development.

Industries within which the impact of WTO accession is unlikely to be so significant include those manufacturing products such as paper and paper-board, washing machines, bicycles, and canned foods. Products where the impact is likely to be greater include sugar, beverages, timepieces, refrigerators, air conditioners, compressors, color film, home appliances, cosmetics and some toys.[9]

(3) Electromechanical industry

China's electromechanical industry is dominated by labor-intensive products, with virtually none of the high-tech products that are just starting to be developed being in any position to compete with advanced foreign products of the same type. Furthermore, the electromechanical industry is characterized by duplication and poor economies of scale. WTO accession will lead to a reorganization of the industry structure and the abandonment of some backward segments of the industry; the impact on the importing and exporting of electromechanical products will also be very significant.

According to statistics produced by the State Bureau for the Electromechanical Industry, WTO accession will result in a 20 percent drop in sales for China's electromechanical industry. Analysis of the 70 main industry segments shows that the affected products fall into the following four categories: (i) Those which will be seriously affected, including mainly high-tech products, the development of which began relatively late, such as semiconductors, video recorders, small passenger cars, computers, photocopying machines and telephone exchanges; (ii) Those which will be affected to a moderate extent, including products with no economies of scale, or those that are not competitive enough in terms of product technology, quality and price. Examples include electrical equipment for industrial use, transformers, broadcasting equipment, forging and pressing equipment, heavy goods vehicles and cranes; (iii) Those products which will suffer relatively little impact, mainly including products developed from technology transfer, where the scale of production is already quite large and the technology level has been raised, but where there is still some way to go in terms of quality, performance and price competition. Examples include motorcycles, bearings, refrigerators and televisions; and (iv) Those products that will be basically unaffected, including products mainly derived from technology transfer where technology, quality and price are almost on a par with foreign products of the same type. Examples include medium to low-priced radios and tape recorders, electric fans, washing machines, tractors, bulldozers and electrical instruments. As the vast majority of electromechanical products will suffer a severe impact after China's entry into the WTO, China may decide that it needs to adopt protective measures.[10]

(4)Automobiles
China is still the world's largest potential market for automobiles; however, China's automobile industry is generally characterized by the problems of excessive dispersal of production and poor organization. Average labor productivity is very low, whilst the cars produced are based on out-dated designs and poor fuel economy and are generally of poor quality. They are also too expensive, ability to provide spare parts is poor and design capability is lacking. As a result, China's automobile industry will not be able to stand up to fierce foreign competition, whether in terms of output, quality or price. The industry has had to rely on the protection provided by tariffs, import permits and quotas, but once China becomes part of the WTO, the resultant reduction in tariffs, higher import quotas and the abolition of the import permit system are all bound to produce a flood of imports from many

different countries. Most of China's 120 car plants will be forced to either cease production, switch over to manufacturing different products, or go out of business altogether; the best they can hope for is to be taken over by one of China's bigger auto manufacturing groups.

The rise in consumer spending will encourage the importation of more cars, which will have a significant impact on the domestic auto industry, particularly with respect to saloon cars, hatchbacks and some car parts. China will continue to protect its auto industry, with the basic principles being to protect the production of entire cars, while opening up the parts sector, and to protect the market for saloon cars while opening up the goods vehicle sector. The Asian financial crisis and the downturn in domestic consumer demand have been an obstacle to growth in the auto industry, which had previously been expected to grow rapidly. It is estimated that it will take at least 5 to 6 years for Chinese auto manufacturers to close the gap between themselves and foreign manufacturers. Over the next few years, therefore, we can expect to see many of China's auto manufacturers as potential collaborative partners before they lose their tariff protection, in an effort to improve their competitiveness.[11]

(5) Chemicals

China's chemical industry has been in receipt of government protection for many years, and not only has this led to problems in terms of quality, product mix and price, but it has also created a situation whereby the development of industry has been unable to meet market needs. As a result, for many products, annual output does not meet demand, and large quantities of chemicals have to be imported from overseas every year. In addition, with the exception of a limited number of export-oriented business groups, the vast majority of enterprises in the chemical industry are still capital-intensive and labor-intensive; the proportion of technology-intensive enterprises is extremely low. Furthermore, there are extremely large numbers of enterprises with small scale of production and high wastage levels; China's chemical producers cannot compete with foreign firms when it comes to production costs. With China inside the WTO, protection from international competition, which the chemical industry has received in the past, will be totally eliminated, and one can only imagine the magnitude of the impact on the industry. The shock will be particularly heavy on those enterprises low on technical skill, with out-dated equipment, unsatisfactory raw material supply channels and extremely small scale of production.

The impact of WTO accession will vary between different sectors within the chemical industry. In the agricultural chemical sector, many of China's smaller manufacturers of chemical fertilizers will go out of business. Imported agro-chemical materials will replace out-dated varieties, placing the domestic product under extreme pressure. There will be a negative impact on the return on investment in China's tire industry, while the survival of the photosensitive materials industry, which is not competitive, will be in doubt if temporary protection is not provided. The dyes industry will be seriously affected by competition from imports, and in the petrochemical sector, local producers of carbolic acid, polyvinyl chloride, glacial acetic acid and acetone will clearly be unable to compete with imports.

The development of China's chemical industry has been heavily dependent on piracy, particularly with respect to advanced chemicals, where around 97–98 percent of products have been developed through piracy. In the case of agro-chemical materials, around 98 percent of products are pirated, while for dyes the figure is around 80 percent. China's WTO accession brings with it the requirement for the protection of intellectual property rights, and the impact on China's advanced chemicals industry will clearly be devastating. The authorities in China are currently formulating plans for the provision of much-needed protection for the industry.[12]

(6) Pharmaceuticals
The reduction in the import tariff for pharmaceuticals will be of no real benefit to imported new drugs, because WTO accession does not mean that China will allow new drugs to be imported without undergoing pharmacological analysis and review. The procedures for importing pharmaceuticals are very complex and the regulations are very strict; it must be demonstrated that the new drug is superior to the equivalent local product before the formal application procedures can even commence. The final right of determination rests with the Ministry of Health's New Drug Review Committee, which is not permanently in session. For all new drugs, competitiveness lies in their effectiveness rather than their price; thus tariff reductions are unlikely to have the effect of significantly increasing imports.

Biotechnology is an industry with strong development potential in the 21st century. So far, the commercialization of biotechnology in China has been largely confined to the area of pharmaceuticals. Around twenty to thirty different medicines and vaccines had been launched by the end of 2000, creating a new bio-medicine industry, with genetic engineering being the area attracting the most attention; however, as a result of policy factors, China lags well behind in terms of pharmaceuticals technology. Equipment is grossly outdated, and manpower quality is low; the overall production level is fully twenty years behind that of the advanced nations, and as a result, product quality is unstable. Once China joins the WTO and high-quality foreign drugs start to be imported, China's domestic pharmaceuticals industry is bound to find its markets threatened; as a result, the whole pharmaceuticals industry will come under threat.

Furthermore, 97 percent of medicines produced in China are pirated. And following WTO accession, once legislation is put in place for the protection of intellectual property rights, the impact on China's pharmaceuticals industry will be considerable.

However, in the case of those Western medicines, traditional Chinese medicines, pharmaceuticals manufacturing equipment and surgical equipment, where production has reached, or is close to, international standards, as well as other medium and low-end products which are at, or near, international standards, WTO accession will create opportunities for development of exports.[13]

The impact upon China's service sector

As a result of the small scale of production in China's service sector,[14] coupled with the low level of application of new technologies and high technology, and the low level of technology and management, the service sector has low international competitiveness. WTO accession will therefore have a considerable impact on this sector. At present, the government's plans are to first open up RMB business within the banking industry, along with the life insurance and property insurance markets, while delaying the opening up of the securities market.

(1) Telecommunications

Taking into consideration the extent to which the markets have already been opened up, the internal market structure and the time that will be needed to adapt to WTO regulations, the impact of WTO accession on China's telecommunications market must be considered separately from the point of view of telecommunications services and telecommunications equipment manufacturing. The telecommunications services sector has received government protection for many years, has low competitiveness and low profits, and fails to make effective use of resources. Added to this, the telecommunications regulatory system, enterprise management system and legal framework do not conform to WTO requirements. Therefore, it is clear that WTO accession will have a serious impact on this sector; for telecommunications services, the threats are greater than the opportunities.

The opportunities will be greater than the threats within the telecommunications equipment manufacturing sector, and thus the impact will not be as great as in the telecommunications services sector. The main reason for this is that to a large extent, the telecommunications equipment manufacturing sector has already been opened up and Chinese enterprises in this sector are already quite competitive. Taking exchanges as an example, those developed independently by Chinese companies have a current market share of 60 percent. On top of this, tariff reductions will push down production costs, making the domestic manufacturers' prices even more competitive. However, those enterprises and products with weak R&D capability and low technology content levels will find it hard to survive in the new environment of fierce competition.[15]

(2) Software

Overall, China's software industry is relatively backward; its total sales in 1997 accounted for only 8.6 percent of the Chinese computer market. Although the nominal tariff rate for software is 15 percent, given that software is usually sold as part of a complete package deal with a new computer, rather than being sold separately, the effective tariff rate is 0 percent. This has created a situation whereby both systems and operating software in China are dominated by foreign companies; Chinese companies are dominant in only application software, owing to language factors. Changes in the tariff will thus have no direct impact on China's software industry.[16]

(3) Banking

China's banking system is directed by the People's Bank of China, the three major policy banks (the State Development Bank, the Export-Import Bank and the Agriculture Development Bank) and the four major state banks. The system includes many stock-type national and regional commercial banks, but is still dominated by the state-owned banks; the level of marketization is limited.[17] China's banks have received protection from the government for many years, and have an excessively high proportion of non-performing loans. It will be extremely difficult to clear up these within five years and this will affect the various banks' competitiveness; faced with a high level of competition from foreign banks, they will have to undergo a period of adjustment. According to World Bank estimates, it will be around ten years before China's banks are able to compete successfully against foreign banks, which is why China has put the financial sector at the bottom of the list of industries to be opened up. In light of the competitive advantage that foreign banks will possess after WTO accession, and the fact that competition for securing talented manpower will become much more fierce, the reconstruction of the banking system and the strengthening of banks' competitiveness has become an urgent task. The main elements in China's strategy are the conversion of debt to equity to solve the problem of non-performing loans, the strengthening of financial sector regulation, the speeding up of bank reorganization, and improvements to bank management.[18]

(4) Securities

In the long term, WTO accession will be highly beneficial to China's securities industry. Not only will it help to ensure economic stability and benefit stock market development, the opening up of the insurance and banking sectors will also help to expand the sources of funds for the stock market. However, there are many securities firms in China, all with similar business structure; their business activity is concentrated in underwriting in the primary market, and they lack their own unique operational characteristics. There is little variety in the methods of competition used, and a lack of order in the competition between firms; internal management systems are unsatisfactory which weakens the ability to respond to change. In the short term, therefore, WTO accession will not benefit the development and stability of China's securities market. In order to deal with the competition that WTO accession will bring, China's securities firms are taking advantage of the impending implementation of the Securities Law to increase their capitalization as rapidly as possible, reviewing their internal asset mix, participating in the inter-bank market and in government bond buyback, and using the stock market to secure funding, so as to expand their assets and improve their competitiveness. They also need to improve the efficiency of capital utilization[19] and strengthen their own asset management. At the same time, they need to strengthen research into potential markets and derivatives.[20]

We have listed some of the key areas relating to the WTO pre-accession negotiations and the industries that will be more seriously affected, in Tables 5.5 to 5.17, in order to provide a more comprehensive picture of the impact of WTO accession on China's industry and the possible response measures.

Table 5.5   The Impact of WTO Accession on China's Industries –
Agriculture

Current situation	* High tariffs. * High subsidies. * Weak infrastructure. * Low overall productivity and labor productivity. * Development of agricultural technology lagging behind. * Insufficient economies of scale.
Commitments[a]	* Tariff reductions. * Abolition of import volume restrictions. * Reduction of the involvement of state-owned trading companies in trade in key products. * Adoption of a tariff quota system in particularly sensitive areas. * Abolition of inappropriate SPS restrictions. * Abolition of export subsidies.
Impact of WTO accession	* Overall, WTO accession will not constitute a serious threat to Chinese agriculture; the possibility of the production system being destroyed is very small. * The impact on fruit farmers will be less than that on those enterprises involved in wheat production. However, those farmers engaged in growing fruit the same as or similar to the main Californian fruit products will suffer more heavily. * WTO accession will have a more significant impact on grain, cotton and milk products. * Exports of vegetable oils, sugar, fruit (with the exception of oranges), vegetables and other cash crops, as well as aquatic products and meat (with the exception of beef) should increase.

Table 5.5   Continued

Response measures[b]	* The government needs to increase the level of professionalism in agriculture, and to expand the cultivation of products which offer high added value and have competitive advantage in international terms.
	* Efforts need to be made to increase agricultural production, processing output and management efficiency, with the establishment of 'Three Highs' model agricultural districts.
	* Effective use should be made of the WTO's Agricultural Agreement.
	* Effective use should be made of the Development Plans (which exempt countries from the obligation to reduce tariffs), in order to maintain agricultural production.
	* Management of SPS inspection, tariff quota and other measures needs to be tightened up.
	* Anti-dumping and anti-subsidy investigations should be strengthened.
	* The government should establish a policy for the provision of support to agricultural subsidies.
	* Technology inputs in agriculture should be increased.
	* Investment in basic agricultural infrastructure should be increased.
	* The foreign trade system for agricultural products should be reformed.

Note: a. Commitments made with respect to WTO accession.
      b. Response measures include both measures which the Chinese government is likely to adopt and suggestions made by academics and industry insiders.

Source: Collated for this study.

Table 5.6 *The Impact of WTO Accession on China's Industries – Manufacturing and Light Industry*

	Manufacturing industry	Light industry
Current situation	* The industry structure and product mix cannot keep up with changes in the consumption structure.	* The industry structure and product mix cannot keep up with changes in the consumption structure.
Commitments[a]	* Opening up of trading and distribution rights. * Tariff reductions. * Abolition of quotas and reduction of other non-tariff measures.	* Opening up of trading and distribution rights. * Tariff reductions. * Abolition of quotas and reduction of other non-tariff measures.
Impact of WTO accession	* The products which will benefit most (through increased exports) will be clothing, textiles, shoes, suitcases, toys, household goods and home appliances. * Imports of autos, electronic products and some high-quality consumer goods will increase. This will place the car-manufacturing, electronics, consumer durable and building materials industries under severe competitive pressure. * The environmental protection industry will find itself entering a golden age.	* Three types of industry will come under heavy pressure from imports: capital and technology-intensive products; those new technologies, industries and products which are just getting off the ground; those industries where there has been duplication and poorly directed development. * Products on which the impact of accession will be less severe include paper and paper-board, washing machines, bicycles, tinned foods, etc. Products on which the impact will be more serious include sugar, beverages, timepieces, refrigerators, air conditioners, compressors, color film, home appliances, cosmetics, and some toys.
Response measures[b]	* Effective use should be made of the Anti-dumping Agreement. * The government needs to reorganize the export system for textiles and light industry products.	* Effective use should be made of the Anti-dumping Agreement. * The government needs to reorganize the export system for textiles and light industry products

Note: a. Commitments meant it made with respect to WTO accession.
       b. Response measures include both measures which the Chinese government is likely to adopt and suggestions made by academics and industry insiders.

Source: Collated for this study.

Table 5.7   The Impact of WTO Accession on China's Industries – Textiles

Current situation	* The technology level is low, and much of the equipment used is out-dated. * Shortage of raw materials restricts the textile industry's development. * The industry's advantages of cheap raw materials and low labor costs are gradually being eroded. * The product mix in the textile industry is inappropriate, and output value is low. * Productivity is low, and product quality is falling.
Commitments[a]	* Opening up of trading and distribution rights. * Tariff reductions. * Abolition of quotas and reduction of other non-tariff measures.
Impact of WTO accession	* WTO accession will present the textile and clothing industries with considerable development opportunities, with particular benefit to clothing exports, which it is estimated will increase four-fold. Textile exports will also increase slightly. * The relatively backward sectors within the textile industry, such as man-made fibers, cotton fabric, printing and dyeing, and textile machinery manufacturing, will be more seriously affected.
Response measures[b]	* Effective use needs to be made of quotas. * Reorganization of the industry structure needs to be speeded up. * A strengthening of international collaboration is needed.

Note: a. Commitments meant it made with respect to WTO accession.
          b. Response measures include both measures which the Chinese government is likely to adopt and suggestions made by academics and industry insiders.

Source: Collated for this study.

Table 5.8   *The Impact of WTO Accession on China's Industries – Auto-manufacturing*

Current situation	* Low technological standard.
	* Small scale of production.
	* Limited product development capability.
Commitments[a]	* Tariff reductions.
	* Abolition of import quotas and reduction of other non-tariff measures.
	* Opening up of trading and distribution rights.
Impact of WTO accession	* The auto industry will be more seriously affected than other industries, particularly with respect to passenger cars.
	* The plans to develop the domestic car industry will be affected.
Response measures[b]	* Initially, the pace of change will be kept to a minimum, and the additional taxation on cars will not be abolished. As a result, car prices may not fall immediately.
	* The industry structure and product mix of the passenger car industry need to be adjusted.
	* The ancillary measures regarding car purchase and use need to be relaxed.
	* The government should encourage mergers within the industry, to create car manufacturing groups.
	* Car manufacturers should seek out foreign manufacturers to collaborate with before they lose tariff protection.

Note: a. Commitments made with respect to WTO accession.
       b. Response measures include both measures which the Chinese government is likely to adopt and suggestions made by academics and industry insiders.

Source: Collated for this study.

*Table 5.9   The Impact of WTO Accession on China's Industries –
Electromechanical*

Current situation	* Most products are labor-intensive. * Hardly any of the hi-tech products currently getting off the ground are capable of competing against advanced foreign products of the same type. * Economies of scale are inadequate, and there is a serious problem with duplication.
Commitments[a]	* Tariff reductions. * Abolition of quotas and reduction of other non-tariff measures.
Impact of WTO accession	* WTO accession is bound to lead to re-structuring of China's electromechanical industry. * Some backward industry sectors will go under. * The impact on imports and exports of electromechanical products will be considerable. * Products that will be seriously affected: Mainly hi-tech products the development of which began late, such as integrated circuits, video recorders, small passenger cars, computers, photocopying machines, telephone exchanges etc. * Products that will be moderately affected: Mainly products which lack economies of scale, or which are uncompetitive in terms of technology, quality and price, such as industrial electrical equipment, transformers, broadcasting equipment, forging and casting equipment, heavy goods vehicles and cranes. * Product that will be only slightly affected: Mainly products derived from technology transfer, where a reasonable scale of production and technical level have already been attained, but where Chinese products still lag behind foreign products somewhat in terms of quality, functions or price, such as motorcycles, bearings, refrigerators, televisions etc. * Products that will be basically unaffected: Mainly products derived from technology transfer, where product technology, quality and price already approach those of foreign products of the same sort, such as medium and low-end tape recorders, electric fans, washing machines, tractors, bulldozers and electrical instruments.
Response measures[b]	* The government needs to encourage diversification of exports. * Exports of electromechanical products to the USA should be increased.

Note: a. Commitments made with respect to WTO accession.
b. Response measures include both measures which the Chinese government is likely to adopt and suggestions made by academics and industry insiders.

Source: Collated for this study.

Table 5.10   *The Impact of WTO Accession on China's Industries –*
              Chemicals

Current situation * The industry has been protected for many years.
                 * The level of technology is low, and the scale of production is
                   small.
                 * The industry's R&D capability is low; product development is
                   largely dependent on piracy, particularly with respect to more
                   advanced technologies.

Commitments[a]   * Tariff reductions.
                 * Reduction of non-tariff measures.
                 * The pharmaceuticals market will be opened up in accordance with
                   intellectual property rights agreements.

Impact of WTO   * The chemical industry will be seriously affected, particularly the
accession   more hi-tech sectors.
                 * Agro-chemical industry: Many of China's small chemical
                   fertilizer manufacturers will go out of business. Imported
                   agro-chemicals will replace out-dated products, putting pressure
                   on the domestic product.
                 * There will be a negative impact on return on investment in
                   China's tire industry.
                 * The photosensitive materials industry is uncompetitive; if
                   temporary protective measures are not adopted, it will be difficult
                   for this sector to survive.
                 * The dyes industry will be seriously affected by imports.
                 * In the petrochemical industry, manufacturers of carbolic acid,
                   polyvinyl chloride, glacial acetic acid and acetone will not be able
                   to compete with foreign products.

Response   * Small manufacturers of chemical fertilizers will be forced to
measures[b]   cease production, merge, or switch over to manufacturing other
                   products. Medium-sized manufacturers will need to improve their
                   technology, and establish large-scale chemical fertilizer
                   manufacturing centers.

Note: a. Commitments made with respect to WTO accession.
         b. Response measures include both measures which the Chinese government is likely
            to adopt and suggestions made by academics and industry insiders.

Source: Collated for this study.

*Table 5.11   The Impact of WTO Accession on China's Industries –
Pharmaceuticals*

Current situation	* The industry has been protected for years. As a result, its technology is backward, its R&D capability is low, and 97% of products are derived from piracy. * The regulations governing the importation of new drugs are very strict, and the procedures complicated. * Equipment is out-dated, and manpower quality is low. * The industry is 20 years behind current international standards.
Commitments[a]	* In accordance with intellectual property rights agreements, China will be required to open up its pharmaceuticals market to a considerable extent. * The tariff on pharmaceutical products will be reduced to 5.5% – 6.5%. * Other non-tariff measures will be reduced.
Impact of WTO accession	* Pharmaceuticals manufacturing firms will be seriously affected. * The price of imported medicines will fall significantly.
Response measures[b]	* The government should encourage enterprises to merge with one another. * Scientific research into Chinese medicine should be stepped up.

Note: a. Commitments made with respect to WTO accession.
       b. Response measures include both measures which the Chinese government is likely
          to adopt and suggestions made by academics and industry insiders.

Source: Collated for this study.

Table 5.12   The Impact of WTO Accession on China's Industries – Service Industries

Current situation	* Low output value. * Limited use of high technology; low technical level and poor management. * High level of government protection.
Commitments[a]	* China has agreed to accept the fundamental multilateral service agreements with respect to telecommunications and financial services. * Abolition of the restrictions on distribution services. * Foreign companies to be permitted to hold majority shares in service providers. * Restrictions on scope of operation to be gradually relaxed. * Geographical restrictions to be gradually lifted. * Quantity restrictions to be gradually lifted.
Impact of WTO accession	* WTO accession will have a significant impact on China's service sector.
Response measures[b]	* Advanced technology, capital and mechanisms of competition need to be introduced from overseas. * The service sector will be opened up step by step. * The government will be opening up the RMB banking business, life insurance and property insurance markets first, leaving the opening up of the securities business till later.

Note: a. Commitments made with respect to WTO accession.
       b. Response measures include both measures which the Chinese government is likely to adopt and suggestions made by academics and industry insiders.

Source: Collated for this study.

Table 5.13   The   Impact   of   WTO   Accession   on   China's   Industries   –   Telecommunications

Current situation	* The percentage of GDP accounted for by the telecommunications sector is increasing at an average rate of 3% per annum. * Posts and telecommunications still account for less than 3% of GDP. * The telecommunications services sector is characterized by low enterprise competitiveness, low profits, failure to make full use of resources, a regulatory system and enterprise management system which do not conform to WTO requirements, and a legal framework which does not conform to WTO requirements. * The telecommunications equipment manufacturing sector has a weak R&D capability.
Commitments[a]	* China has agreed to accept the fundamental multilateral service agreements with respect to telecommunications and financial services. * Abolition of the restrictions on distribution services. * Foreign companies to be permitted to hold majority shares in service providers. * Restrictions on scope of operation to be gradually relaxed. * Geographical restrictions to be gradually lifted. * Quantity restrictions to be gradually lifted.
Impact of WTO accession	* In the telecommunications services sector, the problems outweigh the opportunities. * In the telecommunications equipment manufacturing sector, the opportunities outweigh the problems, although enterprises whose products have low technology content are likely to go under.
Response measures[b]	* Transitional protective measures: Protection should be provided to key hi-tech products and products of great importance to national industrial policy. * Foreign companies will be allowed to rent existing telecommunications networks, rather than establishing new networks. * Telecommunications enterprise structure needs to be adjusted. * The establishment of modern telecommunications infrastructure needs to be speeded up.

Note: a. Commitments made with respect to WTO accession.
         b. Response measures include both measures which the Chinese government is likely to adopt and suggestions made by academics and industry insiders.

Source: Collated for this study.

Table 5.14   The Impact of WTO Accession on China's Industries – Software

Current situation	* Application software tends to be locally produced, whereas system software and operating software are dominated by the leading foreign companies. * While the nominal tariff rate is 15%, the effective tariff rate is 0%.
Commitments[a]	* China has agreed to accept the fundamental multilateral service agreements with respect to telecommunications and financial services. * Abolition of the restrictions on distribution services. * Foreign companies to be permitted to hold majority shares in service providers. * Restrictions on scope of operation to be gradually relaxed. * Geographical restrictions to be gradually lifted. * Quantity restrictions to be gradually lifted.
Impact of WTO accession	* The impact will be limited, and the situation will gradually improve thanks to external pressure.

Note: a. Commitments made with respect to WTO accession.

Source: Collated for this study.

Table 5.15   The Impact of WTO Accession on China's Industries – Banking

Current situation	* The four leading commercial banks which occupy an oligopolistic position in the financial sector are poorly managed.
	* State-owned banks account for too high a percentage of the total; the level of marketization is inadequate.
	* The level of non-performing loans is too high; it will be difficult to clear these up within five years.
Commitments[a]	* China has agreed to accept the multilateral service agreements relating to financial services.
	* Abolition of the restrictions on distribution services.
	* Foreign companies to be permitted to hold majority shares in service providers.
	* Restrictions on scope of operation to be gradually relaxed.
	* Geographical restrictions to be gradually lifted.
	* Quantity restrictions to be gradually lifted.
	* Non-bank financial institutions to be allowed to engage in car loan business.
Impact of WTO accession	* Foreign banks will take business away from China's state-owned banks.
	* Competition for talented manpower between Chinese banks will become fierce.
Response measures[b]	* Debt to equity conversion.
	* Strengthening of financial regulation.
	* Speeding up of bank reorganization, and improvement of bank management.

Note: a. Commitments made with respect to WTO accession.
          b. Response measures include both measures which the Chinese government is likely to adopt and suggestions made by academics and industry insiders.

Source: Collated for this study.

Table 5.16   The Impact of WTO Accession on China's Industries – Securities

Current situation	* There are a large number of different securities firms.
	* There is excessive concentration of securities business.
	* The methods of competition used are not sufficiently diverse.
	* Securities firms' ability to adapt to change is limited.
Commitments[a]	* A limited number of joint venture companies will be allowed to engage in fund management business, enjoying the same treatment as local firms. When the scope of operation of the securities business is expanded, joint venture securities firms will be able to enjoy the same treatment as local firms.
	* Joint venture securities firms will be allowed to underwrite domestic securities, and to underwrite and trade in securities denominated in foreign currency, including both bonds and shares.
	* For joint venture securities firms engaged in fund management, the upper limit on foreign shareholding will be 33%, rising to 49% within three years.
	* For joint venture securities firms engaged in underwriting, the upper limit on foreign shareholding will be 33%.
Impact of WTO accession	* The opening up of the insurance and banking sectors will help increase the sources of funds available to the securities market.
	* WTO accession will not be beneficial to the development and stability of China's securities market.
Response measures[b]	* There is a need for a comprehensive securities issue mechanism, and for better stock market regulation.
	* The management mechanisms of securities firms need to be improved, with an expansion of the scale of operation, a strengthening of internal asset management, and more research with respect to potential markets and derivatives.
	* The securities market will be opened up gradually.
	• Participation by foreign securities firms through provision of trans-national services will be expanded.
	• A considerable measure of control will be exercised over foreign securities firms actually operating within China.
	• In the short term, the establishment of joint venture investment banks on a trial basis will be expanded, through an expansion in the establishment of representative offices by foreign securities firms and investment banks

Note: a. Commitments made with respect to WTO accession.
       b. Response measures include both measures which the Chinese government is likely
          to adopt and suggestions made by academics and industry insiders.

Source: Collated for this study.

Table 5.17   The Impact of WTO Accession on China's Industries – Insurance and Travel

	Insurance	Travel
Current situation	* Since 1997, the annual rate of growth in insurance premium income has exceeded 30%. * The number of service providers in the insurance market has increased, with a move away from monopoly to oligopoly.	* There is a serious problem of oversupply in the hotel industry. * Local hotels lack competitive advantage.
Commitments[a]		* Foreign hotel chains will be allowed free access to the China market. * As soon as China enters the WTO, foreign hotel chains will be allowed to hold a majority share in Chinese subsidiaries. * Foreign companies will be allowed to establish wholly-owned subsidiaries within three years after accession.
Impact of WTO accession	* WTO accession will present China's insurance industry with major challenges.	* Hotel companies will find themselves under serious pressure.
Response measures[b]	* China needs to trade market access for technology, encouraging further participation by foreign insurers, and reducing the level of geographical restrictions, so as to attract capital and technology. * The restrictions on fund use by insurance companies should be relaxed, with a speeding up of the process of marketization.	

Note: a. Commitments made with respect to WTO accession.
            b. Response measures include both measures which the Chinese government is likely to adopt and suggestions made by academics and industry insiders.

Source: Collated for this study.

5.2.2 The Evaluation of WTO Accession for Listed Companies

We now go on to evaluate the impacts of China's accession into the WTO on listed companies, impacts that will clearly vary from industry to industry. Listed companies in labor- and resource-intensive industries, such as textiles, clothing, food, home appliances and the electromechanical industry will benefit considerably; however, they will also find themselves faced with fierce competition. WTO accession will have a more serious impact on the more heavily protected agricultural sector and on capital-intensive industries such as autos, instruments, cotton and wheat. The output from these sectors will fall significantly, with listed companies feeling the full force of the changes and coming under severe pressure.

The key issue here is how industries seek to upgrade themselves. Studies indicate that following accession, the number of enterprises in the car manufacturing, petrochemical processing and metallurgical industries will fall by 27 percent, 3 percent and 16 percent respectively; at the same time, there will be expansion in the average size of enterprises in these sectors. For listed companies in the high-tech sectors, WTO accession does not necessarily mean that prices will fall significantly; however, with competition in the areas of technology and service becoming increasingly fierce, technology, profits and high-quality service will also become increasingly important.

For listed companies in the financial sector, WTO accession will mean that their monopoly will be broken and that local banks and companies will find themselves under heavy pressure from foreign competitors.[21] WTO accession will affect the telecommunications services and telecommunications equipment manufacturing industries in different ways. Listed companies in the telecommunications services industry will be faced with severe competition, while listed companies in the telecommunications equipment manufacturing industry will not only have to contend with the competition resulting from the internationalization of the domestic market, but they will also need to respond to the questions of whether they have to own their own intellectual property rights, and whether they need to expand overseas.

China's listed companies are not as competitive as those of the advanced nations, in terms of management experience, management quality, product pricing, after-sales service and economies of scale. In particular, there is a need for greater regulation in the areas of finance and accounting, credit rating and disclosure. Once China joins the WTO, the level of protection enjoyed by these listed companies will be considerably diminished; their subsidies will gradually be eliminated and market competition will become much more fierce. They will face challenges in terms of raw materials, products, technology, funding, production and management methods, as well as the challenge of meeting international standards and conforming to international practice. This is bound to lead to changes in management status and profit levels.

In concrete terms, listed companies that enjoy comparative advantage, or import large quantities of raw materials, or which are already capable of competing in international markets, will benefit along with some trading companies; those listed companies that do not enjoy comparative advantage, or that are inefficient or insufficiently innovative, will suffer, as will those companies that lack economies of scale. The listed companies enjoying comparative advantage in China are those whose products have a high technology content or which are moderately labor-intensive, such as clothing, shoes, textiles, toys and some appliances. Once China has joined the WTO, these companies will no longer have to deal with the uncertainties created by European and American import quotas; thus they will be able to make use of the advantages they already possess, particularly in terms of cheap labor, to increase their exports to Europe and to the USA. Some examples of this type of listed company are shown in Table 5.18.

In addition, once China joins the WTO, with the fall in import tariffs and the abolition of import quotas, those listed companies which have to import large quantities of raw materials will find that their costs are significantly reduced, removing one of the obstacles to their continuing development. Those listed companies that have already developed the ability to compete on the international stage, and have already established a competitive advantage in international markets, will be in a position to secure future growth despite the fierce competition. WTO accession will lead to an increase in import-export trade, thereby benefiting trading, transportation and port management companies (see Table 5.19).

As regards listed companies which are relatively weak, and which do not enjoy competitive advantage compared to foreign firms, the reason that these listed companies have been able to survive until the present is that China's markets were not open to foreign companies for many years, and in many cases have still not been fully opened up (see Table 5.20). A second factor is that many of China's listed companies were converted from state-owned enterprises. While the low efficiency and inadequate innovation capability of state-owned enterprises constitute an obstacle to the development of listed companies, once China has joined the WTO the impact on inefficient SOEs will be even greater.

In addition, although listed companies in the high-tech sector possess the capability to innovate, as comparison to foreign companies of the same type shows, this ability is still inadequate. Following WTO accession, many of the small high-tech listed companies in China will find themselves facing heavy competition. Furthermore, because of the quota system in China, companies

Table 5.18 Examples of Listed Companies in Industries which Enjoy Comparative Advantage

Industry	Typical listed company	Details
Toys	Hai Xin Ltd.	The value of Hai Xin's annual exports comes to RMB500 million, with toys accounting for three-quarters of this. The company's main export markets are the USA and Europe.
Clothing	Long Tou Ltd. Jiangsu Zong Yi	San Qiang has now been taken over by Long Tou. As a result of quota restrictions, of San Qiang's total exports of US$20 million in 1998, only US$2 million went to the USA. San Qiang anticipates that, once the USA import quotas are abolished after China joins the WTO, the company's exports to the USA will at least double. Jiangsu Zong Yi exports silk clothing to the USA; at present they are hobbled by quota restrictions.
Shoes	Qingdao Shuangxing Lan Sheng Ltd.	30% – 40% of Qingdao Shuangxing's output is exported; WTO accession is sure to improve the company's profits. Lan Sheng is a trading company which controls several shoe manufacturers; shoes are their most important export product.
Chinese medicine	Tai Ji Group Tong Ren Tang	With the USA's Food and Drug Administration having gradually relaxed the restrictions on the importing of Chinese medicine, once China joins the WTO the opportunities for exportation of Chinese medicine should increase steadily.
Metallurgy	Xin Gang Fan Xi Tu High-tech	China continues to enjoy an advantage in international competition owing to its extensive ore resources. Metals of which China has considerable reserves include tungsten, molybdenum, titanium, barium, niobium and tombarthite.

Source: Zhu and Wang (2000).

Table 5.19 Examples of Companies with the Ability to Compete Successfully in International Markets

Industry	Company	Details
Home appliances	Haier Kelong Kang Wa Xia Hua	Haier already exports refrigerators to the USA and washing machines to Japan.
Computers	Lian Xiang	Lian Xiang has overtaken Chang Hong as the number one company in the electronics sector. Lian Xiang Chairman Liu Chuanzhi believes that China's reduction of import tariffs on IT products in 1999 has triggered a period of rapid development for China's IT sector. While initially the increased competition was harmful to Lian Xiang, subsequently Lian Xiang was able to rise to the challenge and establish itself as the China agent for several leading international computer brands, in the course of which Lian Xiang improved its quality management, after-sales service and sales strategy. At present, not only has Lian Xiang become the computer manufacturer with the highest market share in the China market, it has also become one of the most important computer manufacturers in Asia outside Japan; Lian Xiang's share of the Asia Pacific market (excluding Japan) has risen from 3.1% in 1997 to 5.4% today, with only Compaq and IBM having higher market share.
Auto components	Xiang Huo Ju Wan Xiang Qian Chao	Possessing advantages in terms of technology and scale of operations, in 1998 these companies were able to achieve impressive performances despite the poor health of the industry as a whole. Their main products have obtained the necessary certification from the USA, and they have begun to export to the USA on a large scale.

Source: Zhu and Wang (2000).

Table 5.20 Industries and Listed Companies on which WTO Accession Will Have a Severe Impact

Industry (Level of impact)	WTO requirements	Typical listed companies
Timber and paper-making (Great)	The current tariffs of 12% – 18% on imported timber and 15% – 25% on imported paper will be reduced to 5% – 7%.	Dali Paper-making, Jiangxi Paper, Gui Zhi Ltd.
Telecom-munications equipment (Great)	Within six years the import restrictions on pagers and mobile phone handsets, and the geographical restrictions on fixed line service, will be lifted. Within four years, foreign companies will be allowed to hold shares of up to 49% in companies in all telecom sectors, and up to 51% in some sectors. The tariff restrictions on telecommunications equipment will be lifted.	Zhongxing Communications, Datang Telecom, Dongfang Telecom, You Tong Equipment
Computers (Significant)	By 2005, the tariff restrictions on semiconductors, computers and peripherals will be lifted.	Small and medium-sized computer manufacturers, as well as listed companies in other industries which have expanded into computers, will suffer; examples include Hai Xin Electronics and Huadong Computers.
Autos (Great)	By 2005, the import tariff on autos will have been reduced from 80% – 100% to 25%, and the tariff on auto components will have been reduced to 10%. At the same time, the import quotas will be abolished.	There are 34 companies producing autos and auto components listed on the Shanghai and Shenzhen stock exchanges. Shanghai Autos and Hangtian Electromechanical supply parts to Shanghai Dazhong; Dongfeng Instruments supplies parts to Dongfeng and Yi Qi. The fate of these companies is linked to that of the big auto manufacturing groups.

Table 5.20   Continued

Industry (Level of impact)	WTO Requirements	Typical listed companies
Agriculture (Significant)	China has been asked to reduce the average tariff on agricultural products to 17% by 2004, and to reduce the tariff on agricultural products imported from the USA to 14.5%. China has also been asked to lift the import ban on US wheat, meat and oranges.	Feng Le Agriculture, Jin Guo Enterprises, Jia He Ltd., the Ya Sheng Group, Jin Jian Rice (these companies are mainly engaged in the cultivation and processing of grains and fruit); the Ruyi Group, Caoyuan Development, Yi Li Ltd. (these companies are mainly engaged in the processing of meat and milk products).
Pharmaceuticals (Significant)	The import tariff on pharmaceuticals will be lowered to a level similar to that of other WTO member nations, around 5.5% – 6.5% (at present the tariff rate is 20%). China will also be required to ensure that intellectual property rights relating to pharmaceuticals are protected.	Those listed companies, most of whose products are ordinary medicines with low added value, and which have had low profits for many years, will suffer heavily. Once China joins the WTO, companies such as Huabei Pharmaceuticals, Tianmu Pharmaceuticals and Nanjing Pharmaceuticals will see their price advantage disappear. Manufacturers of medical instruments such as Weida Medical Instruments will also be affected.
Petrochemicals (Significant)	The market will be opened up and tariffs lowered. The price of foreign crude oil and gasoline will be at least 30% lower than the domestic product.	Listed companies such as Shiyou Daming and Liaohe Oilfields which are involved in oil drilling, as well as companies such as Hubei Xinghua, Yanhua Gaoxin, Shanghai Petrochemicals and Qilu Petrochemicals which are involved mainly in the sale of gasoline and organic chemical products will all be affected.

Source: Zhu and Wang (2000).

that are comparatively small and weak are still able to secure stock market listing. These companies, which lack the necessary economies of scale, will find it difficult to survive when faced with open markets and fierce competition.

Since the 1990s, the proportion of international capital flows accounted for by indirect financing – in the form of international bank loans – has been declining, while the proportion accounted for by direct financing – in the form of share issues – has been on the increase. The transformation of China's economy has encouraged the country's listed companies to internationalize, by issuing for example, international bonds or B-shares to foreign investors and then trading in these shares on the secondary market. They have also undertaken stock market listing overseas (through the use of H-, N- and S-shares), issuing American Depository Receipts, having Chinese-owned enterprises list overseas, buying and creating shell companies, and so on. However, the fact remains that in order to achieve further development, Chinese enterprises have been circumventing the government's quota restrictions and the requirements of the law in order to secure listing overseas. This clearly shows that the internationalization of China's stock market cannot satisfy the needs of economic development.

The main factor restricting the internationalization of China's stock market is the fact that the management of the stock market has not yet broken away from the planned economy, therefore, the role of government needs to be reviewed. Direct government interference in enterprise operation has caused profits to fall and has exacerbated the problem of instability. The Chinese government has, of course, also adopted a series of policy measures to promote the internationalization of the stock market, including the introduction of new financial accounting systems.

Unfortunately, there are still considerable disparities between these systems and international accounting principles. For example, Chinese financial statements do not have the provision of financial information as their main purpose, and are unable to provide full disclosure. China's accounting standards have also failed to adopt internationally approved standards of soundness, such as bad debt reserve, inventory value and fixed asset calculation methods. As a result, it is difficult for overseas investors to gain a clear picture of an enterprise's operations and prospects; in other words, it is not possible to provide a guarantee of return on investment and this has a negative impact on the issuing of B-shares and on overseas listing (Cao, 1998).

Nevertheless, WTO accession will not be entirely without benefit to China's stock market. Once China becomes part of the WTO, listed companies will be able to improve their operational management through the experience of competition, thereby raising their competitiveness. Listed companies that lack markets or competitiveness will find themselves removed from the stock market, leaving only those enterprises that display strong performance and profitability. In this way, the overall quality of China's listed companies will rise, and the foundations of the stock market will become stronger. At the same time, faced with the challenges that WTO accession will bring, listed companies will be forced to make improvements with respect to accounting, credit rating and disclosure methods; this will also be beneficial to the long-term development of the stock market.

Furthermore, while the entrance of foreign companies will create challenges for the stock market, it will also help the stock market to attract foreign capital. The introduction of foreign capital into the stock market is bound to promote the fusion of the A-share and B-share markets, eliminating the division that has for so long affected the stock market. In addition, the inflow of foreign capital into China will increase the supply of funds available to the stock market, strengthening the market and making more capital available for the issuing of new shares; it will thus speed up the reorganization of the equity structure of Chinese enterprises. What's more, once foreign securities firms begin to participate in the market, bringing with them their advanced management techniques, this will strengthen the competitive mechanisms of Chinese securities firms; these firms will find themselves coming under considerable pressure, which will encourage them to speed up reform, strengthen their management, improve their service quality, and reduce their operating costs.

Finally, in accordance with the principles of the WTO, while China's financial markets will be opened up to foreign competition, foreign markets will also be opened up to Chinese financial institutions. Chinese securities firms will be able to take advantage of this opportunity to expand overseas, establish branches in other countries, learn advanced foreign methods and transmit them back to China, in addition to acquiring financial information, and thereby speeding up the process of internationalization and stimulating the overall development of China's financial sector.

Notes

1. Examples include Guang Da Securities (Hong Kong), Zhong Jin International (a member of the Zhong Jin Group established by Morgan Stanley and the People's Construction Bank of China), and Zhong Yin International (*Commercial Times*, 7 September 2000).
2. For more thorough analyses, see *Ta Kung Pao*, 16 November 1999; *Wen Hui Pao*, 22 October 1999 and *Zhong Xin She*, 20 October 1999.
3. For further discussion, see *Zhong Jing Wang* (1999c, 1999g).
4. See *Zhong Jing Wang* (1999d, 1999h) for some additional discussion.
5. For deliberating discussion, see *Zhong Jing Wang*, 1 June 1999, Li, Xie and Zhang (1999) and Chen, Dong (1999).
6. See Chen, Ge (1999a) and Liao (1999).

7. See Xue and Wang (1998) and Zhang, Hanlin (1999)
8. See *Securities Times*, 10 May 1999.
9. For a related discussion, see *Zhong Jing Wang* (1999f).
10. See Liu and Ding (1999).
11. For discussion of these issues, see *Zhong Jing Wang* (1999a) and *Economic Reference Report*, 11 May 1999.
12. See Ye (1999).
13. See Song and Xu (2000).
14. In 1997, China's service sector accounted for 33 percent of GDP, far less than the 65–80 percent in the advanced nations, and around 10 percentage points lower than the figures for other developing nations such as Indonesia, the Philippines and India.
15. See Zhong Jing Wang (1999f) and China Securities Report, 27 April 1999.
16. See Zhong Jing Wang (1999b).
17. China's four leading state-owned commercial banks are all controlled by the Ministry of Finance, and account for over 90 percent of all bank assets. Shenzhen Development Bank, Shanghai Pudong Development Bank and Minsheng Bank are the only listed banks.
18. See Zhong Jing Wang (1999e), Chen, Dong (1999), Li, Xie and Zhang (1999) and Jiao (2000).
19. The low efficiency of capital utilization in China's securities industry can be seen in the following: (i) Low equity multiplier – although securities firms' debt ratios are not high, they have large amounts of capital tied up in non-financial assets such as real estate which are difficult to liquidate, leading to low liquidity; and (ii) Human resource use efficiency is low.
20. See China Securities Report, 20 April 1999.
21. Statistics indicate that of the different business areas in which Chinese banks are involved, only in 30 percent do they conform to standard international practice; this will have a highly negative impact on trans-national operation and international competitiveness (Huang, Wuxiang 2000).

6. Future Trends in the Evolution of China's Stock Market

6.1 Institutional Prospects of China's Stock Market

Following the establishment of China's securities market, the gradual reform of its operating environment is now under way. The decision was made to rely on 'learning by doing' in the development of the stock market, which resulted in a lack of concrete, long-term development plans; however, in order to ensure that the system of public ownership retains its primacy, shares are divided into state shares, legal person shares and public shares, with only the public shares – which account for a relatively small proportion of the total – being allowed to circulate freely. The government has tried to attract foreign capital while at the same time placing restrictions upon it. In terms of the impact on China's stock market, this has created a dual-track system for the A-, B- and H-shares, each with differing prices.

The fact that the same listed company can have several different categories of shares in existence at the same time, and that state shares and legal person shares, which account for 60 percent of the total, are not easily transferable, makes it difficult to implement transfer of ownership rights and to undertake mergers and acquisitions between enterprises. The securities transaction market is uniform and oligopolistic, which also makes it difficult to establish an effective mechanism for mergers and insolvencies, or a reasonable business management mechanism. As a result, one would have to say that the major obstacle in the way of the development of China's stock market is the traditional planned economy. Within any planned economy, the distribution of resources is directed, rather than being dictated by the market, and institutional transformation can only occur through the replacement of planning by the market mechanism and certain trends favoring the development of a sound stock market.

The marketization of share issues

The marketization of share issues in China refers to the elimination of the current equity structure with its division between state shares, legal person shares and public shares. This kind of equity structure restricts the stock market in its appraisal of enterprise operation, and strengthens the 'soft' restrictions on listed companies' budgets, a situation which does not support the reform of state-owned enterprises. The marketization of share issues involves a switch from management of the number of listed companies to management of the quality of listed companies. At the same time, there will be a move away from demand dominated by individual shareholders to demand dominated by institutional investors, mainly securities investment funds. Although China's inhabitants have already been transformed from the pure consumers of the 1980s into consumer/investors, with the stock market being constantly exposed to this source of capital, it is likely to result in dramatic rises and falls.

The stock market's planned quota controls no longer meet the needs of economic development in the transitional period, so China should abandon the placing of controls on share issue volume, and instead, marketize its market scale. The key task in securities supervision should be rigorous review of applications to issue new shares, in order to render the operations of listed companies more sound (Zhao and Guo, 1998).

The need for multiple transaction levels

The development of China's securities companies is affected by the limited number of market levels and excessive market concentration. The Shanghai and Shenzhen stock exchanges are very similar in terms of listing standards and operational mechanisms, and as the interests of the stock exchange are often closely bound up with those of the local government authorities, stock exchange behavior tends to become regionalized. Although securities exchange centers throughout the country are engaged in securities transactions similar to OTC trading, this has not yet received formal authorization by the government. As a result, the number of market levels is insufficient, which constitutes an obstacle to stock market development.

At the same time, the concentration of the stock market in eastern China has resulted in a large-scale flow of capital and talent towards the east, which is not conducive to balanced regional development. As far as the secondary market is concerned, the introduction of multiple transaction levels would help to increase market liquidity. During the institutional transformation period China could seek to render the internal transactions between the Shanghai and Shenzhen stock exchanges more sound, so that they become a centralized national exchange. China could also develop a legalized off-floor OTC exchange properly regulated by law.

Regional exchanges could also be developed. For example, larger securities transaction centers such as those at Wuhan and Tianjin could be upgraded to become regional stock exchanges; this would help to strengthen the stock market's capital allocation function (Chen, 1998a).

Strengthening of the legal framework

A market is not an abstract supply and demand curve, and the market mechanism is able to function through the use of a set of formal institutional arrangements, rules and practices. Although deep into its period of institutional transformation, China's traditional planned economy has yet to be eliminated, thus, the government continues to engage in frequent interventions in the economy, and as such, the market mechanism has not yet become fully formed. The result of such a situation is that government interference restricts the development of the market system and participants in new economic activities have no choice but to engage in rent-seeking activities in order to obtain further room for development. The existing situation in the stock market is still one in which market scale is small, with rampant speculation and a lack of comprehensive brokerage facilities. The range of products available is not sufficiently broad, the quality of investors is low and the term structure of interest rate is inappropriate. The gap separating China's stock market from the mature markets of the developed nations is extremely wide.

A comprehensive legal framework is the key element in stock market development; however, the lack of progress in the creation of new legislation has been one of China's most notable failings during its period of institutional transformation. As such China will have to speed up the strengthening of its legal system if it is to make real progress. Following the promulgation of the Securities Law and Insurance Law, the government could formulate and improve on, *inter alia*, the Securities Transaction Law, Investment Trust Law, Investor Protection Law, Mergers and Acquisitions Law, the Securities Rating Law, Investment Consultancy Law and Law for the Protection of Securities Investors. At the same time, regulations still need to be drawn up to cover the establishment of a 'second board' for high-tech stocks that would conform to the existing circumstances in China. Revisions and additions are also needed to other pieces of legislation, such as the Company Law, the Criminal Code and the Code of Administrative Procedures, in order to solve the problem of unsatisfactory dovetailing between the different laws, while the deficiencies in the Securities Law should also be addressed. These weaknesses include the problems relating to the transfer of state shares and legal person shares, off-floor transactions and the dual-track system of A- and B-shares, none of which are currently governed by clear regulations.

For a variety of reasons, both objective and subjective, there are weaknesses in terms of the handling of transactions undertaken by companies that have been taken over, and with regard to compensation for civil liability. In addition, the division made by the Securities Law between enterprise responsibility, rights and interest relationships has caused concern among some listed companies. They feel that this kind of separation restricts the room for development available to state-owned enterprises, and will make it difficult for them to compete on an equitable basis as an independent corporate entity. Only with the introduction of a comprehensive legal framework, the creation of a fair, orderly market competition environment and the establishment of transparent 'game rules', can the stock market develop properly (Yu, Hui 2000).

Improved production of financial statements

The development of the stock market during the period of institutional transformation has exposed the inability of the present accounting system to fully reflect enterprises' real financial status, risk and future changes. A number of methods can be used to improve the accuracy of accounting information disclosure, and thereby improve the operational efficiency of the stock market. Comprehensive operational performance reports should be introduced, to be produced separately from the regular financial statements and to serve as a supplement to the income statement. In this way, the income statement will be able to reflect both profit and loss that has already occurred, and that which is likely to occur in the future. Each department of a company should be required to produce comprehensive reports in order to provide supplementary information on the enterprise's opportunities and risks and the structure of the financial statements should be adjusted, with a clear division between core and non-core businesses. In such a way, the direction in which a company is moving, along with its opportunities and risks, can be more clearly portrayed. The auditing activities of accountants should be regulated and registered in order to improve the accuracy of financial information disclosure, thereby improving the operational efficiency of the stock market (Li, 2000).

Strengthening of regulations

There is a need for a set of regulations to govern capital flows, in order to improve the stock markets' transaction, management and regulatory systems.

Improved capital market structure and promotion of financial innovation

Further improvement is needed in the method of issue of new shares, in order to reduce the price differential between the primary and secondary markets.[1] What is needed is a system within which it is possible, on the one hand, to choose between the different methods of issue already in existence, according to what is being issued and market status, while at the same time achieving constant innovation in issue methods, aggressively seeking out new market pricing methods for new share issue; for example, by expanding the price bands for new share issue, making use of the auction method or bringing in strategic investors. The determination of new share issue prices will ultimately be based entirely on the share's inherent investment value along with market supply and demand.

In order to allow more investors to participate in the market, the system governing participation in the B-share market needs to be reformed; for example by encouraging the participation of local and foreign investment funds and by opening up the B-share market to Chinese citizens in a systematic, step-by-step manner. Eventually, once conditions are ripe, the dual-track system of A-shares and B-shares should be abolished.

A new board needs to be established for start-ups in high-risk industries[2] with a complete reorganization of the stock market. If consideration is given only to the encouragement of start-ups and the provision of an 'exit route' for venture capital firms, rather than putting the protection of investors' rights at the heart of stock market development, then the problems of market manipulation that have plagued the main board for so long will also occur in the second board, and investor confidence will gradually evaporate; the second board will find itself in the same awkward position as the second boards in many other countries. A rigorous regulatory mechanism will therefore be necessary for the establishment of the second board, with a higher level of regulation, stricter requirements with respect to disclosure and greater demands placed on listed companies. In this way, the abuses that have commonly occurred in the main board can be kept to a minimum in the second board. Through the strengthening of regulation, the prevention of excessive speculation and market manipulation and the establishment of a mechanism for de-listing, the market can be made to operate properly.

With the increase in the volume of shares issued, the number of bonds issued also needs to be raised. At the same time that an increase in the volume of government bonds issued takes place, the number and variety of bank debentures and corporate bonds issued also needs to be increased, with the introduction of more intermediate product types linking the bond market and stock market, such as convertible bonds, warrants, and so on.

More innovation is needed with regard to the different types of investment products available. On the basis of current market status, it can be estimated that the total amount of funding required for new share issues and allocation in 2001 will be approximately RMB120 billion. A reduction in state share holdings may create the demand for an additional RMB50 billion while the establishment of the second board may produce a further RMB60 billion. Handling fees and stamp tax will account for a further RMB70 billion, giving a total of approximately RMB300 billion. The range of different tasks that need to be performed in order to maintain a balance in terms of the expansion of both capacity and capitalization includes the establishment of the second board, the issuing of new shares on the main board, securitization of loans and reduction in holdings of state shares. Therefore it will be necessary to draw in new funds, and open-end funds will be one of the main sources (Yang et al., 2001). However, with open-end funds, the issues of liquidity and security have to be dealt with; there are also restrictions on the objectivity of the subscription and settlement networks. An even bigger problem is that open-end fund development requires mature investors. By comparison with closed-end funds, therefore, the operation of open-end funds poses considerably greater difficulties. In order to ensure the maintenance of stability, semi-open funds or open-end funds for private subscription could be launched initially, waiting until the conditions are right before launching open-end funds for public subscription. In addition, futures products (such as index futures and futures options) need to be introduced on a trial basis.

To summarize, there is a need for innovation in market systems and financial products; there is also a need for linkage between the primary and secondary markets, between the stock market and the bond market, between the A-share market and the B-share market, and between the spot market and the futures market. Only with such innovation will it be possible to improve the overall efficiency of the capital markets.

The need for appropriate intermediaries

With regard to the principle of maintaining separation between the banking, investment and trust and insurance sectors, there is a requirement for suitable intermediaries such as investment funds to be established, so that the state's capital can flow into the stock market. Article 133 of the Securities Law prohibits bank funds from flowing into the stock market through improper channels; however, looking at this from another angle, it should be possible for bank funds to flow into the stock market without any violation of the law.

In reality, when securities firms use securities as collateral to obtain bank loans, this constitutes away of bank financing flowing into the stock market. Although there is a general prohibition on bank funds entering the stock market directly, it should be possible to allow bank funds to support listed companies' merger and acquisition activities. Therefore, one might ask whether insurance company funds should be allowed to flow into the stock market through (private placement, open-end) investment funds? In the long term, bank funds are likely to be the main source of funding for the stock market, with insurance company funds also becoming an important, permanent source of funds.

The need for improved quality of listed companies

The quality of listed companies needs to be improved in order to strengthen their guiding position in the market, since quality is a precondition for, and foundation of, stock market development. Only when listed companies display good performance and strong growth can the continuing development of the market be assured. In order to improve the quality of listed companies, it is necessary on the one hand to choose for listing, those companies with good performance and strong development potential, which occupy a leading position in their industry, while also encouraging and supporting the entry into the stock markets of high-tech enterprises and enterprises within emerging industries. A further requirement is the need to improve the efficiency of listed companies' fundraising; the activities of listed companies in their efforts to raise capital have to mesh with their asset adjustment and technology upgrading. Listed companies must also undertake a thorough overhaul of their management mechanism, establishing efficient corporate governance and corresponding equity and futures mechanisms. On the other hand, it is necessary to support the operations of listed companies, helping them to use debt-to-equity conversion and refinancing to improve their asset and liability structure, encouraging inter-regional, cross-industry and cross-ownership system mergers, acquisitions and asset reorganizations among listed companies and between listed companies and non-listed companies. This will help to improve their performance and to cultivate a group of large, strong, listed companies that are capable of being competitive in international markets, thereby strengthening the leading role of these listed companies in the stock market and allowing them to function as a force for stability.

Solving the problem of state share liquidity

Multiple methods need to be used to gradually solve the problem of the liquidity of state shares and there are various methods that can be used to achieve this aim. One is to reduce the number of state shares in listed companies, thus reducing the proportion of all shares accounted for by state shares. Secondly, for those industries of vital importance to the nation, which need to be controlled by the state, converting these state shares into transferable shares does not mean that they would be sold immediately; they could remain within state control. Thirdly, in the case of better performing listed companies in the more competitive industries, state shares could be converted into long-term bonds. Furthermore, those listed companies which have abundant funds could be allowed to buy back state shares, while state shares in listed companies could be sold to the general public (this method is in fact already in use).[3]

Achieving the greater liquidity of state shares would help to ensure an appropriate dispersal of equity, strengthening the corporate governance of listed companies and providing an exit route for state capital that conforms to market requirements. Solving the problem of state share liquidity is thus an urgent task.

The development of institutional investors and large securities firms

There is a need to develop institutional investors and to cultivate large securities firms. First of all, the development of investment funds needs to be speeded up and made more comprehensive. Thereafter, the development of different types of investment fund, including securities investment funds, must be speeded up; this would have a major impact in terms of encouraging the application of savings to capital investment. Secondly, the reorganization of securities companies should be promoted, with active cultivation of ultra-large securities firms. In order to respond to the competition that WTO accession will bring, mergers need to be used to create large securities groups. This would also help in the process of state-owned enterprise reform and conversion to joint stock company status, ensuring that resources are allocated in the most efficient manner; the new, large securities firms would be able to serve as financial advisors and investment consultants. The government should encourage securities companies, supporting capital increments by securities firms and providing them with further legal financing channels, while also actively encouraging the establishment of ultra-large securities companies.

Clarifying the definition of 'share price manipulation'

There is a need for clarification of the definition of 'share price manipulation' by state-owned enterprises and state-owned holding companies, in order to open up normal stock investment channels for state-owned enterprises. Article 76 of the Securities Law stipulates that state-owned enterprises and state-owned holding companies may not manipulate share prices. However, there is as yet no clear definition of just what is meant by 'share price manipulation'. Given the background of government policy which opposes share trading by state-owned enterprises and state-owned holding companies, this lack of clarity with respect to 'manipulation' is likely to deter state-owned enterprises from engaging in stock market investment. The definition of 'share price manipulation' therefore needs to be clarified so that state-owned enterprises can participate in stock market investment openly and in a properly regulated manner. The relevant government agencies recently began giving conditional approval for stock market participation by state-owned enterprises, a move which represents a major breakthrough; however, the restrictions on funding sources and the time limits placed on investment still create serious obstacles for state-owned enterprises wishing to invest in the stock market.

6.2 The Globalization of Financial Markets and the Reform of China's Stock Market

Although the pace of stock market liberalization in China has been relatively slow, as the country's economy is opened up and financial sector reform progresses, and particularly after it gains WTO accession, the opening up of China's stock market and the securities industry to international capital is, nevertheless, inevitable. In reality, in the long term, WTO accession should have many benefits for China's stock market. Not only will the economic stability of WTO entry support the development of the stock market, but the opening up of the insurance and banking sectors will also help to expand the funding sources available to the stock market. However, China's stock market does have structural and systemic weaknesses, and in the short term, WTO accession will bring negative impact to the development and stability of the market. In order to meet the challenges of WTO accession, the stock market needs to develop in a number of ways; in precisely what order these measures need to be taken will depend on the severity of the impact.

The equity structure of China's securities firms is unsound; for example, the equity structure of Da Peng Securities and Southern Securities is highly dispersed, with their largest shareholders accounting for only 4.12 percent and 11.3 percent of all shares, and the various other shareholders all holding roughly equal shares. In the case of Guotai Diaoan, Haitong Securities, Guo Tong Securities, Zhong Xin Securities, Guo Xin Securities, Guang Fa Securities, Beijing Securities, Changjiang Securities, Hu Cai Securities, Hua Xia Securities and Lian He Securities, the equity structure is more centralized, with the five largest shareholders holding a combined share of over 40 percent. Either case, an excessively centralized or an excessively dispersed equity structure, is disadvantageous to a securities firm's governance. With excessive centralization, it is easier for large shareholders to interfere in the company's management; whereas, with excessive dispersal, the cost of shareholder supervision of management is increased, affecting shareholders' participation in governance (Huang, 2001).

China's securities firms have had to deal with a buyer's market for a long time, and this, in conjunction with their small scale of operation, their overall low competitiveness and unsound internal management mechanisms, the excessively large number of firms in the industry and the fact that all the different securities firms have a similar structure and lack their own distinguishing characteristics, means that they will be seriously affected by China's WTO accession. They will be forced to compete against the major global securities companies such as Merrill Lynch and Morgan Stanley. Strategies available to China's securities firms in response to WTO accession include: (i) Taking advantage of the implementation of the Securities Law to increase their capitalization as rapidly as possible, reviewing their internal asset structure, participating in the inter-bank market and repurchase of government bonds, and using the stock market to raise capital in order to expand their scale of operation and enhance their competitiveness; (ii) Mergers and reorganization can be used to form large securities groups which would also be beneficial to the reform of state-owned enterprises, helping to ensure that resources are allocated in the most efficient manner; only large securities firms, with their greater scale of operation and resources, would be able to function as a provider of financial information and consultancy services (see Chapter 5 for details); (iii) Increasing the efficiency of capital use and strengthening internal financial management. Securities firms need to adopt strategies to differentiate themselves from other companies in the industry, for example by developing online trading[4] and venture capital business.[5] Some securities firms have already begun planning the development of asset securitization business, international collaboration, and so on, as a means of differentiating themselves; however, the legal framework for these business areas is not yet comprehensive, which means that for the moment, their efforts are unable to move beyond the planning stage; (iv) The securities business is an industry heavily reliant upon talent; in the future, the main focus of competition within the industry will be on competition for human resources. Thus, securities firms will need to gain the ability to cultivate their own high quality staff; and (v) China can use its WTO special clause to restrict competition from foreign securities firms and thereby protect Chinese securities firms. It can encourage foreign investment banks and securities firms to participate in the issuing of B-, H- and N-shares, and open up sectors where Chinese securities firms and investment banks cannot meet demand, such as mergers and acquisitions (particularly transnational asset reorganization), securitization of assets, financial consultancy services and other business areas where there is a high level of innovation. The Chinese government can also encourage foreign companies to participate in the reorganization of state-owned enterprises. A reasonable degree of protection should be given to those sectors in which Chinese securities firms are capable of service provision, such as underwriting of government bonds, issuing of A-shares, packaged listing and underwriting service and brokerage business in the secondary market, in order to reduce the impact of foreign competition (Chen, Yiqin 2000)

The Chinese government has traditionally adopted a very cautious attitude to the listing of financial enterprises. Their main concern has been that if companies in the financial sector were listed without proper internal controls being in place, without full transparency with respect to disclosure and with insufficient regulation of enterprise governance, this would be likely to produce a high level of risk. At present, China's stock market has only seven listed financial enterprises, a major disparity with the advanced nations. The situation is particularly serious for banks, with Shenzhen Development Bank, Shanghai Pudong Development Bank and Minsheng Bank currently being the only listed banks. Faced with the competition from foreign financial institutions on WTO accession, China's financial institutions will need to strengthen themselves and overhaul their systems.

With many Chinese banks and insurance companies currently seeking stock market listing, in November 2001 the China Securities Regulatory Commission will be promulgating the Regulations Governing Disclosure by Firms Which Have Issued Securities Through a Public Offering, containing special provisions regarding disclosure by listed companies in the financial sector. This will make it significantly easier for financial institutions to secure stock market listing. At present, non-state-owned enterprises account for over 70 percent of China's economy and in terms of GDP, over 60 percent is derived from the non-state sector. However, at least 80 percent of bank loans and 70 percent of all credit go to state-owned enterprises and, as a result, the flourishing private sector is starved of capital; this is the background against which the private sector has to operate. Nevertheless, as of early November 2000, of the total loans authorized by Minsheng Bank (currently China's only privately run bank), over 60 percent went to small and medium enterprises, thus demonstrating the importance of privately run banks to small and medium enterprises development (Yang et al., 2001).

In terms of globalization of financial markets, China's stock market itself needs to be reformed as rapidly as possible in order to establish sound market systems and structure, increase the level of stability and reduce speculation and risk. The main areas where reform is urgently needed are: (i) Further competition should be promoted in financing, that is to say, enterprises should be able to decide for themselves, the financing method, cost, quantity and timing, in accordance with the market mechanism. Interest rate controls should be abolished and; interest rates should be decided by enterprises in accordance with credit ratings and their ability to repay; (ii) The government should relax the restrictions on derivatives, such as index futures, in order to ensure that the full range of market functions are provided; (iii) The government should speed up the marketization of interest rates, in order to facilitate financial reform and ensure an effective response to WTO accession; (iv) Reform of the financial system must be speeded up, establishing a sound banking system so that the authorities can effectively monitor the state of foreign capital flows; and (v) As regards opening up the market to foreign capital, the Qualified Foreign Institutional Investor (QFII) system could be adopted in the A-share market, so that prior to the lifting of exchange restrictions on the Yuan, foreign investors would be able to exchange foreign currency for Renminbi, for investment in Chinese enterprises. This would impact on the stock market in several ways: market capacity would be further increased, competition would become more fierce, a higher level of market regulation would be required and investor behavior would become more rational.

Notes

1. For a total of 8,659,600 shares issued by 23 listed companies, the underwriters secured RMB108.26 million in profit; this means that for each company, with an average of 376,500 shares listed, the underwriters secured a profit of RMB4.7 million. The quantity of new shares allocated in the secondary market accounts for only 12.89 percent of all shares issued in initial public offerings. The likelihood of actually being allocated shares is only 0.1027 percent, two-thirds the figure for on-line subscription (Zhu, 2001).
2. Venture capital companies, which have been growing steadily in number, will be the main force behind the new board. There are already several hundred venture capital companies in China, with almost twenty in Shenzhen alone, including Shenzhen Venture Investment, in which the government has a share. Further investment companies have been established by securities firms and listed companies, which have been investing in companies planning to list on the second board. Many of these hope to be among the first to list on the new board themselves (*Zhong Jing Wang*, 10 January 2001).
3. Buyback of state shares refers to listed companies repurchasing 'state shares' in their company from the holders of those shares. However, the process of buying back state shares is not an open transaction, and does not involve trading within the market; the purpose is to improve the company's equity structure (Xiao, Bing 1999).
4. Thirty-three securities firms have already launched online brokerage services; these include Hua Tai Securities, Hua Rong Investment and Trust, Min Fa Securities, Guangdong Securities, Guotai Junan, Southern Securities, Xing Ye Securities, Henan Securities, Shandong Securities, Hua Xia Securities, Hua Tai Securities, Hua An Securities, Huanghe Securities, Suzhou Securities, Zhong Fu Securities and Xinjiang Securities.
5. Guo Tong Securities and Southwestern Securities have participated in the establishment of venture capital companies. Guo Xin has established a venture capital division, seeking to build up its venture capital business beyond the departmental level. Other firms, such as Hai Tong and Guotai Junan, have established venture capital consultancy services; however, on 18 April 2001, the China Securities Regulatory Commission announced that securities firms would no longer be permitted to engage in venture capital business, either directly or through the holding of shares in venture capital companies (*Zhong Jing Wang*, 18 April 2001; Huang and Zhang, 2001).

References

Arthur, W. B. (1989), 'Competing Technologies, Increasing Returns, and Lock-in by Historical Events', *Economic Journal*, **99** (394), March, 116–31.

Beck, T., R. Levine and N. Loayza (2000), 'Finance and the Sources of Growth', *Journal of Financial Economics,* **58** (1/2), October/November, 261–300.

Cai, Wenhai (1999), 'The Reasons Why Repeated Prohibitions Have Failed to Halt Securities Fraud in China', *Hong Kong Economic Journal Monthly*, **272,** November, 18–27.

Cao, Fengchi (1998), *The Development, Normalization, and Globalization of Chinese Security Market (Zhongguo Zhengquanshichang Fazan Guifan yu Guochifa)*, Beijing: Zhongguo Jinrong Press.

Chen, Chaoyang and Qin Wu (2000), 'Perfection of Hypothecation Financing to Promote the Stable Development of the Stock Market', *Zhongguo Jinrong (China Finance)*, **3**, 35.

Chen, Dong (1999), 'Facing the Challenge of International Financial Unification: The Impact of WTO Accession on China's Financial Sector and Possible Response Measures', *Securities Times*, 10 May.

Chen, Dongsheng (1999), 'The B-share Market and Its Investment Opportunities', in Yupen Chen (ed.), *China's Securities Market at the Millennium (Shichizijiao de Zhonggou Zhengquan Shichang)*, Beijing: Jingji Kexue Press, 119–27.

Chen, Ge (1999a), 'WTO Accession Means Problems and Progress for Chinese Agriculture', *Securities Times*, 13 April.

Chen, Ge (1999b), 'Listed Companies and the Modern Enterprise System', *Jingji Lilun yu Jinggi Guanli (Economic Theory and Business Management)*, **3**, 22–4.

Chen, Haowu (1998a), *China's Capital Markets in the Era of Institutional Transformation (Tizhi Zhuangui Shiqide Zhongguo Ziben Shichang)*, Beijing: Jingji Kexue Press.

Chen, Haowu (1998b), 'Government Regulation of the Stock Market', *Jinrong Yanjiu (Journal of Financial Research)*, **7**, 17–22.

Chen, Qiumin (1999), 'Regulation of the Relationship Between China's Money Market and Capital Markets', *Touzi Yanjiu (Investment Research)*, **9**, 19–22.

Chen, Xiaoyun (1997), *China's Stock Market (Zhongguo Gupiao Shichang)*, Hong Kong: Shang Wu Press.

Chen, Yehua (2000), 'The Development of the Stock Market in China – Economic Foundations and Systems', *Caimo Jingji (Finance & Trade Economics)*, **1**, 56–60.

Chen, Yiqin (2000), 'WTO Accession and the Development of China's Stock Market', *Caimo Jingji (Finance & Trade Economics)*, **1**, 52–5.

Chen, Yupen and Ping Zhou (1999), 'Securities Firm Development and Market Intermediary Theory', in Yupen Chen (ed.), *China's Securities Market at the Millennium (Shichizijiao de Zhonggou Zhengquan Shichang)*, Beijing: Jingji Kexue Press, 1–6.

Chen, Zhengrong (2001), 'The Inevitability of Internationalization for China's Securities Market – Strategic Considerations Regarding the Participation of Foreign Enterprises in the Stock Market', *Shanghai Securities Report website http://www.ssnews.online.sh.cn/*, 1 February.

Chen, Zhiyuan (2001), 'China Securities Regulatory Commission Vice Chairman Shi Meilun Notes That Venture Capital Funds in China Still Have Considerable Room for Development', *Shichang Bao*, 1 May.

China Macroeconomic Issues Project Team (1998), 'The Development of the Capital Markets and the Reform of State-owned Enterprises', *Guanli Shijue (Management World)*, **5**, 77–85.

China Securities Regulatory Commission (1998, 1999, 2000), *China Securities and Futures Statistical Yearbook*, Beijing: Zhongguo Caizheng Jingji Press.

China Securities Regulatory Commission Website, *http://www.csrc.gov.cn/*.

China Securities Report (1999), 'Theoretical Analysis: The Impact of WTO Accession on Securities Firms', 20 April.

China Securities Report (1999), 'Theoretical Analysis: Varying Impact – The Effects of WTO Accession on China's Telecommunications Industry', 27 April.

Chow, G.C., Z.Z. Fan and J.Y. Hu (1999), 'Shanghai Stock Prices as Determined by the Present-Value Model', *Journal of Comparative Economics* **27** (3), September, 553–61.

Commercial Times (2000), 'Mainland China's Second Board Is Making a Big Splash Even Before It Gets Off the Ground', 22 August.

Commercial Times (2000), 'Foreign Companies Will Be Permitted to Underwrite A-shares from the End of This Year', 7 September.

Da Peng Securities Project Team (2000), 'The Participation of Commercial Insurance Funds in the Securities Market – Policy and Strategies', *Jinrong yu Boxian (Finance and Insurance)*, **2**, 33–42.

Dan, Ruyong (1999), 'An Empirical Study of the Relationship Between Financial Development and Economic Growth in China', *Jingji Yanjiu*

(Economic Research Journal), **10**, 53–61.

Devereux, M.B. and G.W. Smith (1994), 'International Risk Sharing and Economic Growth', *International Economic Review,* **35** (3), August, 535–50.

Economic Daily News (2000), 'A Wave of Mergers Among Securities Firms in Mainland China', 5 July.

Economic Daily News (2001), 'Germany's Dresdner Bank to Collaborate With Chinese Securities Firm', 20 January.

Economic Reference Report (1999), 'The Auto Industry Still Has a Future on the International Stage', 11 May.

Fama, E. F. (1970), 'Efficient Capital Markets: A Review of Theory and Empirical Work', *Journal of Finance,* **15** (2), May, 383–417.

Fama, E. F. (1991), 'Efficient Capital Markets: II', *Journal of Finance,* **48** (5), December, 1575–617.

Fei, Wuwei, Yao Fu and Shuangli Wu (2001a), 'Future Development Trends in China's Securities Market', *Ta Kung Pao*, 15 February.

Fei, Wuwei, Yao Fu and Shuangli Wu (2001b), 'Securities Regulation in China Displays New Features', *Ta Kung Pao*, 15 February.

Fei, Wuwei, Yao Fu and Shuangli Wu (2001c), 'The Impact of the Tightening Up of Regulatory Policy on the Stock Market', *Zhong Jing Wang* http://www.cei.gov.cn/, 15 February.

Greenwood, J. and B. Smith (1997), 'Financial Markets in Development and the Development of Financial Markets', *Journal of Economic Dynamics and Control,* **21** (1), January, 145–86.

Han, Zhiguo, Gang Fan, Wei Liu and Yang Li (1998), *Reform in China and Institution Response (Zhongguo Gaige yu Fazhan de Zhidu Xiaoying)* (Part Two), Beijing: Jingji Kexue Press.

He, Shunwen and Xing Liu (2000), 'The Management and Equity Structure of Listed Companies in China', *Hong Kong Economic Journal*, 18 May.

He, Xiaoping and Qifeng Zhu (1999), 'The Reorganization of China's Stock Market and Its Development Trends', *Jinrong Yanjiu (Journal of Financial Research)*, **8**, 34 –9.

Holmstrom, B. and J. Tirole (1993), 'Market Liquidity and Performance Monitoring', *Journal of Political Economy,* **101** (4), August, 678–709.

Hou, Juan (2000), 'A Review of Securities Market Regulation Measures', *Zhong Jing Wang* http://www.cei.gov.cn/, 28 December.

Hu, Jizhi (1999), *The Evolution of the Chinese Stock Market and Institutional Change (Zhongguo Gushi de Engjin yu Zhidu Bianqian)*, Beijing: Jingji Kexue Press.

Hu, Meng and Jiahua Xiang (1999), *Securities Investment Fund Practice (Zhungquan Touzi Jijin Shiwu)*, Beijing: Shehui Kexue Wenxian Press.

Huang, Shunxiang (2001), 'The Equity Structure of Chinese Securities Firms and Rational Choice', *Jingji Daokan (Economic Herald)*, **2**, 40–4.

Huang, Wuxiang (2000), 'Analysis of the Strategies Adopted by China's Listed Financial Enterprises in Response to WTO Accession', *Zhong Jing Wang http://www.cei.gov.cn/*.

Huang, Yexuan and Jun Zhang (2001), 'Differentiation Among Securities Firms in China – Current Status and Future Development Trends', *Ju Cao Zixun Wang http://www.cninfo.com.cn/*, 21 March.

Huang, Yuncheng (2000), 'China's Securities Market – Moving Steadily Towards Marketization', *Zhongguo Jinrong (China Finance)*, **9**, 42–3.

Jiang, Shuncai (1999), 'Where to Look for Gold When the Sand Has Been Blown Away? – Analysis of the Overall Competitiveness of China's Securities Firms in the Primary and Secondary Markets, 1996–1998', in Yupen Chen (ed.), *China's Securities Market at the Millennium (Shichizijiao de Zhonggou Zhengquan Shichang)*, Beijing: Jingji Kexue Press, 37–57.

Jiang, Weijun (1999), 'Analysis of Financial Asset Purchase in China', *Caimo Jingji (Finance and Trade Economics)*, **5**, 21–7.

Jiang, Yihong (2001), 'Comparison of the Double Disclosure of Net Profits by Companies Listed on the Shenzhen and Shanghai Stock Exchanges for B-shares', *Touzi yu Zhungquan (Investment and Securities)*, **3**, 76–9.

Jiao, Jinpu (2000), *The WTO and the Future of China's Financial Sector (Shimaozhuzu yu Zhongguo Jinrongye Weilai)*, Beijing: Zhongguo Jinrong Press.

Jin, Tehuan (2001), 'An Important Step Towards Bringing the Securities Market into Step With International Practice', *Ta Kung Pao*, 26 February.

Jin, Yunhui and Cungao Yu (1998), 'An Empirical Study of the Relationship Between China's Stock Market and the National Economy – Part Two', *Jinrong Yanjiu (Journal of Financial Research)*, **4**, 41–6.

Kyle, A.S. (1984), 'Market Structure, Information, Futures Markets, and Price Formation', in G. Storey, A. Schmitz and H. Sarris (eds), *International Agricultural Trade: Advanced Readings in Price Formation, Market Structure, and Price Instability,* Boulder, Co.: Westview.

Lau, L.J., Y. Qian and G. Roland (2000), 'Reform without Losers: An Interpretation of China's Dual-Track Approach to Transition', *Journal of Political Economy,* **108** (1), February, 120–43.

Levine, R. (1991), 'Stock Markets, Growth, and Tax Policy', *Journal of Finance,* **46** (4), September, 1445–65.

Levine, R. (1997), 'Financial Development and Economic Growth : View and Agenda', *Journal of Economic* Literature, **35** (2), June, 688–726.

Li, Changhong (1998), *History and Development of China's Securities Markets (Zhongguo Zhengquan Shichang Lishi yu Fazhan)*, Beijing: Zhongguo Wuzi Press.

Li, D., S. Lin and C. Li (1997), 'The Impact of Settlement Time on the Volatility of Stock Markets', *Applied Financial Economics,* **7** (6), December, 689–94.

Li, Geping and Pin Huang (1999), 'The Transfer of State Shares and Improving the Corporate Governance Structure of Listed Companies', *Caimo Jingji (Finance and Trade Economics)*, **8**, 36–42.

Li, Kang (1999), *Regulation and Analysis of Fluctuation in China's Stock Market (Zhongguo Gushi Bodong Guilu Jiqi Fenxifangfa)*, Beijing: Jingji Kexue Press.

Li, Kemu, Fudan Xie and Xiaoji Zhang (1999), *The WTO and China's Strategy for Opening Up Its Capital Markets (Shimaozhuzu yu Zhongguo Ziben Shichang Kaifancelei)*, Beijing: State Council Research and Development Center.

Li, Liying (2000),'Accounting and Disclosure Policy in the Reform of the Capital Markets', *Liaoning Daxue Xuebao (Journal of Liaoning University)*, **28** (3), May, 31–2.

Liao, Zequn (1999), 'The Heavy Wings of Agriculture', *Securities Times*, 13 April.

Lin, Haochang (1999), 'Structural Problems Affecting Listed Companies in China', *Touzi Yanjiu (Investment Research)*, **6**, 19–23.

Lin, Yifu (2001), 'Four Problems Concerning China's Stock Market', *Touzi Daobao (Investment Reporter)*, 12 March.

Liu, Hua and Yafeng Cui (2000), 'The Impact of WTO Accession on China's Securities Industry and Possible Response Measures', *Touzi Yanjiu (Investment Research)*, **4**, 31–4.

Liu, Ming and Guoliang Yuan (1999), 'Debt Financing and Sustainable Development for Listed Companies', *Jinrong Yanjiu (Journal of Financial Research)*, **7**, 34–9.

Liu, Shoufen and Geng Hu (2000), 'Mechanisms for the Prevention of Securities Crime', *Touzi yu Zhungquan (Investment and Securities)*, **5**, 13–9.

Liu, Shufeng and Wenjie Ding (1999), 'The Structure of the Electromechanical Industry Will Need to Be Reorganized When China Joins the WTO', *China Economic Times*, 5 May.

Liu, X., H. Song and D. Romilly (1997),'Are Chinese Stock Markets Efficient ? A Cointegration and Causality Analysis', *Applied Economics Letters,* **4** (8), August, 511–15.

Lucas, R.E. (1988), 'On the Mechanics of Economic Development', *Journal of Monetary Economics,* **22** (1), July, 3–42.

Ma, Ruohong (2000),'Report on Stock Market Operations in the First Half of 2000', *Zhongguo Jinrong (China Finance)*, **9**, 46–8.

Mao, Chunbo (2000), 'An Analysis of the Impact of the Start-up Board on the

Main Board', *Zhong Jing Wang http://www.cei.gov.cn/*, 11 October.

Mao, Zhenhua (1998), 'The Reform of State-owned Enterprises and the Capital Markets', *Guanli Shijue (Management World)*, **5**, 86–91.

Mayer, C. (1988), 'New Issues in Corporate Finance ', *European Economic Review*, **32** (5), June, 1167–83.

Mookerjee, R. and Q. Yu (1995) ,'Capital Market Reform on the Road to a Market-Oriented Economy: The Case of Stock Markets in China', *Journal of Developing Areas*, **30** (1), October, 23–40.

North, D.C. (1991), *Institutions, Institutional Change and Economic Performance*, New York: Cambridge University.

North, D.C. (1994), 'Economic Performance Through Time', *American Economic Review*, **84** (3), June, 359–68.

Obstfeld, M. (1994), 'Risk-Taking, Global Diversification, and Growth', *American Economic Review*, **84** (5), December, 1310–29.

Qin, Dazhong and Danfeng Kong (1999), 'Analysis of the Big Four Banks and the Macro-environment – The Problems Affecting China's Stock Market and Their Causes', *Touzi Yanjiu (Investment Research)*, **7**, 19–22.

Qu, Baozhong and Xiaoping Zhao (1999), *Stock Market Expansion and Opportunities in China (Zhongguo Gushi Dakuolong Dachiyi)*, Beijing: Zhongguo Caizheng Jingji Press.

Renmin Ribao (People's Daily) (2001), 'Two New Sets of Regulations From the China Securities Regulatory Commission', 3 April.

Renmin Ribao (People's Daily) (2001), 16 November.

Robinson, J. (1979), *The Generalization of the General Theory and Other Essays*, New York: St. Martin's Press, 1–76.

Schumpeter, J.A. (1934), *The Theory of Economic Development,* Cambridge, MA: Harvard University Press.

Securities Statistics Compendium 1998, Taipei: Ministry of Economic Affairs, 1998.

Securities Times (1999), 'Industry Analysis: The Impact of WTO Accession on the Textile Industry', 10 May.

Shanghai Securities Report (2001), 'Wu Bangguo Says that Government Policy Regarding the Listing of Foreign Companies Will Gradually Be Relaxed', *Zhong Jing Wang http://www.cei.gov.cn/*, 19 April.

Shanghai Securities Report Website, *http://www.ssnews.online.sh.cn/*.

Shanghai Stock Exchange Website, *http://www.sse.com.cn/*.

Shao, Yizhi (2000), 'Some Views on the Regulation of China's Securities Market', *Touzi yu Zhungquan (Investment and Securities)*, **4**, 48–51.

Smyth, R. (1998),'New Institutional Economics in the Post-Socialist Transformation Debate', *Journal of Economic Surveys*, **12** (4), September, 361–98.

Song, Haibo and Rong Xu (2000), *The Impact of WTO Accession for China on Listed Companies (Ahongguo Jiari Shimaozjuzu Duishangshikongsi de Engxiang)*, Beijing: Qiye Gunli Press.

Song, Songxing and Weigen Jin (1995), 'An Empirical Study of the Efficiency of the Shanghai Stock Exchange', *Jingjixuejia (Economist)*, **4**, 107–13.

Song, Yan (1999), 'Securities Regulation in China and Overseas – Comparison, Analysis and Future Prospects', *Touzi Yanjiu (Investment Research)*, **7**, 42–6.

Southwest Financial and Economic University Project Team (1999), 'The Securities Market in China – Stages of Development and the Establishment of Systems', *Caijing Kexue (Finance and Economics)*, **5**, 35–40.

Stiglitz, J.E. (1985), 'Credit Markets and the Control of Capital', *Journal of Money, Credit and Banking,* **17** (2), May, 133–52.

Stiglitz, J.E. (1994), 'The Role of the State in Financial Markets', in *Proceedings of the World Bank Annual Conference on Development Economics*, Washington, D.C.; World Bank.

Su, Yuezhong (2001), 'An Analysis of the Asset Reorganization Market', *Jingji Daokan (Economic Herald)*, **2**, 36–9.

Sun, Jie and Weiming Zhang (2001), 'Speeding Up in Share Financing in the First Quarter', *Zhong Jing Wang http://www.cei.gov.cn/*, 15 May.

Sun, Q. and W.H.S. Tong (2000), 'The Effect of Market Segmentation on Stock Prices: The China Syndrome', *Journal of Banking & Finance*, **24** (12), December, 1875–902.

Ta Kung Pao (1999), 'China and the USA Sign a WTO Pre-accession Agreement', 16 November.

Taiwan Stock Exchange Website, *http://www.tse.com.tw/*.

Tam, O.K. (1991), 'Capital Market Development in China', *World Development,* **19** (5), May, 511–32.

Wang, Guogang (2000), 'Analysis of the Relationship Between Trends in China's Stock Market and Trends in the Economy as a Whole', *Caimo Jingji (Finance and Trade Economics)*, **1**, 46–51.

Wang, Guoming (2001), 'The Prospects for China's Second Board', *Touzi yu Zhungquan (Investment and Securities)*, **1**, 92–6.

Wang, Jianguo (1999), 'Change in China's Subsidiary Capital System and the Establishment of New Models of Financing', *Touzi Yanjiu (Investment Research)*, **1**, 19–23.

Wang, Kaiguo (2001), 'The Strategic Concept Behind the Establishment of China's Second Board', *Touzi yu Zhungquan (Investment and Securities)*, **3**, 83–91.

Wang, Wanshan and Kezhong Yuan (1999), 'The Development of the Capital Markets and the Reform of State-owned Enterprises', *Touzi Yanjiu (Investment Research)*, **8**, 19–22.

Wang, Yi (1999), 'Using the Securities Market to Promote the Development of State-owned Enterprises', *Jingjixuejia (Economist)*, **3**, 39–42.

Wen Hui Pao (1999), 'Both China and the USA Are Willing to Hold Further Negotiations Regarding WTO Accession for China', 22 October.

Wu, Jinglian (2001), 'China's Financial Sector – Improving the Governance Structure of Listed Companies', *Ta Kung Pao*, 20 February.

Wu, Youchang and Xiao Zhao (2000), 'From Debt to Equity: Governance Theory and Policy Analysis', *Jingji Yanjiu (Economic Research Journal)*, **2**, 26–33.

Xiao, Bing (1999), 'The Repurchase of State Shares and the Improvement of the Efficiency of Stock Market Regulation', *Touzi Yanjiu (Investment Research)*, **8**, 32–6.

Xiao, Yu (1999), *China's Bond Market (Zhongguo Guozai Shichang)*, Beijing: Shehui Kexue Wenxian Press.

Xu, C.K. (2000), 'The Microstructure of the Chinese Stock Market', *China Economic Review,* **11** (1), 79–97.

Xu, Gang (1998), 'A Discussion of the Stock Market's Weaknesses and Securities Legislation', *Guanli Shijue (Management World)*, **6**, 40–8.

Xu, Weiguo (1999), 'Securities Firm Finance and the Multiplier Effect', in Yupen Chen (ed.), *China's Securities Market at the Millennium (Shichizijiao de Zhonggou Zhengquan Shichang)*, Beijing: Jingji Kexue Press , i–vii.

Xu, X. and Y. Wang (1999), 'Ownership Structure and Corporate Governance in Chinese Stock Companies', *China Economic Review,* **10** (1), 75–98.

Xu, Yan (1997), 'The Development of the Capital Markets and the Improvement of Funding Allocation Segmentation', *Jinrong Yanjiu (Journal of Financial Research)*, **9**, 13–8.

Xue, Rongjiu and Xiaojiang Wang (1998), *The Challenge for China – The Benefits and Disadvantages of WTO Accession (Zhongguo Mianlinzongji – Jiari Shimaozhuzu de Xi yu You)*, Beijing: Shijue Zishi Press.

Yang, Dayong, Qingju Luo, Hanming Huang and Juan Hou (2001), 'The Financial Markets in 2001 – Forecasts and Prospects', *Zhong Jing Wang http://www.cei.gov.cn/*, 2 January.

Yang, Feng and Chunling Shih (1999), 'The Establishment of a Legal Framework and Stock Market Efficiency', *Jinrong Yanjiu (Journal of Financial Research)*, **8**, 40–8.

Yang, Zhishu and Liyan Wang (2000), 'Lessons from the NASDAQ Trading System for the Establishment of China's Second Board', *Jinrong Yanjiu (Journal of Financial Research)*, **10**, 78–84.

Yao, Xiaoping and Yong Sun (1997), 'The Establishment of a Sound Regulatory System for the Stock Market in China', *Touzi Yanjiu (Investment Research)*, **12**, 27–30.

Ye, Weiping (1999), *The Impact of WTO Accession and Risk Avoidance Strategies (Zhongguo Rishi yu Bixian Cuoqiang Duice)*, Beijing: Zhongguo Jingji Press.

Yu, Hui (2000), 'WTO Accession and Reform in China', *Hong Kong Economic Journal Monthly*, **278**, May, 39–43.

Yu, Qiao (1994), 'Market Efficiency, Periodic Abnormalities and Share Price Fluctuations', *Jingji Yanjiu (Economic Research Journal)*, **9**, 43–50.

Yu, Yimin (2000), 'A Discussion of the Unification of the National Share Registration and Settlement System', *Zhongguo Jinrong (China Finance)*, **3**, 30–2.

Yuan, Guoliang and Xuqiang Ho (2000), 'Promoting Stable Securities Market Development Through the Strength of Institutional Investors', *Zhongguo Jinrong (China Finance)*, **7**, 43–5.

Yuan, Guoliang, Wei Lou and Lianfeng Hao (2001), 'Innovation to Attract Foreign Companies to Invest in the A-share Market', *Touzi yu Zhungquan (Investment and Securities)*, **1**, 26–8.

Yuan, Wei (2001), 'Establishment and Perfection of the De-listing Mechanism for China's Securities Market', *Touzi yu Zhengquan (Investment and Securities)*, **1**, 13–7.

Zeng, Rongsheng and Qin Mei (2000), 'The Improvement of China's Securities Tax System', *Touzi yu Zhungquan (Investment and Securities)*, **6**, 36–40.

Zhang, Changcai (1999), *Financing Methods in China (Zhongguo Rongzi Fan Shi Yanjiu)*, Beijing: Zhongguo Caizheng Jingji Press.

Zhang, Dongsheng and Jiandiao Liu (2000), 'A Discussion of the Organizational Structure of Venture Capital Funds in China and the Legal Framework', *Jinrong Yanjiu (Journal of Financial Research)*, **6**, 1–10.

Zhang, Hanlin (1999), *The WTO and China's Future (Shimaozhuzu yu Weilai Zhongguo)*, Beijing: Zhongguo Wujia Press.

Zhang, Kaiping (1999), 'Constructing Long-term Forecasts for Securities Investment', *Zhongguo Gongye Jingji (China Industrial Economy)*, **2**, 26–31.

Zhang, Yongheng (2000), 'Systemic Innovation in China's Stock Market', *Jinrong Yanjiu (Journal of Financial Research)*, **2**, 92–7.

Zhang, Yujun (1998), *Institutional Analysis of the Development of the Securities Market in China (Zhongguo Zhengquan Shichang de Zhidu Fenxi)*, Beijing: Jingii Kexue Press.

Zhao, Haikuan and Tianyong Guo (1998), *Reforms of Chinese Financial Institutions in Twenty Years (Zhongguo Jinrong Gaige 20 Nian)*, Henan: Zhongzhou Press.

Zhao, X. (1999), 'Stock Prices, Inflation and Output: Evidence from China', *Applied Economics Letters,* **6** (8), August, 509–11.

Zheng, Yaodong (1999), *An Analysis of China's Capital Markets (Zhongguo Ziben Shichang Fenxi)*, Beijing: Zhongguo Caizheng Jingji Press.

Zhong Huan Zixun (2000), 'Seven Categories of Business Will Have Access to the Second Board Delayed', *Zhong Jing Wang http://www.cei.gov.cn/*, 6 August.

Zhong Jing Wang http://www.cei.gov.cn/ (1999), 'Opening Up the Service Sector for WTO Accession', 1 June.

Zhong Jing Wang http://www.cei.gov.cn/ (1999a), 'China's Auto Industry Faces Up to the Challenge', 9 June.

Zhong Jing Wang http://www.cei.gov.cn/ (1999b), 'The Impact of WTO Accession on China's Software Industry Will Not Be Particularly Great', 9 June.

Zhong Jing Wang http://www.cei.gov.cn/ (1999c), 'Experts Discuss the Sino-American Agreement for Collaboration on Agriculture', August.

Zhong Jing Wang http://www.cei.gov.cn/ (1999d), 'Seven Sectors Which Will Be Particularly Hard Hit', August.

Zhong Jing Wang http://www.cei.gov.cn/ (1999e), 'The WTO and China's Financial Sector – Challenges and Opportunities', August.

Zhong Jing Wang http://www.cei.gov.cn/ (1999f), 'The WTO and China's Telecommunications Industry', August.

Zhong Jing Wang http://www.cei.gov.cn/ (1999g), 'The WTO and Chinese Agriculture', August.

Zhong Jing Wang http://www.cei.gov.cn/ (1999h), 'The WTO and Chinese Industry', August .

Zhong Jing Wang http://www.cei.gov.cn/ (2000), 'Vice Minister Deng Nan Points Out the Trend for Venture Capital Funding Sources to Become More Diversified', 18 December.

Zhong Jing Wang http://www.cei.gov.cn/ (2001), 'Investment Companies' Attention Has Shifted to the New Board', 10 January.

Zhong Jing Wang http://www.cei.gov.cn/ (2001), 'The China Securities Regulatory Commission Prohibits Securities Firms from Involvement in Venture Capital Business', 18 April.

Zhong Jing Wang http://www.cei.gov.cn/ (2001), 'Ten Case Studies of Mergers Among Chinese Enterprises in 2000', 26 April.

Zhong Xin She (1999), 'Jiang Zemin Discusses China's Three Positions Regarding WTO Accession', 20 October.

Zhong Yin Wang http://www.cfn.com.cn/ (2001), 'The Participation of Social Insurance Funds in the Stock Market – Systems and Regulation', 25 April.

Zhong Yin Wang http://www.cfn.com.cn/ (2001), 'The Ancillary Measures for Reducing Holdings of State-owned Shares Are the Participation of Insurance and Social Insurance Funds in the Stock Market', 9 May.

Zhou, Peisheng (2000), 'Economic Analysis of Rent-seeking In China's

Stock Market and Its Causes', *Touzi yu Zhungquan (Investment and Securities)*, **3**, 4–7.

Zhu, Shengqiu (2001),'Change Brings New Opportunities – Forecasts for the Overall State of the Primary Market in 2001', *Shanghai Securities Report*, 1 February.

Zhu, Yu and Wenjuan Wang (2000), 'Analysis of the Impact of WTO Accession on China's Listed Companies and Securities Market', *Touzi yu Zhungquan (Investment and Securities)*, **4**, 39–44.

Zou, Yang and Guochun Lin (1997), 'Government Intervention in the Stock Market', *Caijing Wenti Yanjiu (Research on Financial and Economic Issues)*, **6**, 73–6.

Index

acquisitions 45, 77, 78, 112, 158,
  160, 164, 167
allocation of resources 1, 47, 52–4,
  80
American Depository Receipts (ADR)
  108, 155
analysis of variance (ANOVA) 86
anti–dumping 121, 124, 136–7
Arthur, W.B. 2
Asian financial crisis 51, 84, 107–8,
  130

bad debts 7, 77
Beck, T. 80
bonds
  corporate 8, 11, 28, 58, 63, 108,
    115–6, 162
  government 9, 11–2, 21, 25, 27–8,
    54, 134, 162, 167
  treasury 11, 25, 63, 115–6
brokerage and dealing business 112
brokerage–type securities firms
  70–2
business cycle 81, 107

Cai, Wenhai 61
Cao, Fengchi 59, 155
capital accumulation 80
capital–deficit sector 7
capital–intensive 130, 149
capital–surplus sector 7
centrally planned economy 1, 5–6,
  9, 61
Chen, Chaoyang 59
Chen, Dong 156–7
Chen, Dongsheng 29
Chen, Ge 75, 156
Chen, Haowu 23, 68
Chen, Qiumin 46
Chen, Xiaoyun 62, 64
Chen, Yehua 60
Chen, Yiqin 167
Chen, Yupen, 45

Chen, Zhengrong 21, 114
Chen, Zhiyuan 22

China Macroeconomic Issues Project
  Team 76
China Securities Association 72–3
China Securities Regulatory
  Commission (CSRC) 12, 15–7,
  19–20, 22–3, 25–7, 29–30,
  33, 36, 58–9, 64, 66–7, 71–2,
  114, 168–9
China Securities Report 157
Chi–square method 81, 86, 98,
Chow, G.C. 75
closed–end funds 115–6, 163
cointegration test 60–61
Company Law 13, 23, 68–9, 72, 78,
  160
corporate governance 15, 78–9, 108,
  164
Cui, Yafeng 110

Da Peng Securities Project Team 22
Dan, Ruyong 81
debt–to–equity conversion 164
de–listing 20, 42, 66–7, 70, 162
Devereux, M.B. 80
Dickey–Fuller test 60
Ding, Wenjie 157
domestic investors 19, 28,30, 33

Economic Daily News 115
Economic Reference Report 157
economic reform 4, 6
economies of scale 2, 42, 51, 127,
  129, 150
effect
  coordination 2
  diffusion 17
  learning 2
efficient market hypothesis 60
equity structure 28, 33, 35–6, 52,
  166, 169

export — orientation 126

Fama, E.F. 55, 59
Fan, Gang 28
Fan, Z.Z. 75
Fei, Wuwei 14, 67 — 8
financial indicators
    growth 81, 83, 92, 99 — 101, 107
    liquidity 81 — 2, 87, 94, 98 — 101,
    107
    management performance 81 — 2,
    90, 92, 98 — 101, 107 — 8
    profitability 81 — 2, 86, 94, 99 — 101,
    107
    stability 81 — 2, 87, 90, 92, 98 — 101,
    107
financial ratios
    current ratio 82
    debt ratio 7, 20, 77, 82
    earnings per share (EPS) 21, 52,
    82, 106
    price / earnings ratio (PER) 33
    quick ratio 82
    return on net assets (ROE) 52, 82
    return on total assets (ROA) 82
financial reform 10, 47, 168
financial statements 34, 59, 66, 78,
    84, 106, 161
financing
    bank 4 — 5, 10, 163
    direct 3, 77 — 8, 80
    diversified 4, 8
    fiscal 4 — 6
fiscal burden 6
fiscal subsidies 7
forced saving 5 — 6
foreign investors 3, 19, 22 — 3, 25,
    30, 54, 115 — 6, 169
Fu, Yao 14, 67 — 8
function approach 80

GARCH model 61
GATT 117, 126
gender 41
globalization 166, 168
gradual reform 3, 158
Granger causality test 61
Greenwood, J. 80
Growth Enterprise Market (GEM) 17
Guo, Tianyong 64, 159

Han, Zhiguo 28
Hao, Lianfeng 116
He, Shunwen 107
He, Xiaoping 72
high — tech 17 — 8, 23, 50, 127, 129,
    160, 164
Ho, Xuqiang 42
Holmstrom, B. 80
Hong Kong Stock Exchange 24
Hou, Juan 52, 67, 163, 168
Hu, Geng 72
Hu, J.Y. 75
Hu, Jizhi 23, 58
Hu, Meng 43
Huang, Hanming 52, 163, 168
Huang, Pin 106
Huang, Shunxiang 166
Huang, Wuxiang 157
Huang, Yexuan 169
Huang, Yuncheng 34

income structure 7, 40
income tax 113 — 4
independent board directors 15
information disclosure 15, 23, 59,
    161
Information Technology Agreement
    (ITA) 120, 125
initial public offering (IPO) 27, 34,
    65, 73, 106, 108, 169
insider trading 68, 107
institutions
    formal constraints 12 — 3
    informal constraints 9, 12
    institutional change 1 — 2, 8 — 9,
    12, 14, 23
    institutional innovation 2, 10
    institutional investors 22, 27,
    37 — 9, 42, 67 — 8, 112, 115 — 6,
    159, 165
    institutional transformation 1 — 4,
    7 — 8, 37, 48, 61, 68, 73, 76, 81,
    158 — 61
    path dependence 2, 14
    self — enforcing mechanism 2, 14
Insurance Law 21 — 2, 160
Insurance Regulatory Commission 22

Jiang, Shuncai 47
Jiang, Weijun 57

Jiang, Yihong 33
Jiao, Jinpu 157
Jin, Tehuan 20
Jin, Weigen 60
Jin, Yunhui 80

Kong, Danfeng 38
Kyle, A.S. 80

Labor — intensive 127
Lau, L.J. 3
learning by doing 3, 158
Least Squares Means (LSM) 86
Levine, R. 80
Li, C. 61
Li, Changhong 28
Li, D. 61
Li, Geping 106
Li, Kang 39, 40 — 41, 94
Li, Kemu 156
Li, Liying 161
Li, Yang 28
Liao, Zequn 156
Lin, Guochun 22
Lin, Haochang 48
Lin, S. 61
Lin, Yifu 108
listed companies 1, 11, 13 — 8, 20,
    23 — 4, 26 — 8, 34 — 6, 38, 42, 45,
    48, 50 — 3, 56, 59 — 61, 63, 65 — 70,
    72, 74 — 5, 79, 81 — 4, 86 — 7, 90,
    92, 95, 98 — 107, 109, 111, 114, 117,
    151 — 6, 159, 161 - 5, 168 — 9
Liu, Hua 110
Liu, Jiandiao 18
Liu, Ming 77
Liu, Shoufen 72
Liu, Shufeng 157
Liu, Wei 28
Liu, X. 60
Liu, Xing 107
loans
    bank 6, 33, 42, 78, 112, 163, 168
    government 6
    non — performing 133, 146
Loayza, N. 80
Lou, Wei 116
Lucas, R.E. 80
Luo, Qingju 52, 163, 168

Ma, Ruohong 14

Mao, Chunbo 77
Mao, Zhenhua 17
market
    bond 3, 9, 27 — 8, 162 — 3
    capital 8, 10, 22, 24 — 5, 38,
        77 — 8, 113, 161, 163
    money 24, 113
    primary 17, 22, 24, 28, 45, 47,
        53 — 4, 66, 112, 115 — 6, 134
    secondary 11 — 2, 17, 22, 24, 28,
        30, 35, 44 — 5, 47, 53 — 4, 57, 65,
        111 — 2, 115 — 6, 159, 161, 163,
        167, 169
market liquidity 159
marketization 1, 17 — 8, 133, 158-9,
    168
Mayer, C. 80
Mei, Qin 58
Mergers 15, 44 — 5, 47, 52, 71, 77,
    112, 139, 158, 160, 164 — 5, 167
Mookerjee, R. 60
moral hazard 7, 17, 106
most favored nation (MFN) 110

non — state — owned enterprises 168
North, D.C. 1–2
null hypotheses 99 — 100

Obstfeld, M. 80
off — floor transactions 160
open — end funds 22, 115 — 6, 163
operating revenue from core business
    83, 94
operational efficiency 12, 55, 161
over — the — counter (OTC) 10 — 11,
    13, 159

particular treatment (PT) 20, 66
pension fund 22, 38, 115
People's Bank of China (PBC) 8, 10,
    25, 42, 59, 61 — 3, 133
policy banks
    Agricultural Development Bank of
    China 6
    Export — Import Bank of China 6
    State Development Bank of China 6
pricing efficiency 55
private placement 163
property rights 2, 6 — 7, 10, 54, 76 — 7,
    130 — 31, 142
Qian, Y. 3

Qin, Dazhong 38
Qu, Baozhong 48 − 51
Qualified Foreigner Institutional
    Investor (QFII) 22, 114, 168

regional distribution 48 − 9, 27, 52,
    86, 99
regulatory dialectic 14
Renmin Ribao 67
rent − seeking 57, 61, 160
Robinson, J. 80
Roland, G. 3
Romilly, D. 60

savings ratio 6
Schumpeter, J.A. 79
Securities Committee of the State
    Council 63
securities firms 1, 10, 23, 27, 34, 38,
    42, 44 − 7, 53 − 4, 58 − 9, 61,
    66 − 73, 111 − 5, 123, 125, 134,
    147, 157, 163, 165 − 7, 169
Securities Law 26, 34, 46, 68 − 73,
    133, 160–61, 165, 167
Securities Times 157
Securitization 3, 22 − 3, 55 − 6, 163,
    167
self − regulation 64, 72 − 3
Shanghai Stock Exchange 1, 17, 21
Shao, Yizhi 42
share price manipulation 38, 45, 58,
    165
shareholder equity turnover 83
shares
    A− 3, 17, 19, 24, 28 − 30, 33, 36,
        52 − 3, 55, 58, 83, 89, 98 − 100,
        114, 162, 167
    B− 3, 19, 24 − 6, 28, 30, 33, 36 − 7,
        53, 58, 83, 86 − 7, 90, 92, 95,
        98 − 100, 114 − 6, 155–6, 160, 162
    H− 3, 24 − 5, 28, 30, 36 − 7, 53,
        108, 158
    internal employee 35 − 6
    legal person 23, 25, 35 − 7, 53,
        158 − 60
    N− 24, 28, 30, 167
    public 35, 37, 53, 158 − 9
    state 35 − 7, 53, 56, 74, 106 − 8,
        158 − 60, 163 − 5, 169
    state − held 16 − 7
Shenzhen Stock Exchange 1, 3, 8,

    13 − 4, 17, 20, 23 − 6, 33, 42 − 3,
        46, 48 − 50, 54 − 5, 57 − 8, 63, 72,
        81, 86 − 7, 90, 92, 94, 98 − 107, 114,
        159
Shih, Chunling 69
shock therapy 2
single tax rate 58
small and medium enterprises
    (SMEs) 18, 168
Smith, B. 80
Smith, G.W. 80
Smyth, R. 3
social insurance fund 22, 115
Song, H. 60
Song, Haibo 157
Song, Songxing 60
Song, Yan 75
Southwest Financial and Economic
    University Project Team 22
Special Economic Zones 44
special treatment (ST) 20 − 21, 66, 75
stamp tax 158, 162
standardization 81 − 3
State Council 12, 22, 25 − 6, 33, 63 − 5,
    68, 71 − 2, 74
State Council Securities Committee
    12, 25 − 6, 63 − 5, 68
State Economic and Trade
    Commission 15
state − owned banks
    Agricultural Bank of China 7
    Bank of China 7
    Industrial and Commercial Bank
        of China 7 − 8, 11, 26
    People's Construction Bank of
        China 7, 26
state − owned enterprises 5 − 8, 14,
    35, 42, 45, 47, 51, 54, 73, 76 − 9,
    106, 114, 159, 161, 165 − 8
Stiglitz, J.E. 80
stock market efficiency 59
    semi − strong form 60
    strong form 60
    weak form 60
Su, Yuezhong 21
Sun, Jie 24, 33
Sun, Q. 23, 54
Sun, Yong 69, 75
system
    accounting 20, 33, 161
    dual − track 158, 160, 162

financing 1, 4 – 10
household responsibility 8
incentive 9
monitoring 67
regulatory 13, 55, 61 – 2, 64, 68,
    73 – 4, 132, 161
settlement 58
trading 53, 57 – 8, 128

Ta Kung Pao 156
Tam, O.K. 54
tariff quota 117 – 9, 135 – 6
tariff rate 117 – 8, 120, 124, 133, 146
technology – intensive 127 – 8, 130,
    137
term structure of interest rate 160
Tirole, J. 80
Tokyo Round 117, 126
Tokyo Stock Exchange 24
Tong, W.H.S. 23, 54
total asset turnover 83
total factor productivity 80
Trade Related Investment Measures
    (TRIMs) 126
transaction costs 10, 13, 27, 58 – 9,
    80
transparency 3, 15, 66, 69, 78, 110,
    167

Uruguay Round 117,

Wang, Guogang 59
Wang, Guoming 17
Wang, Jianguo 6
Wang, Kaiguo 17
Wang, Liyan 18
Wang, Wanshan 77
Wang, Wenjuan 151 – 2, 154
Wang, Xiaojiang 157
Wang, Y. 37
Wang, Yi 77
Wen Hui Pao 156
World Bank 133
World Trade Organization (WTO) 47,
    110 – 2, 114 – 5, 117 – 8, 122 – 3,
    125 – 56, 165 – 8
Wu, Jinglian 16, 23, 108
Wu, Qin 59
Wu, Shuangli 14, 67 – 8
Wu, Youchang 79, 107

Xiang, Jiahua 43
Xiao, Bing 169
Xiao, Yu 28
Xie, Fudan 157
Xu, C.K. 54
Xu, Gang 69
Xu, Rong 157
Xue, Rongjiu 157
Xu, Weiguo 45, 54
Xu, X. 37
Xu, Yan 5

Yang, Dayong 52, 163, 168
Yang, Feng 69
Yang, Zhishu 18
Yao, Xiaoping 69, 75
Ye, Weiping 157
Yu, Cungao 80
Yu, Hui 161
Yu, Q. 60
Yu, Qiao 60
Yu, Yimin 58
Yuan, Guoliang 42, 77, 116
Yuan, Kezhong 77
Yuan, Wei 20

Zhang, Changcai 4, 6
Zhang, Dongsheng 18
Zhang, Hanlin 157
Zhang, Jun 169
Zhang, Kaiping 69 – 70
Zhang, Weiming 24, 33
Zhang, Xiaoji 156
Zhang, Yongheng 57
Zhang, Yujun 22
Zhao, Haikuan 64, 159
Zhao, X. 81
Zhao, Xiao 79, 107
Zhao, Xiaoping 48 – 51
Zeng, Rongsheng 58
Zheng, Yaodong 73
Zhong Huan Zixun 23
Zhong Jing Wang 23, 115, 156, 169
Zhong Yin Wang 22
Zhou, Peisheng 34
Zhou, Ping, 45
Zhu, Qifeng 72
Zhu, Yu 151 – 2, 154
Zhu, Shengqiu 169
Zou, Yang 22